IMAGES
of America

COACHELLA

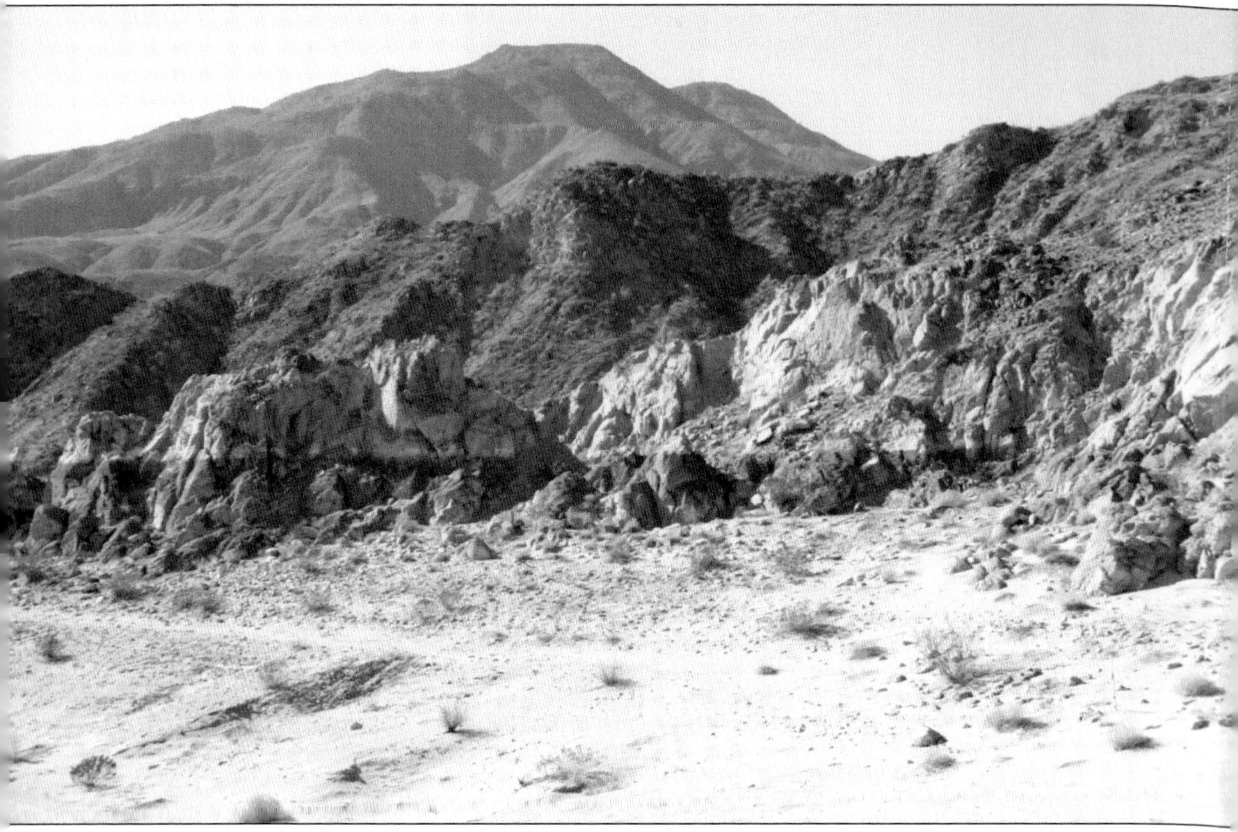

The waterline for the Ancient Cahuilla Lake can be seen in the mountains surrounding the Coachella Valley in this photograph. The light white line is evidence of the tremendous size of this ancient lake. The periodic flooding of the valley created the lake, which attracted a diverse assortment of wildlife, both aquatic and land-based, to this arid desert. (Courtesy of the Coachella Valley Water District.)

On the Cover: This photograph was taken in 1962 during a Coachella Valley Pioneer's Society picnic at the Coachella Valley High School. The Coachella Valley Pioneer's Society worked toward preserving the history of the Coachella Valley and establishing a museum. It would be the successor to the Coachella Valley Pioneer's Society, the Coachella Valley Historical Society, that would establish a museum in 1984. (Courtesy of the Coachella Valley History Museum.)

IMAGES
of America

COACHELLA

Erica M. Ward

ARCADIA
PUBLISHING

ISBN 978-1-4671-3266-4

Published by Arcadia Publishing
Charleston, South Carolina

Printed in the United States of America

Library of Congress Control Number: 2014942177

For all general information, please contact Arcadia Publishing:
Telephone 843-853-2070
Fax 843-853-0044
E-mail sales@arcadiapublishing.com
For customer service and orders:
Toll-Free 1-888-313-2665

Visit us on the Internet at www.arcadiapublishing.com

To the younger generations, may you be as inspired to preserve, study, and discuss the ever-evolving history of Coachella as those who have preceded you.

Contents

Acknowledgments

Residents of the Coachella Valley who volunteer throughout the valley to preserve the history of the city of Coachella and surrounding cities are invaluable in the preservation of historical photographs and other artifacts that relate to and tell the history of Coachella. I extend my gratitude to these volunteers for their important work benefiting the people of the Coachella Valley.

I also wish to thank my editor, Alyssa Jones, for all her assistance during this project. I specifically want to thank Robert Tyler, Kathy Bartlett, Sarah Seekatz, and the Breakfast Club for their support and guidance while researching and writing this book. To Patricia Laflin, who was a wonderful resource on the history of Coachella and a great source of support and encouragement, thank you. I also want to thank Dr. Thomas Long, who advised and encouraged my love of history early on and continued that support during this project. Finally, I want to extend a special thank-you to my husband, Victor Ward, our children, and my family. Thank you for your support and love throughout my educational journey and my continued adventures in history.

Introduction

The city of Coachella was once an arid desert occupied by the Cahuilla Indians. The Cahuilla, for centuries, had migrated between the valley floor and the surrounding mountains in reaction to the flooding of the valley by the Ancient Lake Cahuilla. By 1600, the lake had dried up, and some of the Cahuilla Indians established the Coachella Valley as their home; they are known as the Desert Cahuilla. They were accomplished well-diggers and expertly dug out walk-in wells with ramps or stairs without the assistance of modern machinery. They harvested natural vegetation and hunted local game, including rabbits and birds. The Desert Cahuilla's cultural and social beliefs were a major focus of everyday life. Often, important knowledge of the people was passed through oral stories or games. The stories and games taught the people about their landscape and environment. Their cultural traditions include singing about different aspects of life. Some of the songs still sung in the 21st century are the creation songs, death or burial songs, and songs known as bird singing.

Spanish explorer Juan Bautista De Anza made the first non–Native American expedition through an area of the Coachella Valley, later called Palm Springs, in 1774. It was not until the expedition led by Capt. José Romero in the 1820s that more of the Desert Cahuilla come in contact with Europeans. As more surveys and expeditions passed through the Coachella Valley, so did the slow arrival of non–Native Americans. The Desert Cahuilla as a result lost the large territories they once freely lived on and became more restricted throughout the years. During the time of the Spanish and Mexican eras of governing California, the Desert Cahuilla living in the Coachella Valley were recorded on maps within a mission or *rancheria*, respectively. After the transfer of California to the United States from Mexico with the signing of the Treaty of Guadalupe Hidalgo in 1848, the United States began governing California, including the areas occupied by the Desert Cahuilla. The US government established the Agua Caliente Reservation in 1876, the Augustine Reservation in 1891, the Cabazon Reservation in 1876, and the Torres Martinez Reservation in 1876.

Jason L. Rector, the founder of Coachella, was the first recorded non–Native American to occupy the area. Rector would remain in Coachella and become very influential in the political development of the town until his later years, when he moved to Los Angeles. The area that was established as Woodspur in 1876 and later named Coachella in 1901 was next to the area where the Cabazon Reservation was established. The town of Coachella would grow from a desert landscape to a thriving agricultural community. The residents had access to general stores, bars, churches, and schools in the early years. As the town grew, so did the social organizations. Women formed the Coachella Valley Women's Club and actively participated in the social and economic development of the town while they maintained their households, and some also worked on the farms and ranches owned by their families.

As the agricultural industry continued to grow in the Coachella Valley, Coachella was established as a city in 1946. Due to the large Hispanic population, which by the year 2000 was more than 96 percent of the city population, Coachella was an area of social and political activism during the 1960s and 1970s regarding fieldworkers' rights. Coachella was one of the areas visited by social and political activist César Chávez during the fieldworkers' rights movement.

Coachella would again be an area of political activism in the 21st century. This time, the issue was deporting illegal immigrants. The City of Coachella declared itself a safe haven for illegal migrant immigrants in 2006. Joining other cities across the United States, Coachella declined to use local resources, such as police, to investigate and detain illegal immigrants for transfer to the US Customs and Border Patrol and eventual deportation.

In addition to the important regional and national roles Coachella has had in the social and political debates over agriculture and immigration, the city also has international recognition for the city of Indio's Coachella Valley Music and Arts Festival, commonly known as the Coachella Fest or just Coachella. The Coachella Valley Music and Arts Festival started in October 1999 as a two-day concert/festival. Attendees had the opportunity to hear multiple musicians in one day, with a focus on rock music. Organizers took a year off, and in April 2001, relaunched the festival. By 2007, the event had expanded to three days. This successful music festival gained international recognition, with music fans eagerly awaiting the release of the band list each year.

Even with the international name recognition Coachella has received, day-to-day life in Coachella has a rich history of social, political, and community changes. The Cabazon Band of Mission Indians tribe, whose reservation is within the city, has established several successful businesses, including the Fantasy Springs Casino and Resort. They also preserve and honor their ancestors and cultural traditions. Annually, the Cabazon Band of Mission Indians hosts the Indio Powwow, bringing together different Native Americans to celebrate their culture and traditions while allowing non–Native Americans to experience some Native American traditions, such as powwow dancing and singing.

The rich history and multifaceted culture of Coachella were influenced by the Desert Cahuilla who lived in the area prior to the development of Coachella, and by the early residents of Coachella. The local community was further shaped by the continued expansion and development of the city of Coachella and its growing population. The Coachella of the 21st century is a dynamic area where people of many cultures and traditions live side by side while reshaping the arid desert landscape into a thriving city focused on its people and the community.

One

The People of the City of Coachella

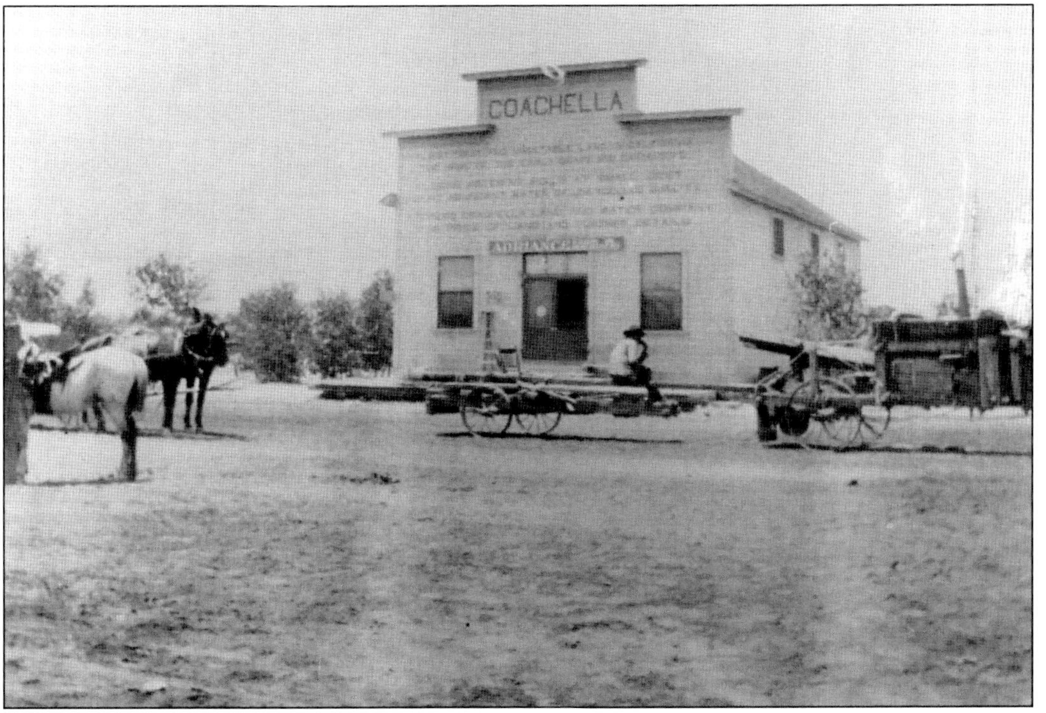

Otho Moore, an early white resident of the Coachella Valley area, took this 1904 photograph. It shows the first general store in Coachella, which would later become known as the Huntington Store. Originally the town's name was Woodspur, but in 1903 it was changed to Coachella. (Courtesy of the Coachella Valley Water District.)

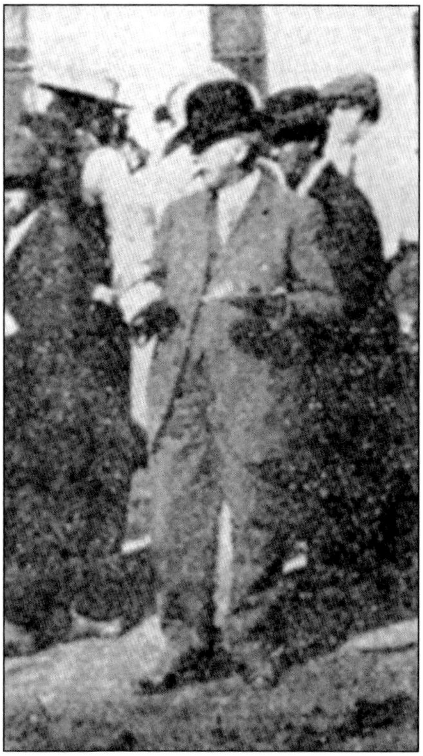

The photograph at left of town founder Jason L. Rector was taken in the late 1800s and is the only known image of him in existence. Rector was born in Iowa and moved to San Diego in 1884, working in the local cattle industry there. After being employed by the Southern Pacific Railroad to clear wood from the area later known as Coachella, Rector moved to the Coachella Valley. He established the wood siding terminal for the Southern Pacific Railroad next to the railway and began clearing the wood, mostly mesquite. The siding and surrounding new town became known as Woodspur. Rector and his brother Lon B. Rector dug the town's first water well, which was completed in November 1900. With the availability of fresh water, people began arriving and settling in. Rector also established and managed the Coachella Valley Produce Association in 1902 and the first precooling plant in the valley, Coachella Valley Refrigerating Company, in 1904. He remained actively involved in the town's development until his death on September 24, 1919. Rector is listed in the 1907 directory below (near bottom right) as manager of the ice plant. (Left, courtesy of the City of Coachella; below, courtesy of Ancestry.com.)

438 RIVERSIDE COUNTY DIRECTORY

Espy Rev Herbert P pastor United Presbyterian Ch
Eyer Clarendon B pres Beaumont Land & Water Co r Los Angeles
Eyraud Fredk F section foremn S P Co
Farnum Arthur H pumper S P Co
Fisher Martha M (wid Almond A)
Frady Chas L lab
Frady Halleck C clk J A Gray
Frady Ulysses L blksmith
French Ralph S editor Beaumont Independent
Gilbert-Dean Mercantile Co (M P Gilbert, I M and W H Dean) gen mdse tel Home 268
Gilbert Fredk H lab
Gilbert Matthew P (Gilbert-Dean Mercantile Co)
Gobin John M real est
Gonzales Jose lab
Gould Geo firemn S P Co
Gray John A gen mdse tel Home 253
Green Saml eng S P Co
Greig Jas M artist
Guthrie Edgar M
Hayes Louis A eng S P Co
Holbrook Frank E lab
Hotel Edinburgh David Cochrane prop tel Home 254
Heaney Robt eng S P Co
Henderson Wm eng S P Co
Jenkins Robt T carp
Jenkins Sidney A carp
Johnson Wm A stablemn W B Warren
Johnston Wm T eng S P Co
Kelly Ben lab
KELLY JAMES A postmaster
Laird Martha G (wid John S)
Lawrence Amaro rancher
Lovren John N constable
McCarty Eugene C eng S P Co
McCormick Alex
McCoy John J undertaker and contr tel Home 262
McCue Jos B agt S P Co
McDermott Parnell firemn S P Co
McDonald Chas A eng S P Co
McKenzie David P lab
McKenzie Harry T clk J A Gray
McKenzie Wm A
McNevin Michael pumper S P Co
Maddocks Henry C clk Hotel Edinburgh
Maguire John J emp S P Co
Martin Fredk C emp S P Co
Mason Benj F hostler S P Co
Mathers Geo W rancher
Maynard Harry rancher
Mellen Thos J orchardist
Meyer Max A signal man S P Co
Mungia Thos S lab
Murray Robt F plasterer
Osgood Chas R eng S P Co
Ostrom John G lab
Park Martin V
Percy Walter L agt Beaumont Land & Water Co
Petty Mrs Lydia
Phillips Luke D sec Beaumont Land & Water Co r Los Angeles
Porter Frank J
POSTOFFICE J A Kelly postmaster
Powers Pleasant A rancher
Presbyterian Church Rev W M Barrett pastor
Rawlings Saml L meatctr J A Gray
Roach Patrick J rancher
Roberts Horace J rancher
Roberts H Leslie rancher
Roberts Jos E rancher
Royce Ansil G boarding
Samson Jas rancher
School Board—Rev Herbert P Espey, H J Roberts, Fred C Martin
Scott Geo S tel opr S P Co
Sears Wm J rancher
Sharpe John C mach S P Co
Sheets Clyde firemn S P Co
Shepard Walter shop clk S P Co
Shore Edmund M barber
Smith Sylvester K rancher
Smoot Clement E agt Beaumont Land & Water Co
Southern Pacific Co J B McCue agt
Stewart Emery R rancher
Stewart Regnor P rancher
Sullivan Jas S bkpr Gilbert-Dean Mercantile Co
Summit Hotel Mrs Katinka Bassler prop

RIVERSIDE COUNTY DIRECTORY 439

Swan Andrew rancher
Thomas Livingston S
Toutain Chas S lab
Toutain Lewis D emp S P Co
Twiss Chas C
United Presbyterian Church Rev H P Espy pastor
Veale Clinton A signal foremn S P Co
Waffle Melvin S rancher
Wallace David H rancher
Warren Herbert A poolroom
Warren Wilson B livery
Watson Chas H emp S P Co
Watson Wm justice of the peace
Watson Wm W apiarist
West Chas E
West Clarence E rancher
Whelan Mary tchr Beaumont Sch
Whitten S D firemn S P Co

BEAUMONT CLASSIFIED BUSINESS DIRECTORY

Apiarists
Bliss Frank
Watson W W

Barbers
Shore E M

Billiards and Pool
Warren H A

Blacksmiths
Frady U L

General Merchandise
Gilbert-Dean Mercantile Co
Gray J A

Hotels
Hotel Edinburgh
Summit Hotel

Livery Stables
Curler B H
Warren W B

Newspapers
Beaumont Independent

Real Estate
Beaumont Land & Water Co
Durgee L H
Gobin J M

Water Companies
Beaumont Land & Water Co

COACHELLA

Baker Jos P farmer
Beach Geo M farmer
Bell Walter H blksmith
Bird Frank C farmer
Black Chas A farmer
Caldwell Frank C oil and distillate
Cawthon Chas R farmer
Coachella Valley News C Paulsen Visal editor
Dillman Allen E engineer
Dillman Levi W farmer
Dilworth Albt E farmer
Dilworth John N farmer
Dudley Frank E meat mkt
DeuPree John T farmer
Estle Chas B constable
Goodrich Alvin E farmer
Goth Edwin A farmer
Goth Oscar A real est
Gridley C S farmer
Griffin Jas H engineer
Hall Chas L farmer
Hansen Neils C farmer
Hardison Franklin I farmer
Hayward A O poultry raiser
Hobbs Wm I farmer
Holeway F E farmer
HUNTINGTON GEORGE E postmaster and gen mdse
Hyde Claud N farmer
Ingraham Geo farmer
Jeffries C B & Co fruit growers and shippers
Lamb Horace G phys
Lolmaugh J M farmer
Lolmaugh J W farmer
Lolmaugh P C farmer
McCarroll Roy dep constable
McDonald Chas & Co gen mdse
Massingale Calvin F farmer
Mawby Chas E real est and notary
Metzler Chas L pool
Payne Jess B farmer
Payne Wm J farmer
Peterson Frank hotel
Rector Jason L mgr ice plant
Robertson Christopher C farmer
Robertson Jas R contr
Rose Homer D farmer

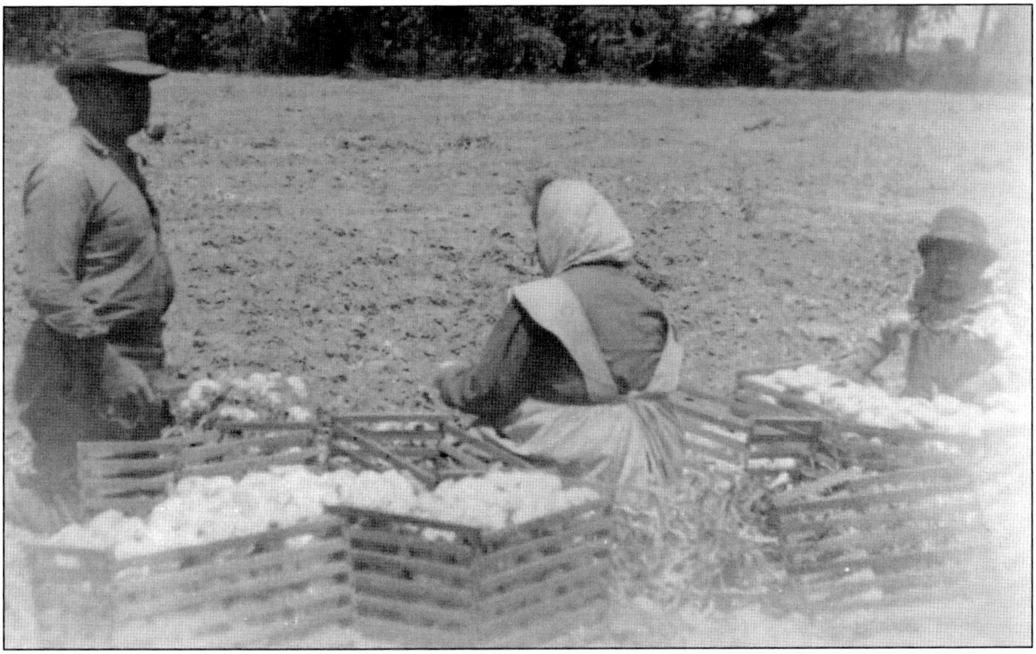

Juan Siva, his wife, and their daughter posed for the above photograph in 1925 while picking onions at the Proctor ranch in Coachella. The Siva family and other Cahuilla Indians were the first to settle in the Coachella Valley, hundreds of years before Europeans settled in the Americas. As the white settlers moved to the Coachella Valley, they often employed the local Desert Cahuilla on their ranches and farms and purchased Desert Cahuilla handmade items. Below, Desert Cahuilla Indian Mary Kintano teaches Coachella Valley High School students how to weave baskets in the Desert Cahuilla style as Mrs. August Tomas interprets for the students and school personnel. (Both, courtesy of the Coachella Valley History Museum.)

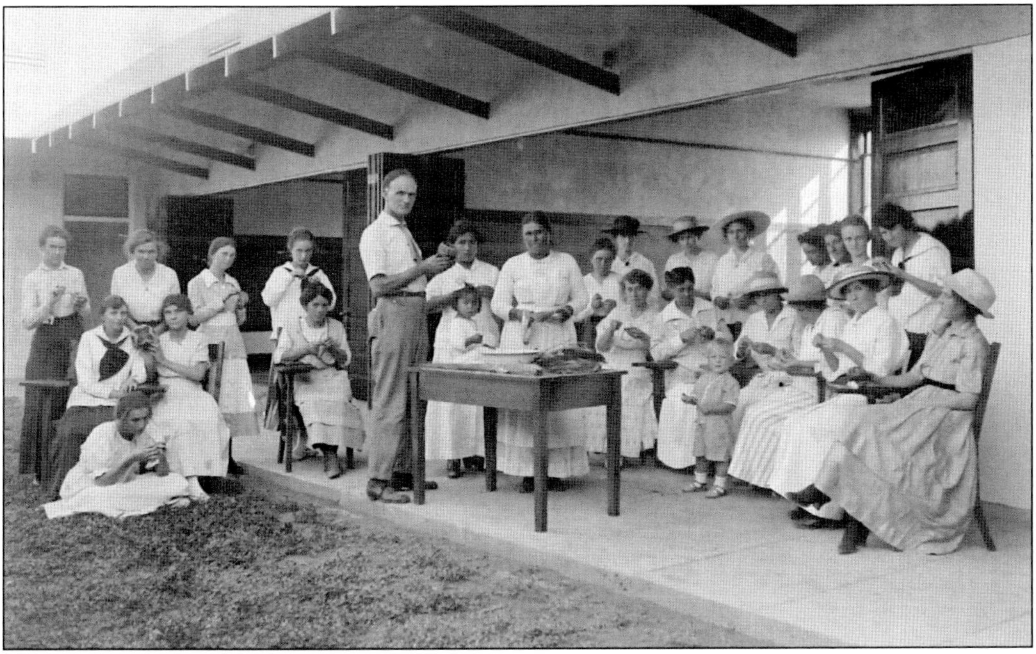

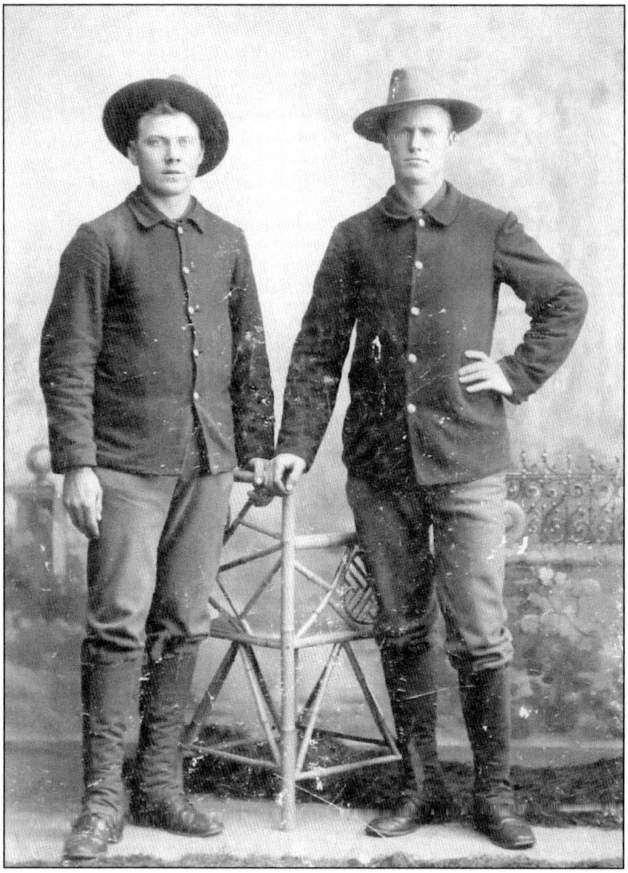

Otto (left) and Oscar Goth are shown in this 1897 portrait. The brothers moved to Coachella in 1897 where Otto "Ed" and his wife ran a hotel on Seventh Street. Oscar, also called "Buck," was a well digger. Their jobs were part of the early development of Coachella from a barren desert to the agricultural industry of today. (Courtesy of the Coachella Valley History Museum.)

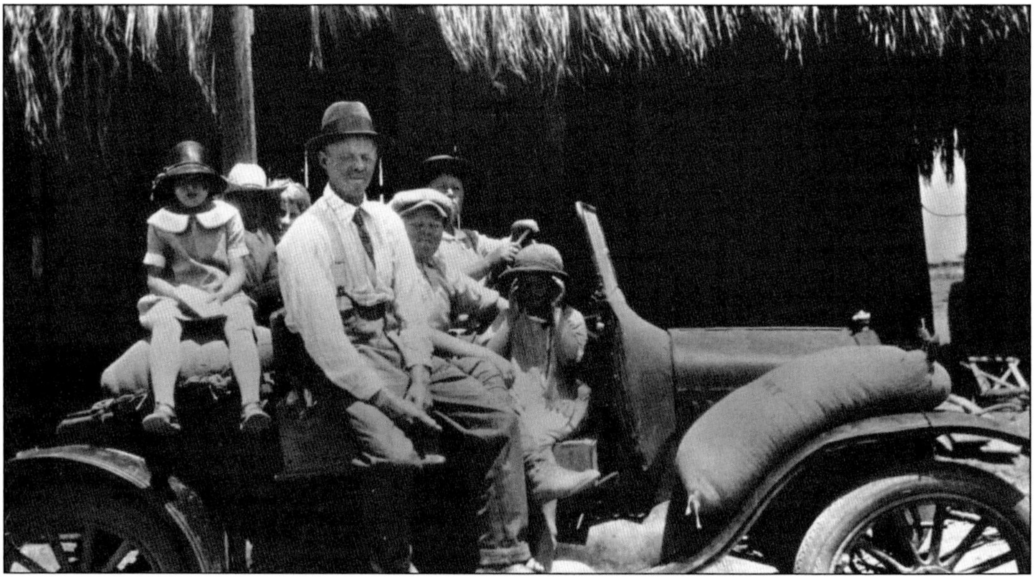

Squinting in the intense desert sun, the Leach family is shown here in 1916 posing on their vehicle. Standing or sitting still long enough for a photograph under the unforgiving sun was no easy task during this time. (Courtesy of the Coachella Valley Water District.)

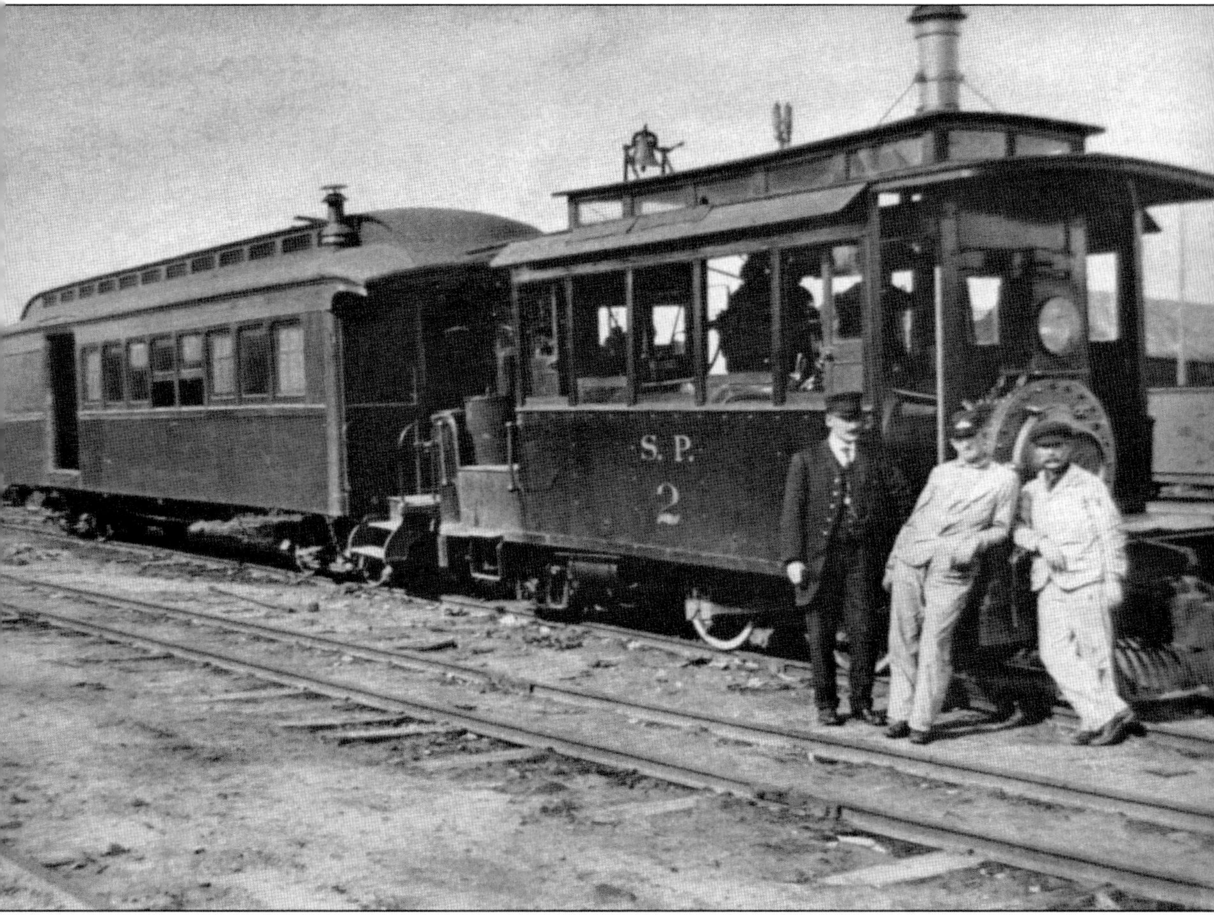

The development of the Southern Pacific railway through the Coachella Valley drew many settlers into the southern part of the Colorado Desert known as the Coachella Valley. Many settlers worked for the railroad or developed businesses such as hotels or farms that depended on the railroad and its workers. The conductor and two train employees (most likely the engineers) lean against Southern Pacific Engine No. 2 as they pose for this early 1900s photograph. The Southern Pacific Railroad Company established the Indio train depot as it built a line from Yuma, Arizona, to Los Angeles. Indio was the midway point between the two cities, so a depot was built there. Steam engines would replenish their water supply there, and the passengers could venture out to explore the depot, which boasted a restaurant and an area where people could lie down and relax. (Courtesy of the Coachella Valley Water District.)

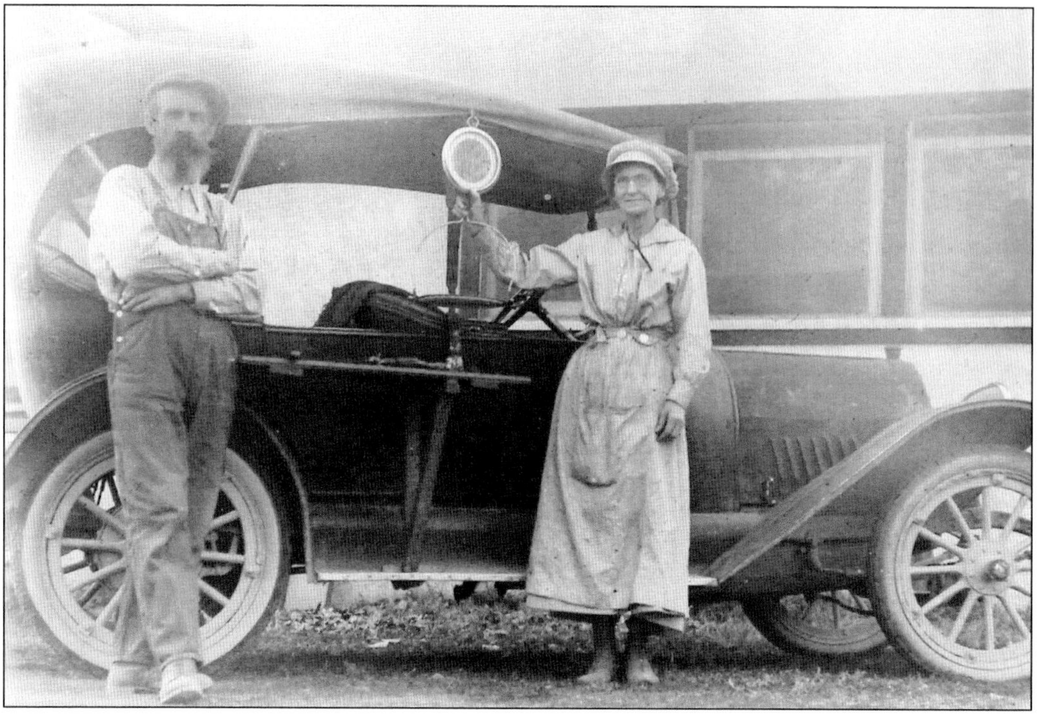

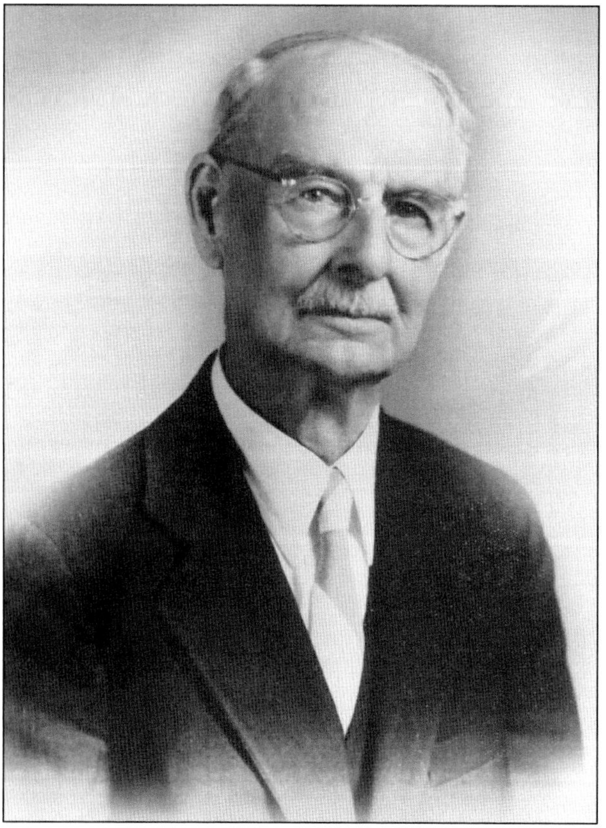

Henry W. and Margaret McKay used their 1913 Chevrolet to deliver meat to residents in the Coachella Valley, pictured here in 1919. The service provided by the McKays allowed families to purchase meat without having to travel to the store, since settlers often lived spread out. Henry McKay is credited with naming the main streets in the Coachella Valley after US presidents. (Courtesy of the Coachella Valley History Museum.)

This early 1900s portrait of Harry A. Westerfield was taken in Coachella. Westerfield was a cofounder of the First National Bank in Coachella. He also participated in the early city government; today, there is a street in Coachella bearing his name. (Courtesy of the Coachella Valley History Museum.)

The photograph at right shows Coachella Valley High School students Fern Draper and Arthur M. Westerfield in 1915. Westerfield's father, Harry Westerfield, and uncle John M. Westerfield founded the First National Bank of Coachella in 1912. In the early 1900s, a first bank was established but was later destroyed in a fire. As retold by John W. Westerfield, a second bank opened, but the two bank owners robbed the wooden vault of its contents and left. Arthur M. Westerfield, pictured below, also worked for the family bank. In December 1946, the town of Coachella became an incorporated city, and Arthur Westerfield's brother John W. Westerfield became the mayor. He continued as mayor until April 1950. (Right, courtesy of the Coachella Valley Water District; below, courtesy of the Coachella Valley History Museum.)

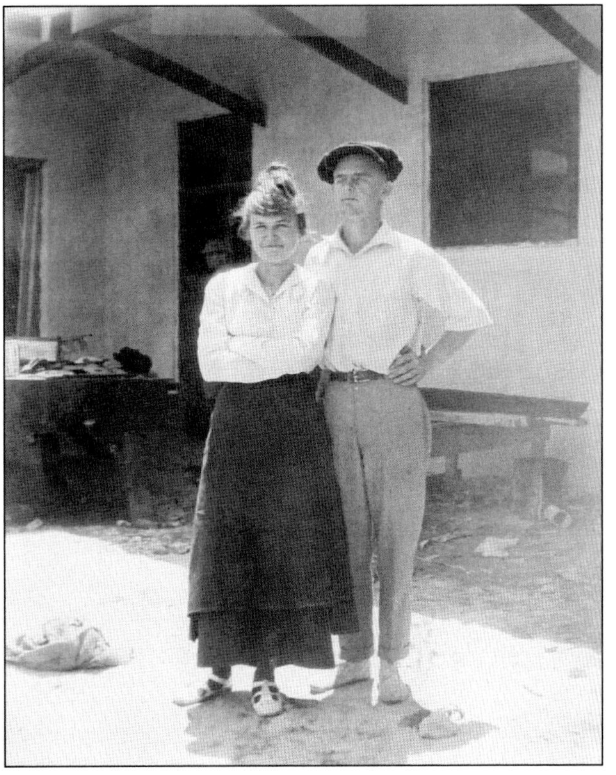

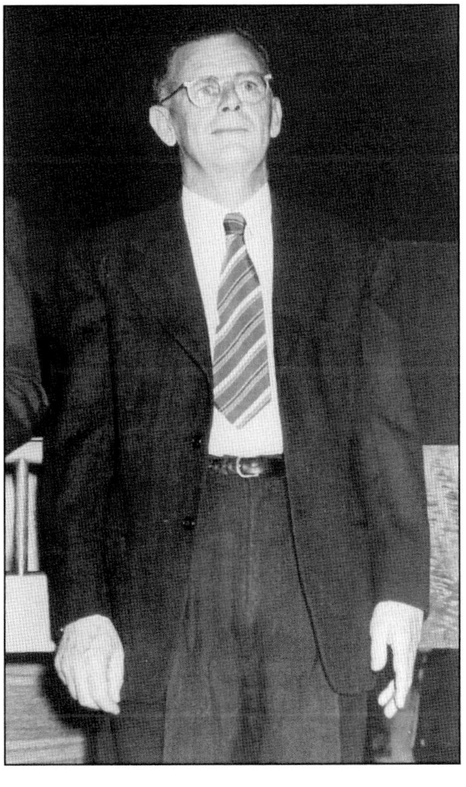

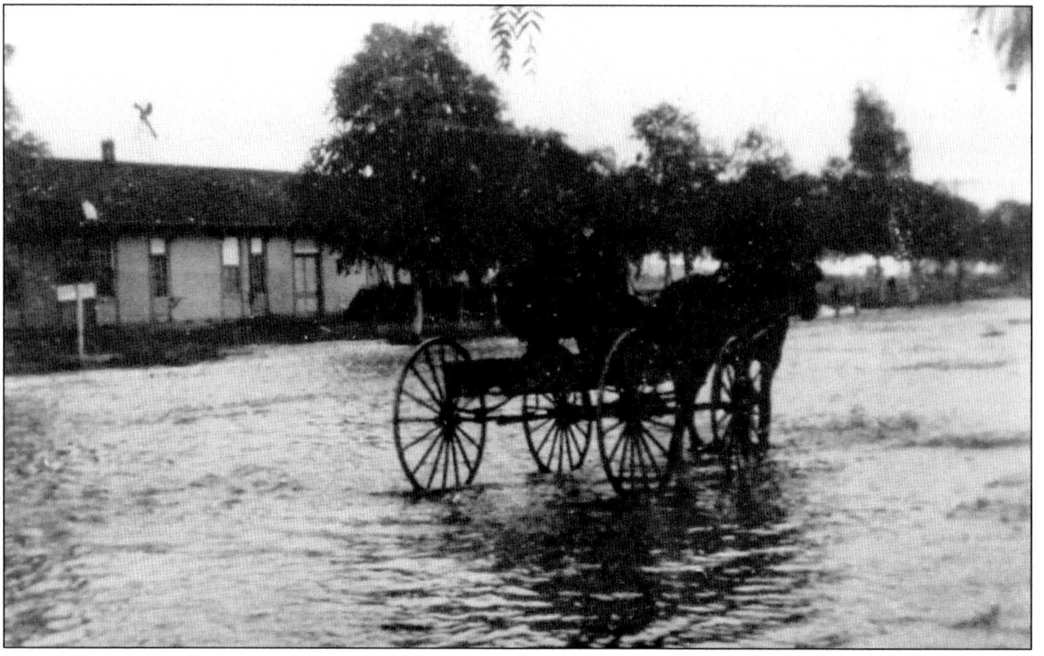

This 1908 photograph shows Highway 99 in Coachella. A man is driving a wagon through flooded streets. The 1908 flood was one of many that Coachella residents dealt with. The desert soil was unable to absorb large amounts of rain or runoff coming from the surrounding mountains. (Courtesy of the Coachella Valley History Museum.)

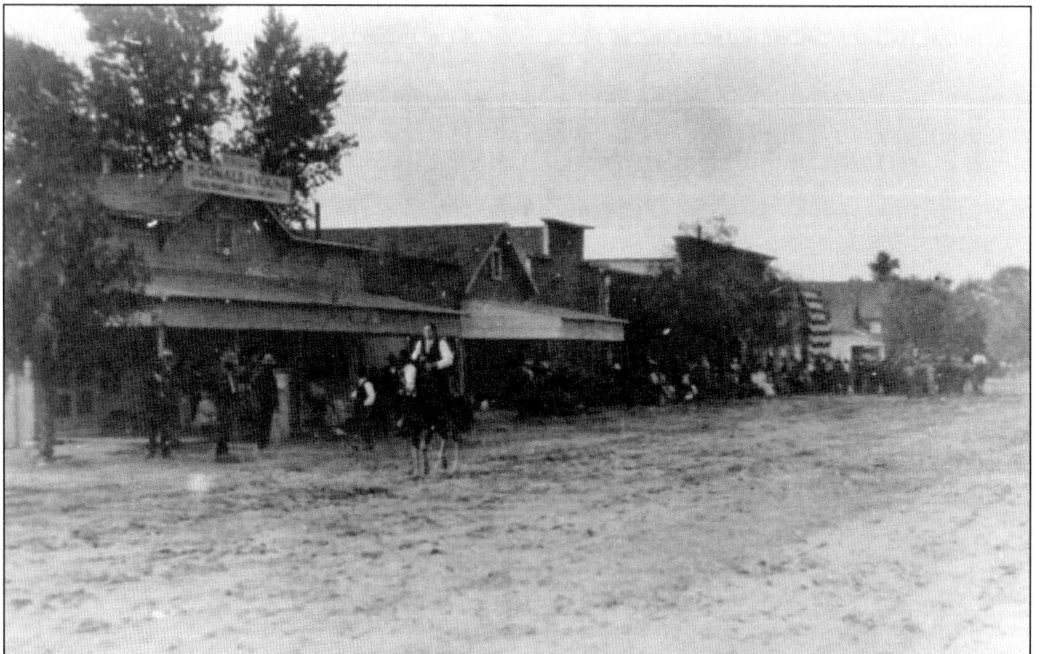

The people of Coachella came together to celebrate Christmas with a parade in 1909. Community efforts like this parade provided a time for residents to socialize when they otherwise were busy tending to ranches and farms. (Courtesy of the Coachella Valley History Museum.)

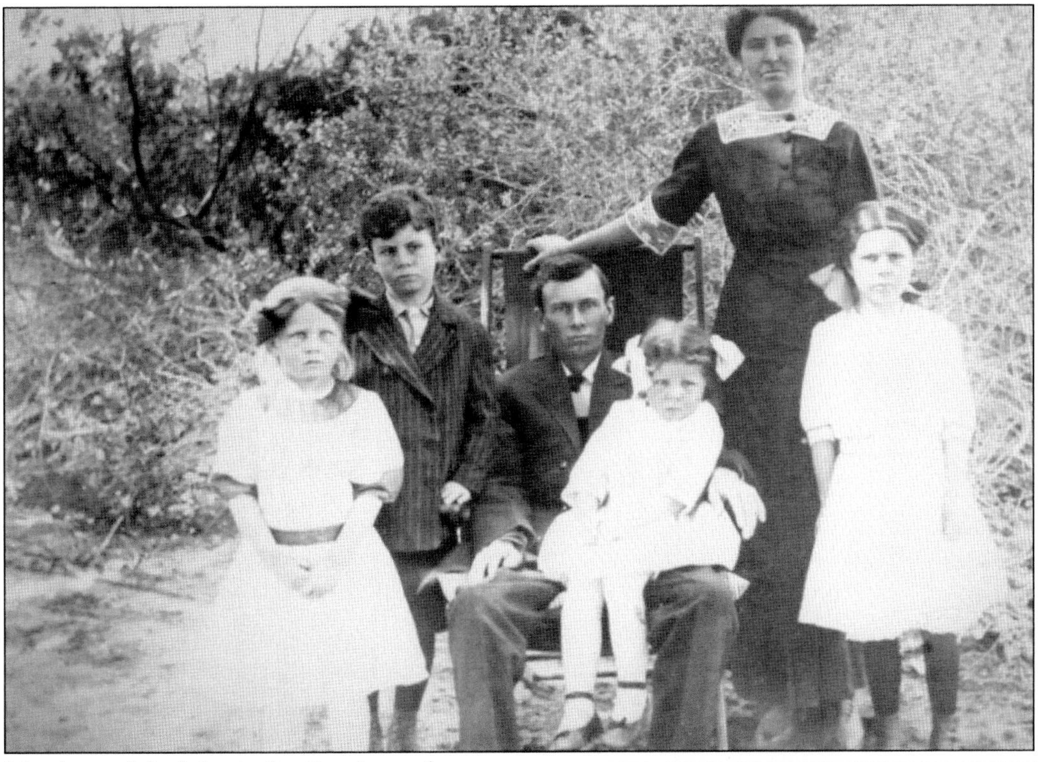

Members of the Martin family, pictured above in 1920, are, from left to right, Edith Martin, Bryant Martin, Mr. Martin, Thelma Martin, Mrs. Martin, and Ethel Mae Martin. As with many families, the Martins dressed in their best clothes for the photograph. In a time when owning many clothes was a luxury, people often had one outfit for dressy occasions, while the rest of their clothing was for everyday use. The photograph at right was taken in 1928 on the Proctor ranch. The women are from the local bridge club. (Above, courtesy of the Coachella Valley Water District; right, courtesy of the Coachella Valley History Museum.)

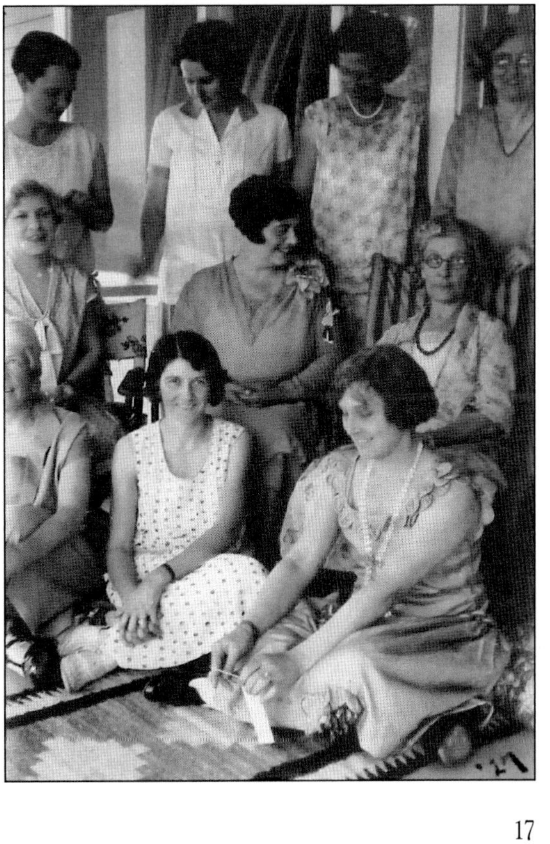

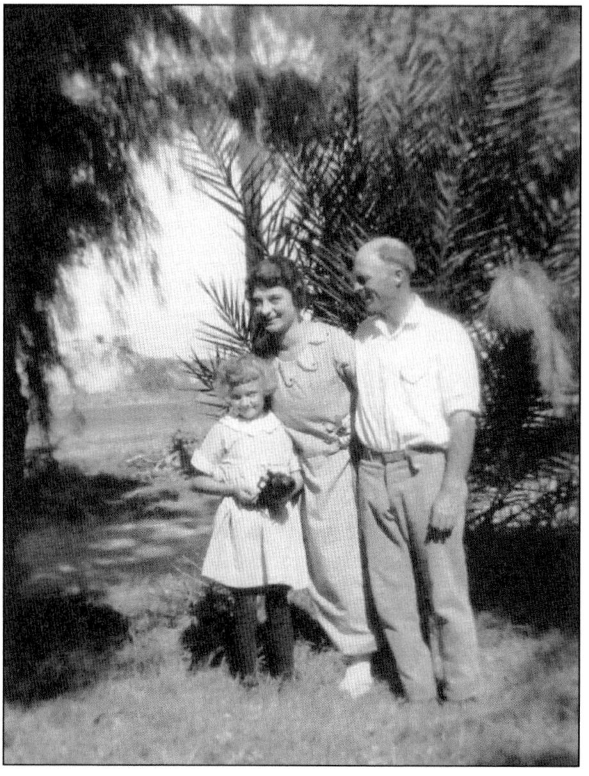

The Proctor family was made up of prominent Coachella ranchers. Pictured at left are, from left to right, Margaret, Grace, and Hugh Proctor. The February 1924 photograph was taken on the Proctor ranch. Margaret Proctor, shown in the 1927 photograph below, would later marry Dr. John Tyler, who became the local dentist. According to Margaret Proctor Tyler, it was love at first sight when she and John Tyler met. The Tylers purchased a house in Indio from the Smiley family, and in 1984, the City of Indio purchased the house from the Tyler family. The Smiley-Tyler house is now part of the Coachella Valley History Museum campus. (Both, courtesy of the Coachella Valley History Museum.)

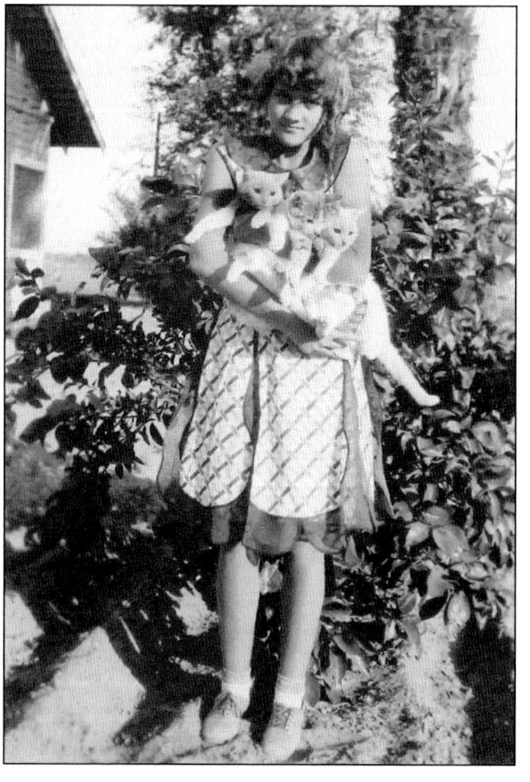

Two

Communities in a Harsh Land

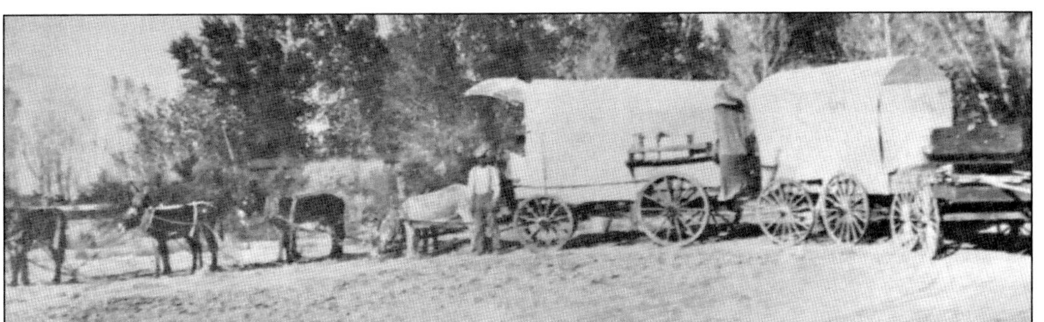

The early mode of arrival for settlers required traveling by wagon, as seen here. Travel by wagon was treacherous. People traveled through areas where there was no help available if there were an emergency. Once settlers arrived, there was little to no infrastructure, which meant they had to dig a water well and build their homes. (Courtesy of the Coachella Valley Water District.)

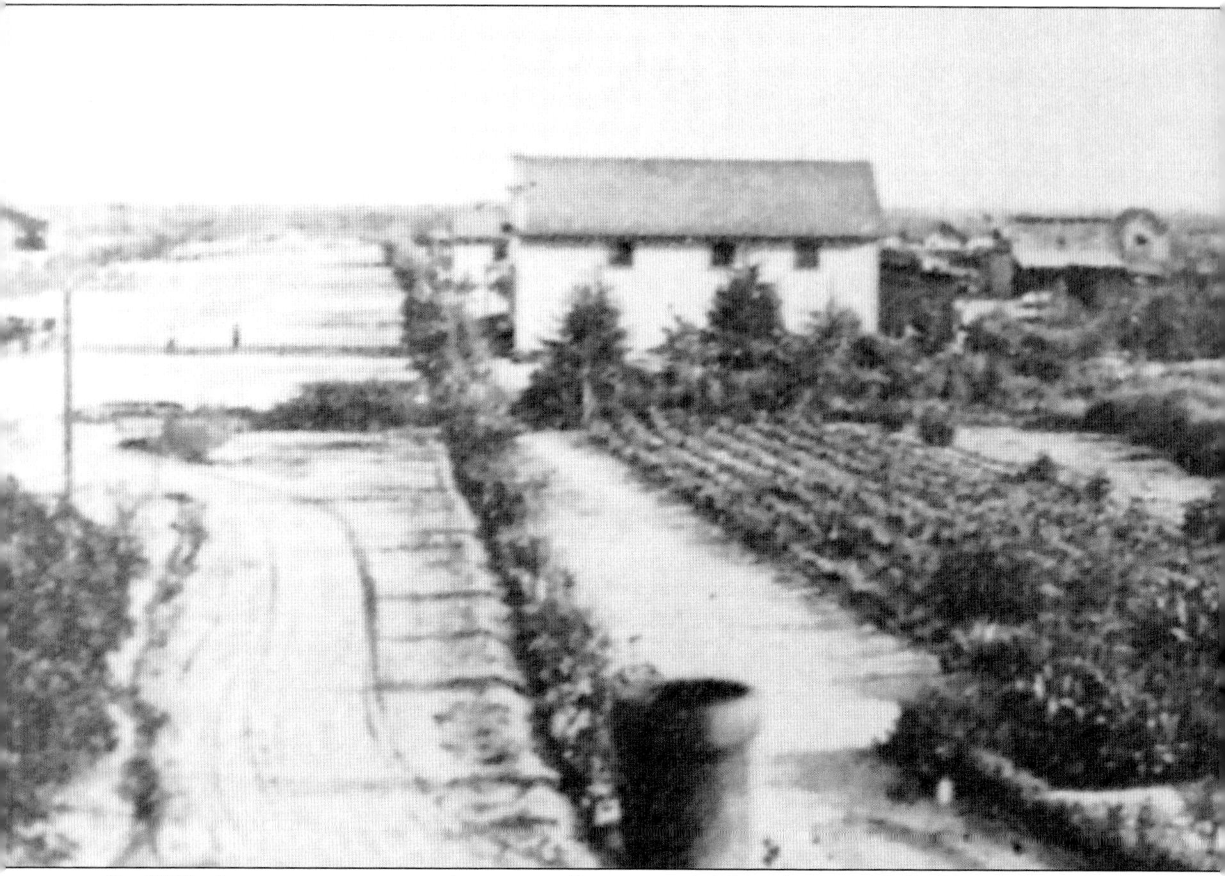

By 1903, the town was growing but was still very rural. This photograph looks south on Front Street (now Grapefruit Boulevard) in the center of Coachella. The well dug in 1900 by town founder Jason L. Rector and his brother Lon B. Rector is in the center of Grapefruit Boulevard.

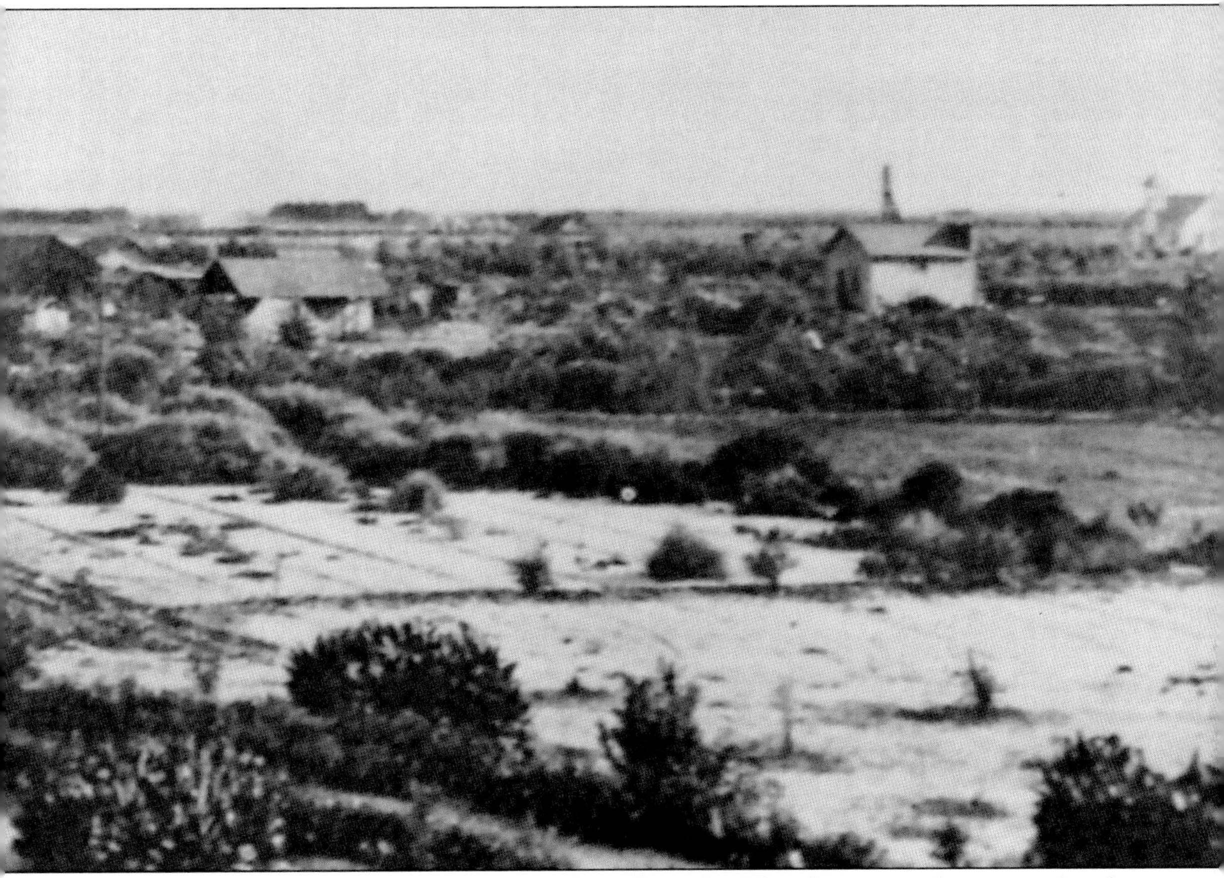

The first school in Coachella is also visible at far right. The change in the geographical landscape from an arid desert to an agricultural town had begun. (Courtesy of the Coachella Valley Water District.)

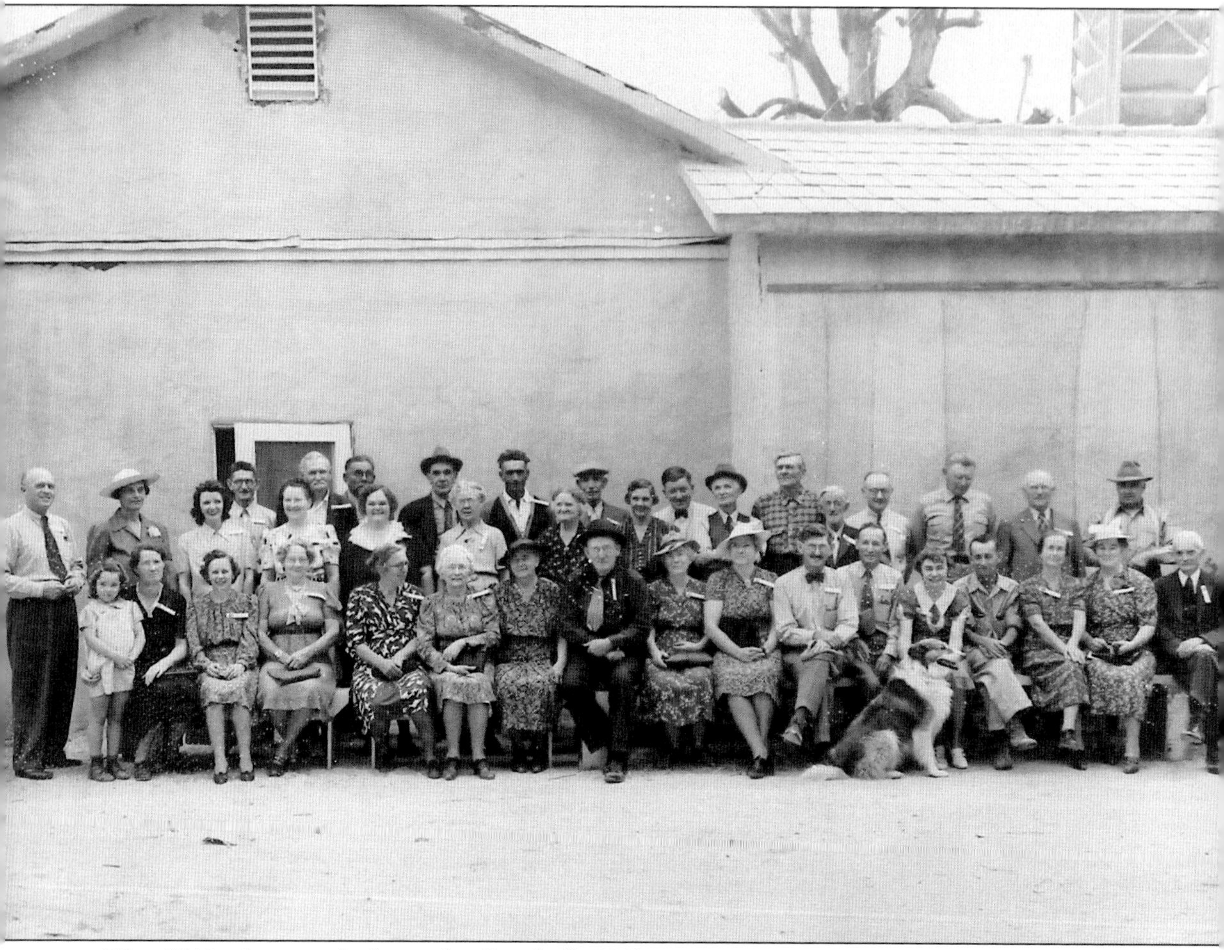

This 1940s photograph shows the Coachella Valley Pioneer's Society, of which valley resident George White was a member. He is believed to be in the back row, fifth from the left. White recounted a Woodspur town meeting in the summer of 1901 that he attended with his parents; the meeting was regarding changing the town name from Woodspur. There are varying accounts about who suggested the name Conchilla, which means "little shells" in Spanish. Some sources report town founder Jason L. Rector made the suggestion after declining the honor of having the town named Rector after him. Others report that early Indio resident, Southern Pacific Railroad man, and merchantman Albert G. Tingman recommended the name. Regardless of how the name came about, the people of Woodspur voted, and Conchilla was filed on the prospectus papers with the printer; however, at the printer's shop, the name was misread and filed as Coachella, which had no meaning in any language. The townspeople, after discovering the mistake, decided to not pursue changing the name, and the town became Coachella. (Courtesy of the Coachella Valley History Museum.)

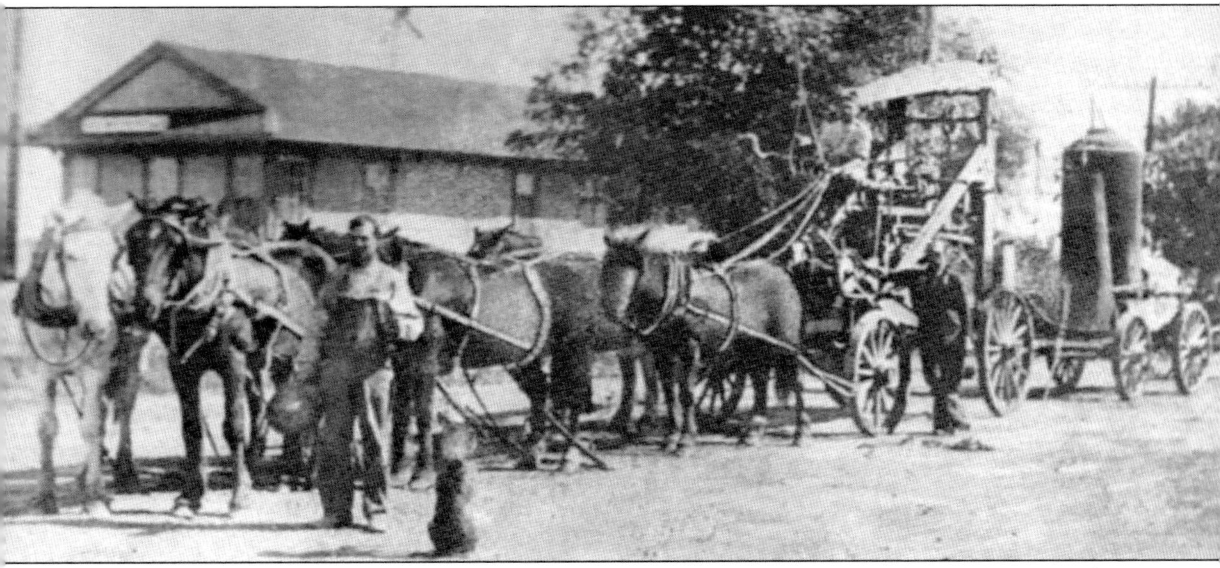

This early 1900s photograph was taken on Front Street in Coachella. Note the Southern Pacific depot in the background. The horse-drawn steam well drill shown is how early non–Native American settlers dug water wells. This horse team and drill belonged to C.B. Estel, an early resident. The well dug by Jason L. Rector and his brother took a reported eight months to complete. During this time, the water table in the Coachella Valley was fairly close to the surface, making most wells fairly shallow. In this arid desert surrounded by mountains, having a nearby sustainable water source was an absolute necessity. Prior to settlement, the Native Americans (the Cahuilla Indians) in the Coachella Valley dug water wells using the help of wood and stone implements. The Cahuilla were master well diggers—often digging walk-in water wells with sloping ramps or stairs going into the well. All of that was done without steam or metal instruments in the sandy, desert soil. (Courtesy of the Coachella Valley History Museum.)

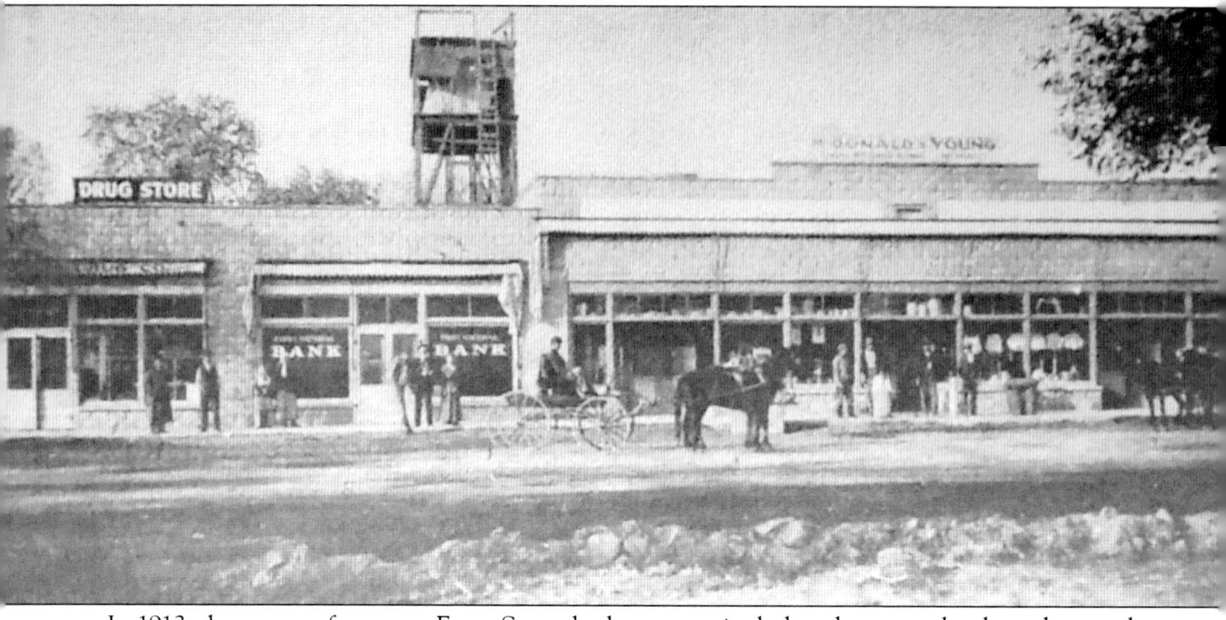

In 1913, the center of town on Front Street had grown to include a drugstore, bank, and general store. Horse-drawn wagons were still the primary mode of transportation for most residents. The drugstore was owned by Dr. English, and later by Dr. Schwartz. The bank pictured is the First National Bank of Coachella, and to the right was where the first Coachella Valley County Water District offices where. The McDonald & Young business was the general store, as well as the hardware and implement store. Front Street was renamed Cantaloupe, and in the 1970s it became Grapefruit Boulevard. These buildings still stand today. (Courtesy of the Coachella Valley Water District.)

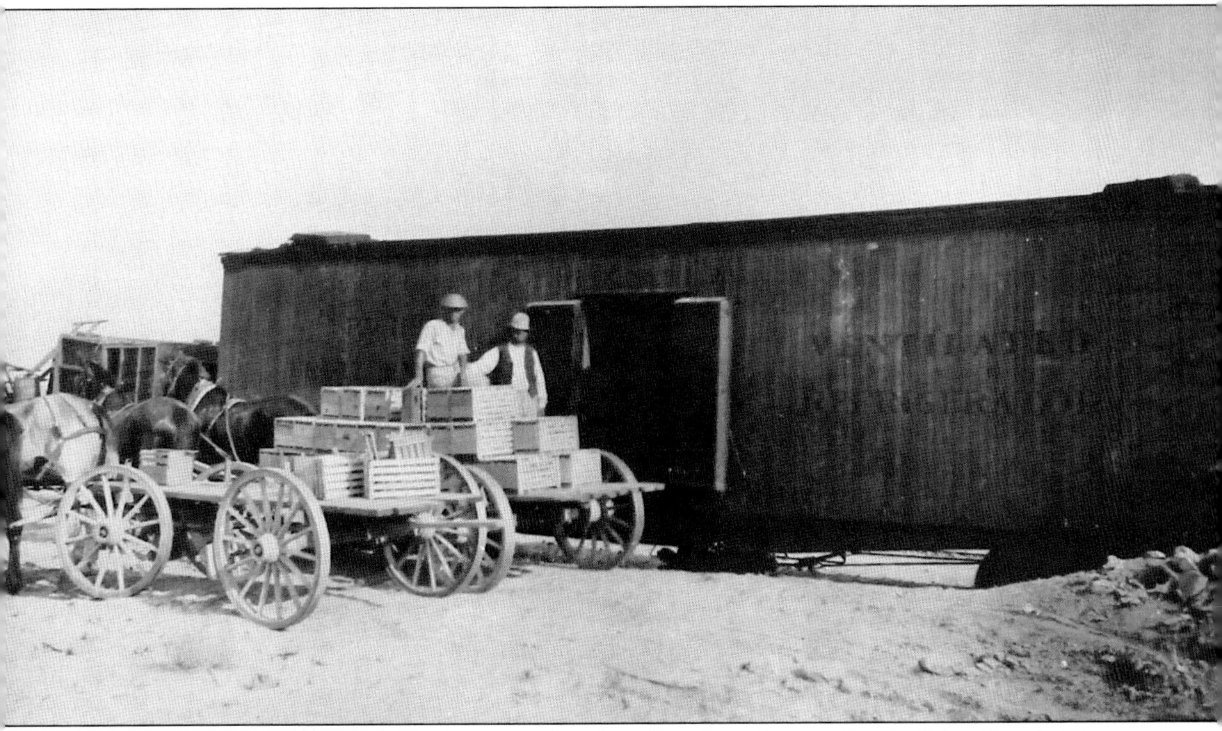

Workers are pictured loading onions into a Southern Pacific railcar at Coachella's railroad siding in the early 1900s. As clearing opened up the area to settlement and agriculture, Jason L. Rector surveyed the area, and with the help of his brother Lon B. Rector, dug the first artesian water well in the Coachella area. Once people heard of the available water supply, they settled in the area. By 1901, the town name was changed to Coachella, and the townsite officially recorded. The Southern Pacific train station in Indio, on the west of Coachella, was the primary location where people arrived and exited the Coachella Valley, whereas the Coachella siding was where goods, such as the local agricultural products, were loaded onto the train. (Courtesy of the Coachella Valley History Museum.)

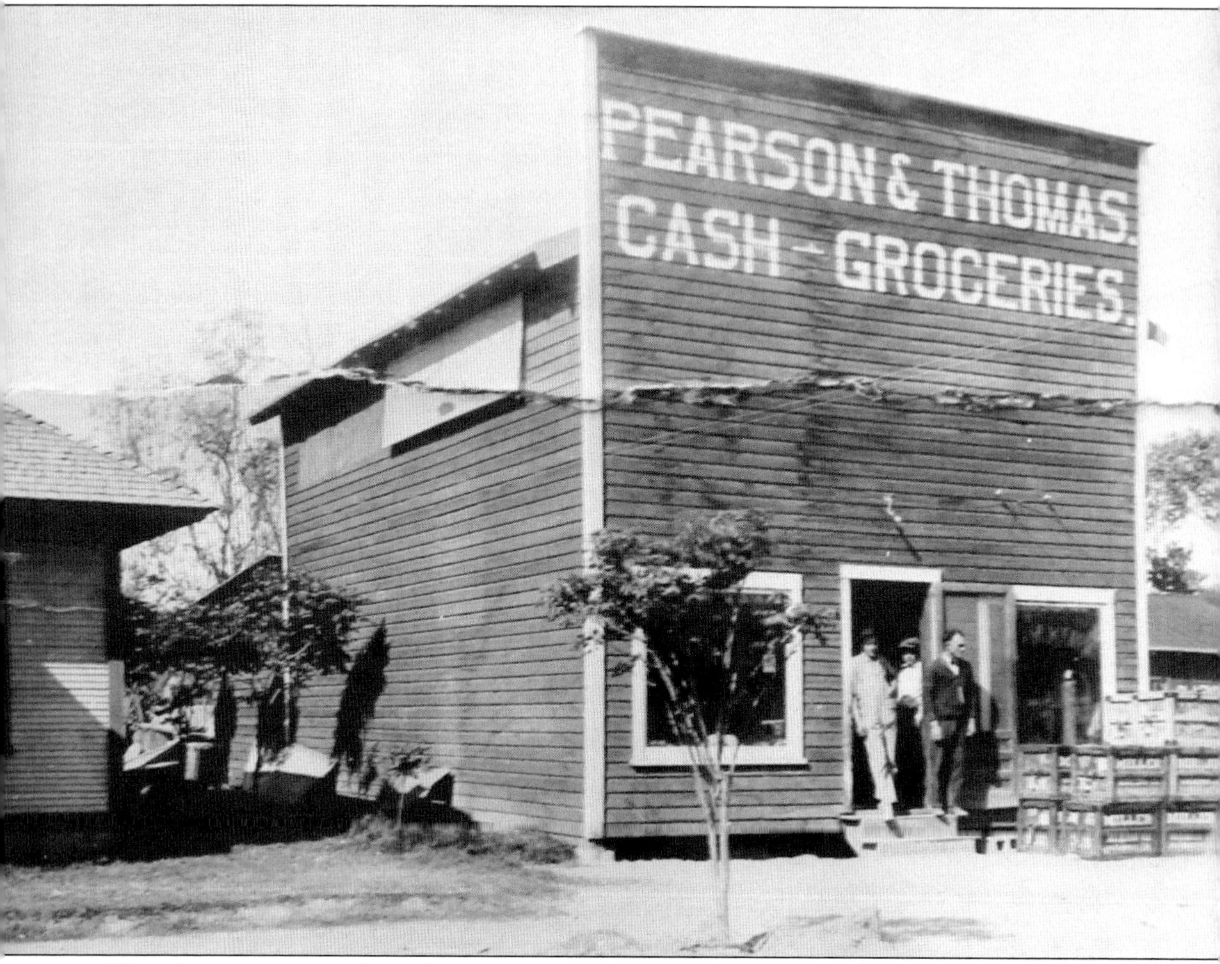

This photograph was taken after the Pearson & Thomas Store opened in 1917. Residents could get their cash and groceries there. The Pearson family was one of the influential families in the early development of Coachella. This store, like many of the early stores, carried a variety of items and often offered various services. (Courtesy of the Coachella Valley History Museum.)

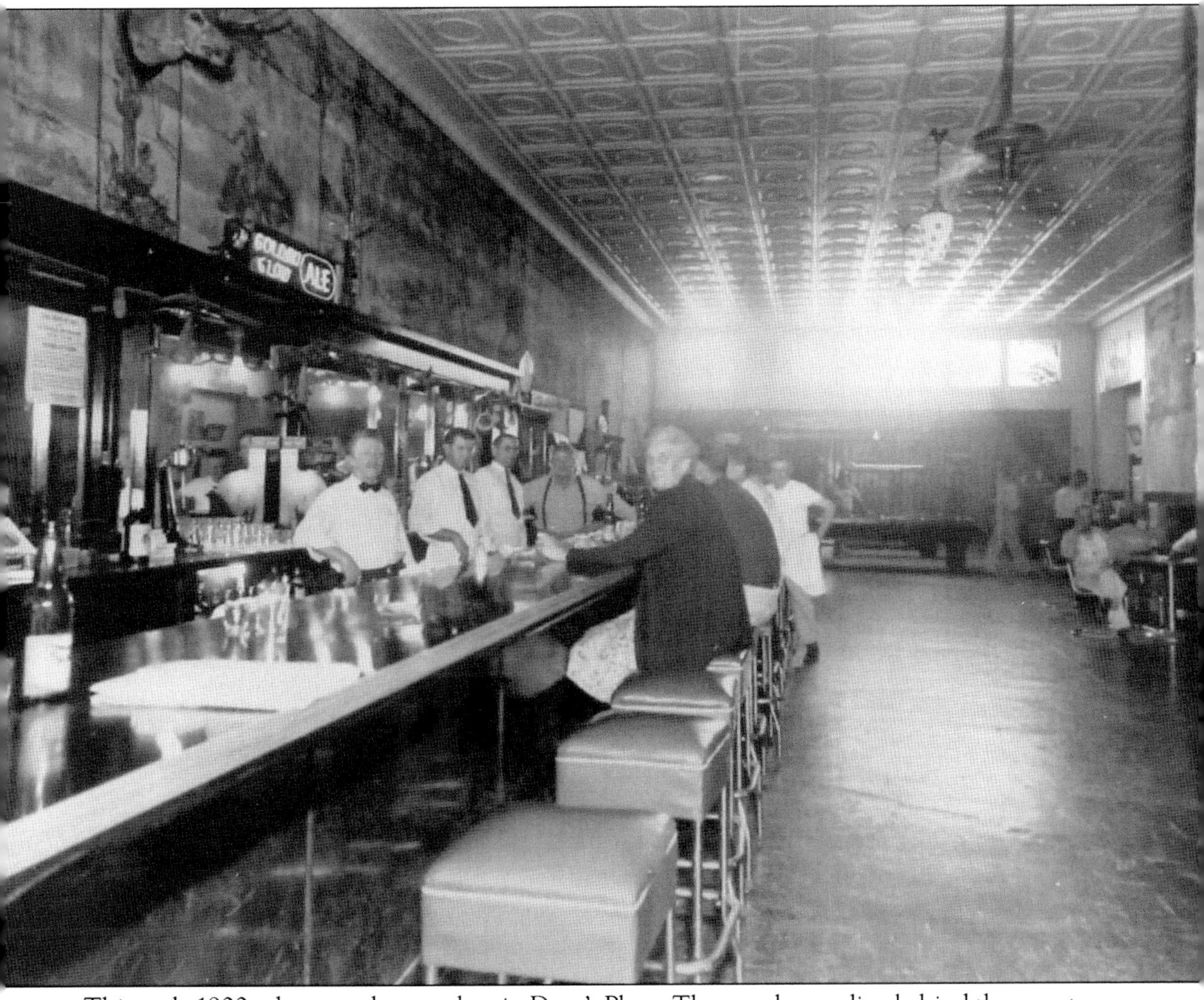

This early 1900s photograph was taken in Dave's Place. The people standing behind the counter are, from left to right, Charley Estel, "Mutt" Bullard, unidentified, and Dave Estel. The customers are unidentified. The ceiling tiles are similar to those found in the Indio train depot and the 1909 Indio Schoolhouse. (Courtesy of the Coachella Valley Water District.)

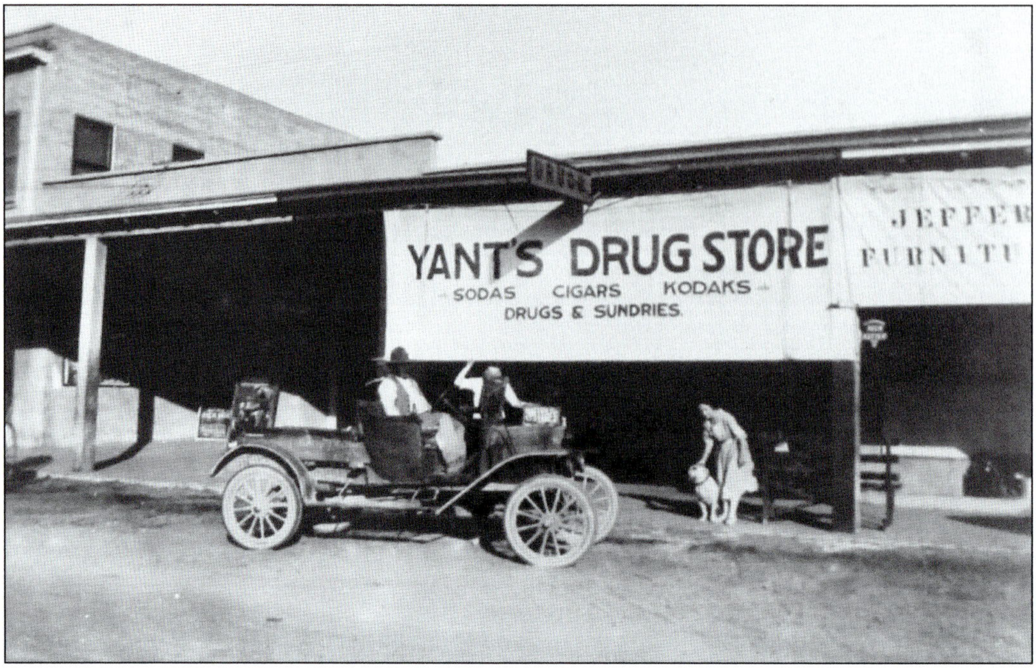

Yant's Drugstore featured retail merchandise and was also a place for residents to get sodas while they shopped. This was often a treat for the children, who did not have movie theaters, malls, or other such entertainment. The above photograph shows the outside of the store, while the interior is shown below. The people pictured below are, from left to right, Nickloas Lopez, unidentified, and W.E. Yant. As the town developed, more retail businesses opened, providing services and products beyond just the necessities. (Both, courtesy of the Coachella Valley Water District.)

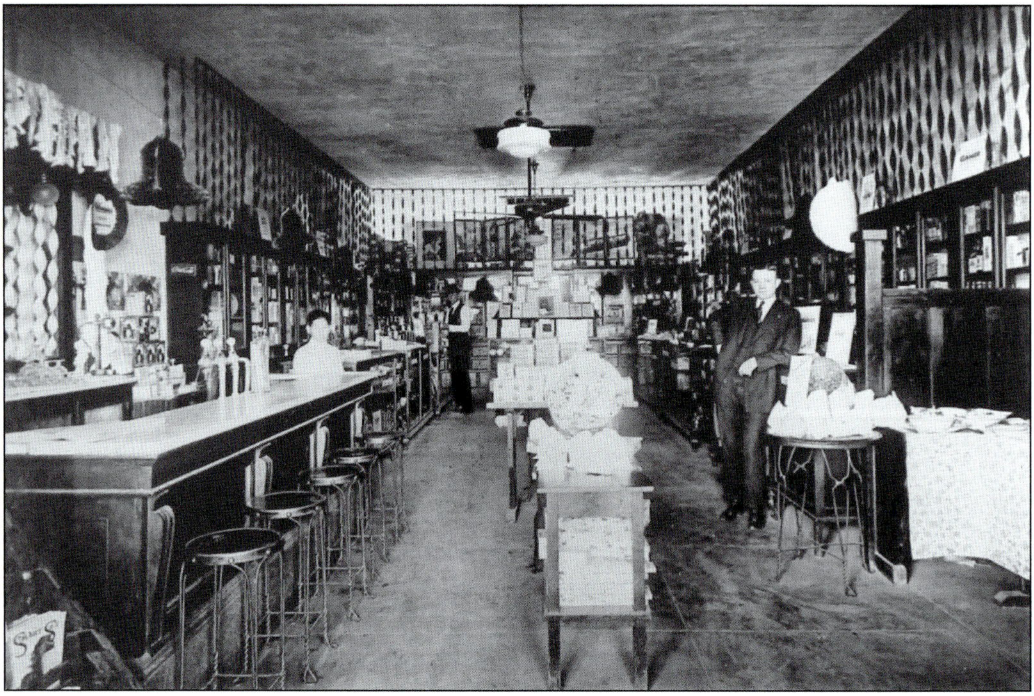

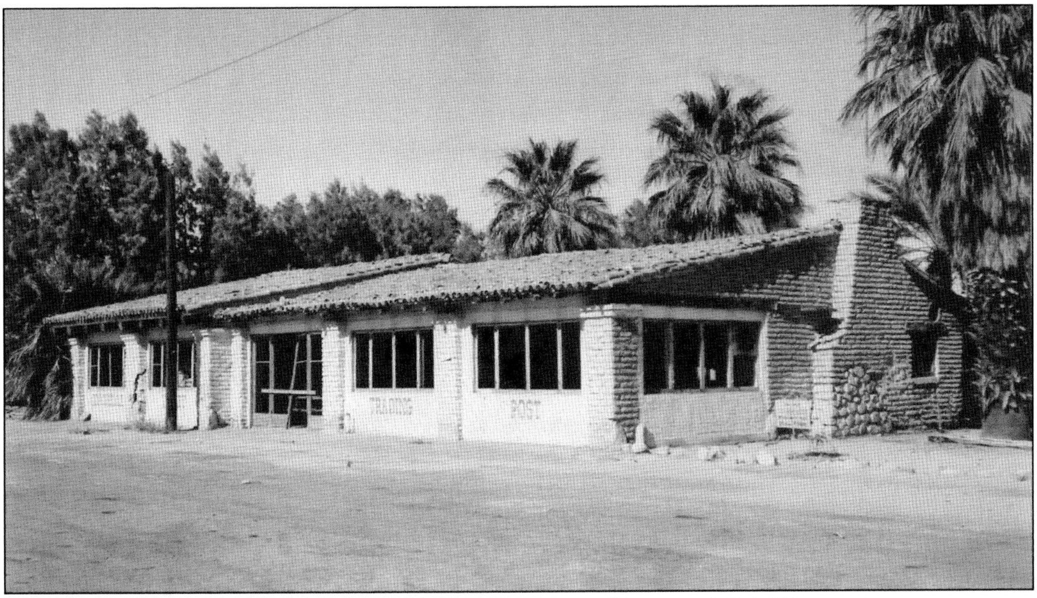

Kenneth Peck built the Coachella Trading Post, pictured here in 1926. This trading post was on Highway 99 (now known as Harrison Street) when this picture was taken in early 1926. Local residents enjoyed the trading post's recreation center and public swimming pool. Until the 1950s, this was the only public swimming pool. (Courtesy of the *Indio Daily News*.)

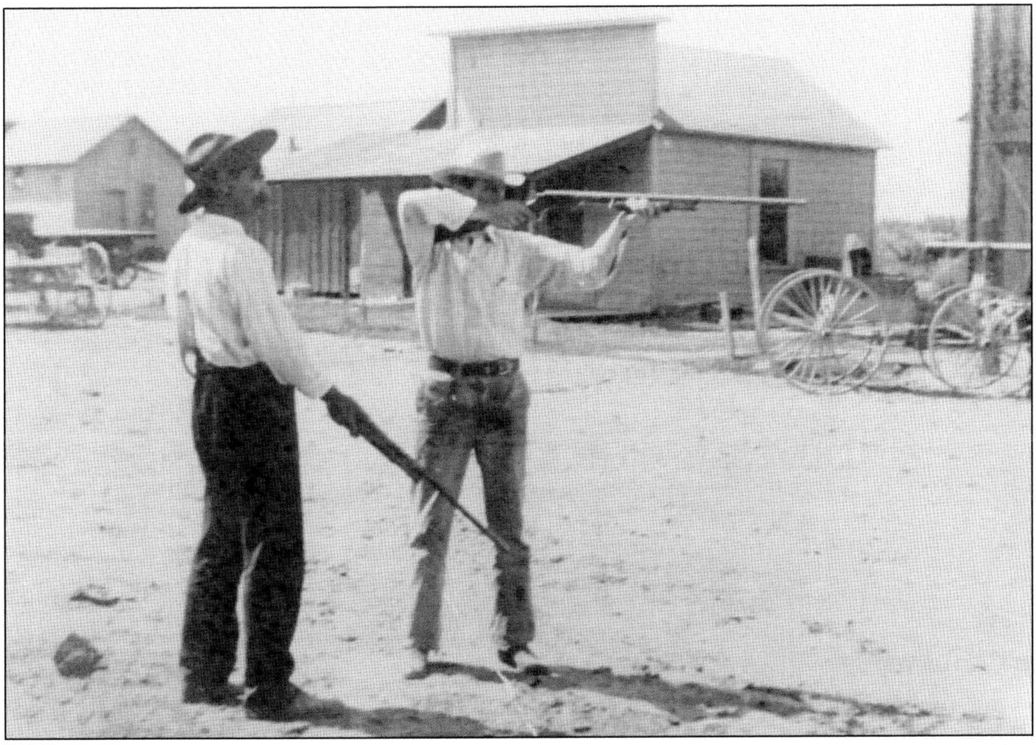

Charlie Estel (left) and E. Roderick are shooting their shotguns in the middle of the street in this photograph taken in 1902, long before many of the firearms rules and regulations were passed. (Courtesy of the Coachella Valley History Museum.)

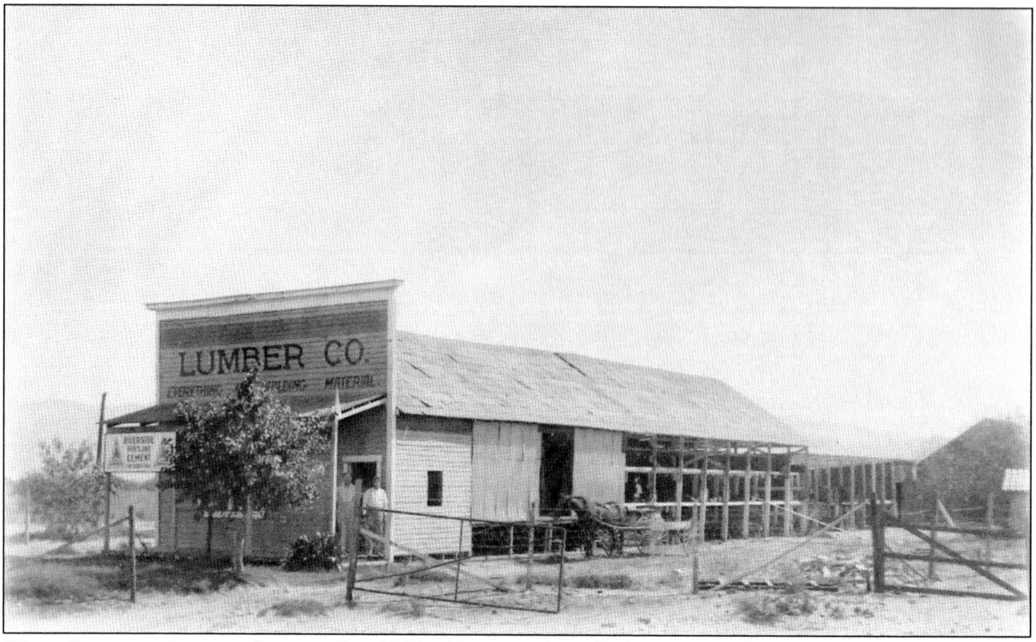

This photograph was taken in the 1910s. Two unidentified men are shown in front of Hayward Lumber Company. This early business was one of the few places new arrivals could get products for building their houses and other structures. (Courtesy of the Coachella Valley History Museum.)

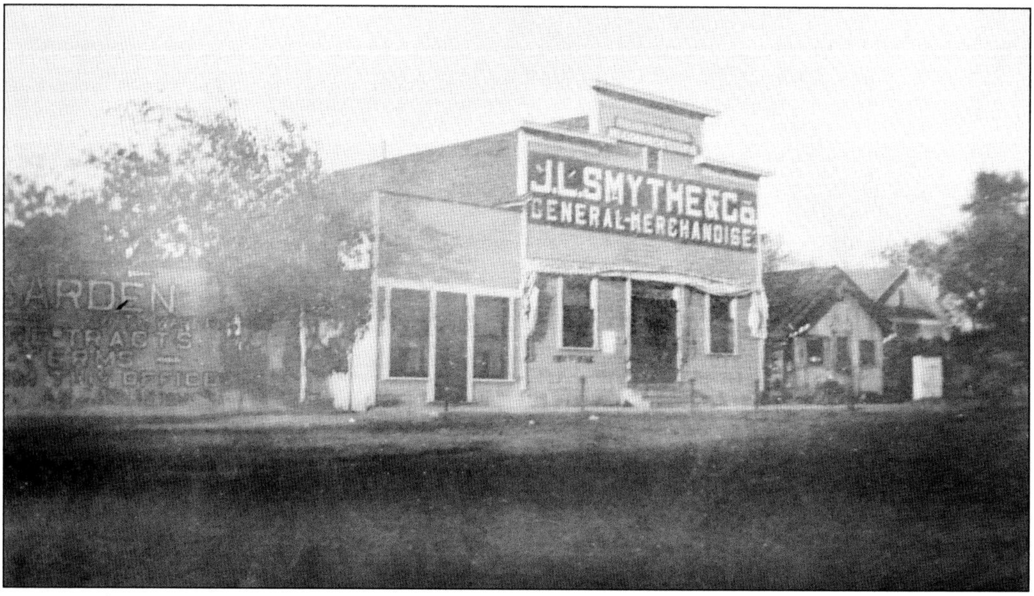

J.L. Smythe & Company was a general merchandise store in Coachella. This photograph was taken in the early 1900s. To the left of the store is a sign pointing to the small building next door. The sign advertises lots with water for sale at this office. (Courtesy of the Coachella Valley History Museum.)

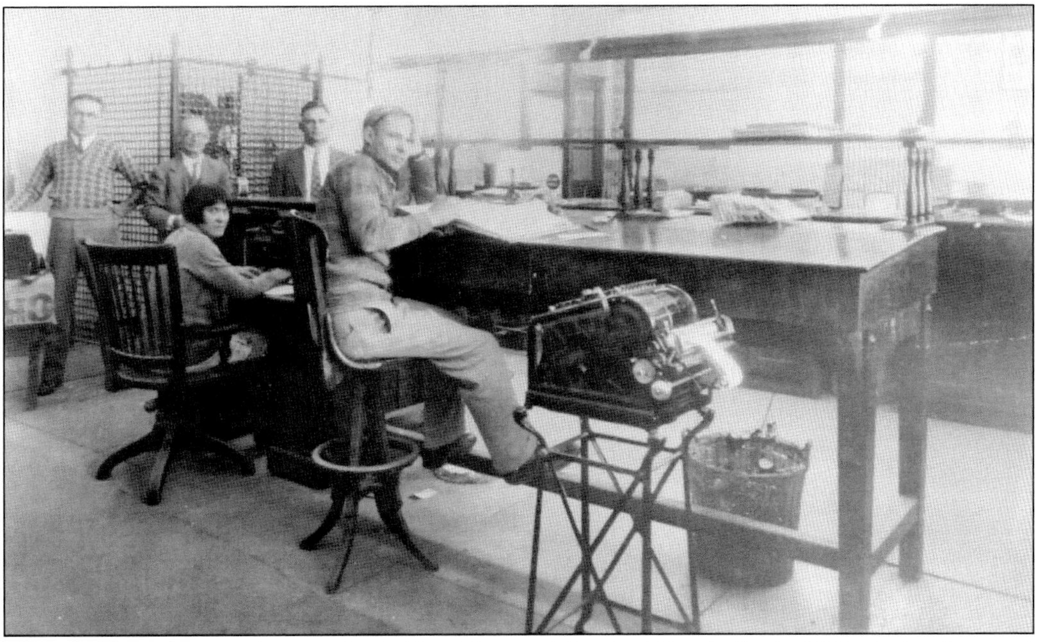

This photograph was taken inside the First National Bank of Coachella. In 1920, the bank moved to this building, then on Sixth Street and Vine Avenue, from its original location on Front Street. The bank would move once more, to the building shown below on Orchard Avenue and Sixth Street, in 1948. It merged with Valley Independent Bank in 1992. In 2002, Valley Independent merged with Rabobank, and the Rabobank in Coachella still resides in the same building on Orchard Avenue and Sixth Street. Lopes Hardware currently occupies the building on the corner of Sixth Street and Vine Avenue. (Both, courtesy of the Coachella Valley History Museum.)

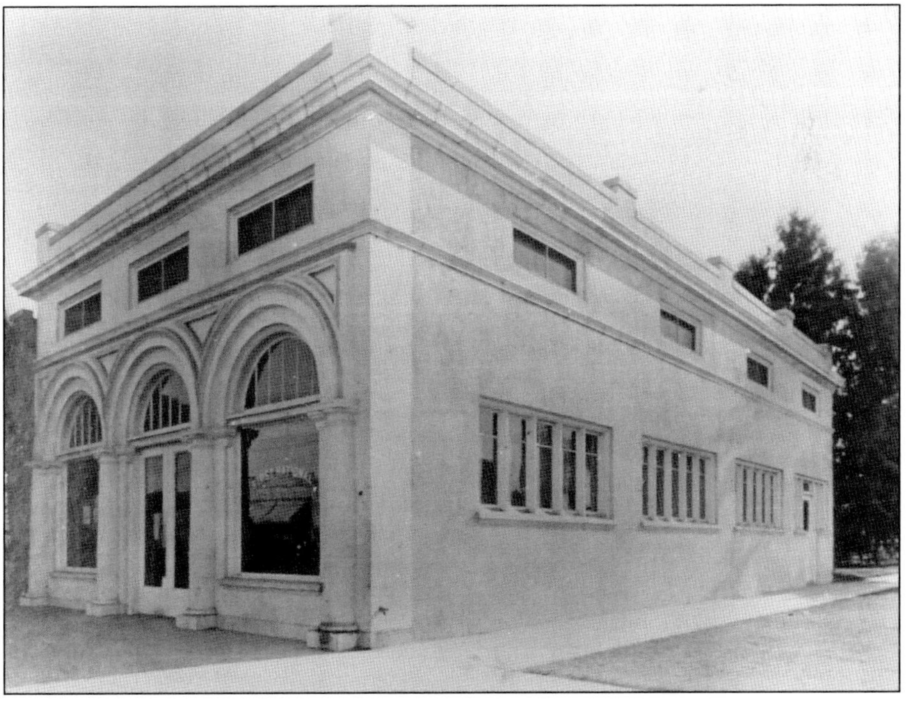

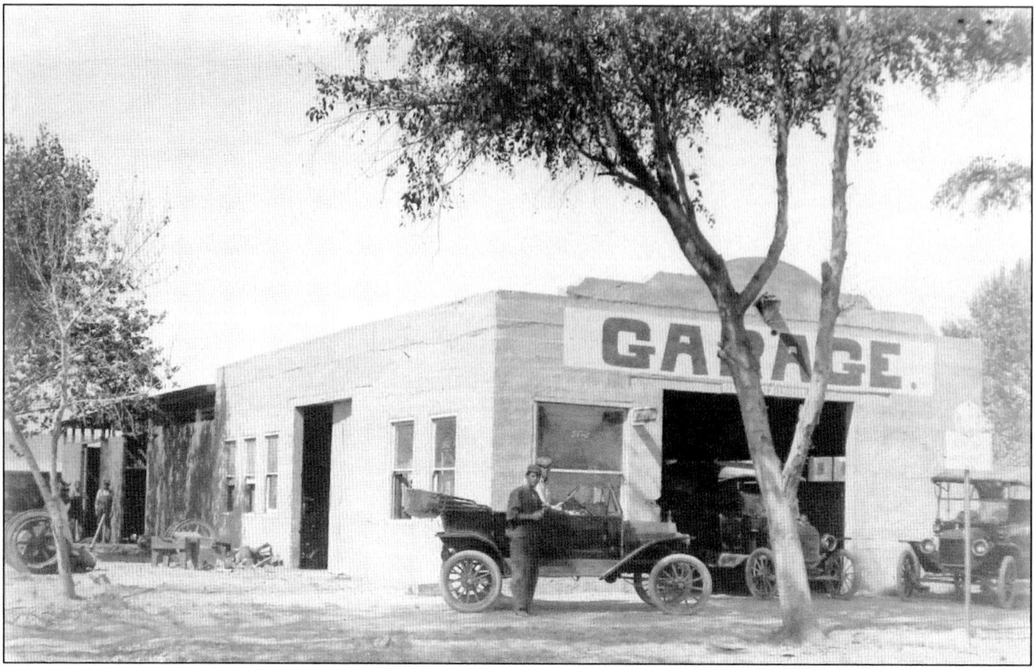

As vehicles became more affordable and popular, garages, like the one shown above, became common in towns and cities. This was originally George Phelps's garage and was later sold to a man named Eddie. It was located next to the Covalda Date Packinghouse. Pictured below in 1926 is the Triangle Service Station, which was off of the state highway. In the background is the Covalda Date Packinghouse, and at center right is the Eddie James Restaurant. (Both, courtesy of the Coachella Valley History Museum.)

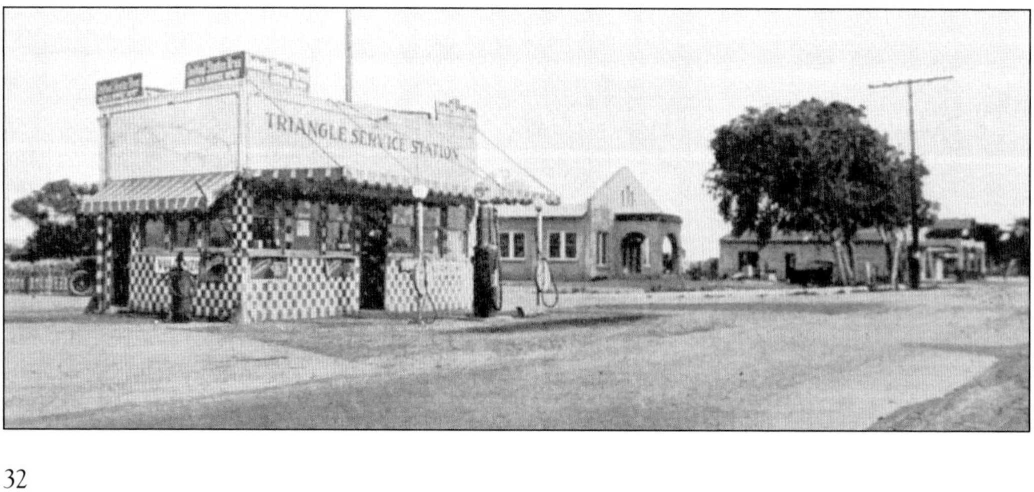

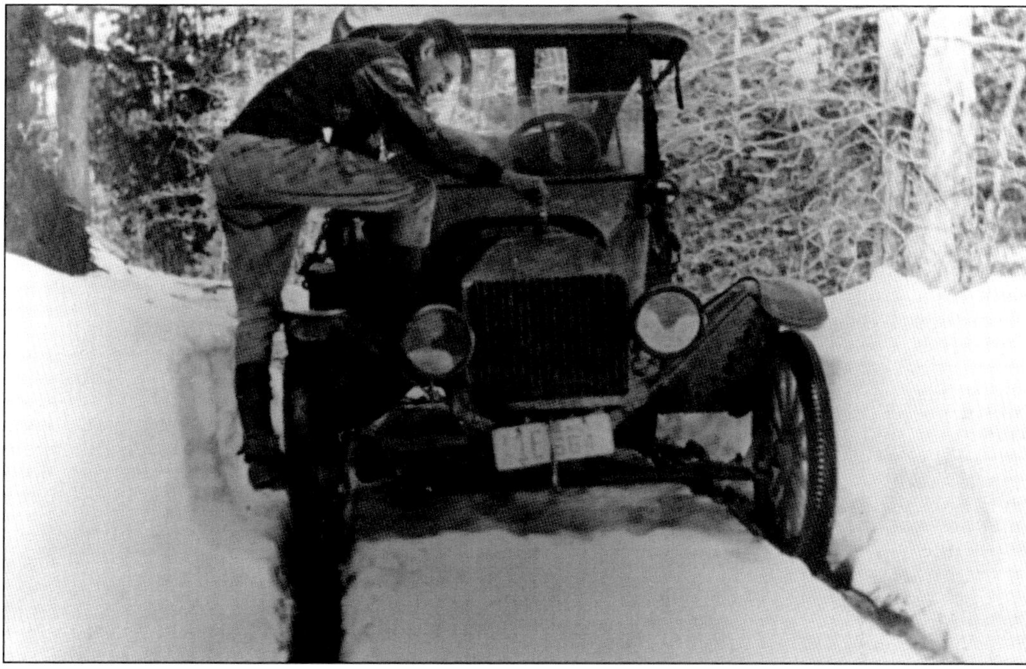

In 1922, E.N.T. Burnett is working on his vehicle during a winter trip from Idylwild to Banning. This was the first reported automobile to go between Idylwild and Banning despite the snowdrifts. Burnett was a resident of Coachella, where he worked his ranch. (Courtesy of the Coachella Valley Water District.)

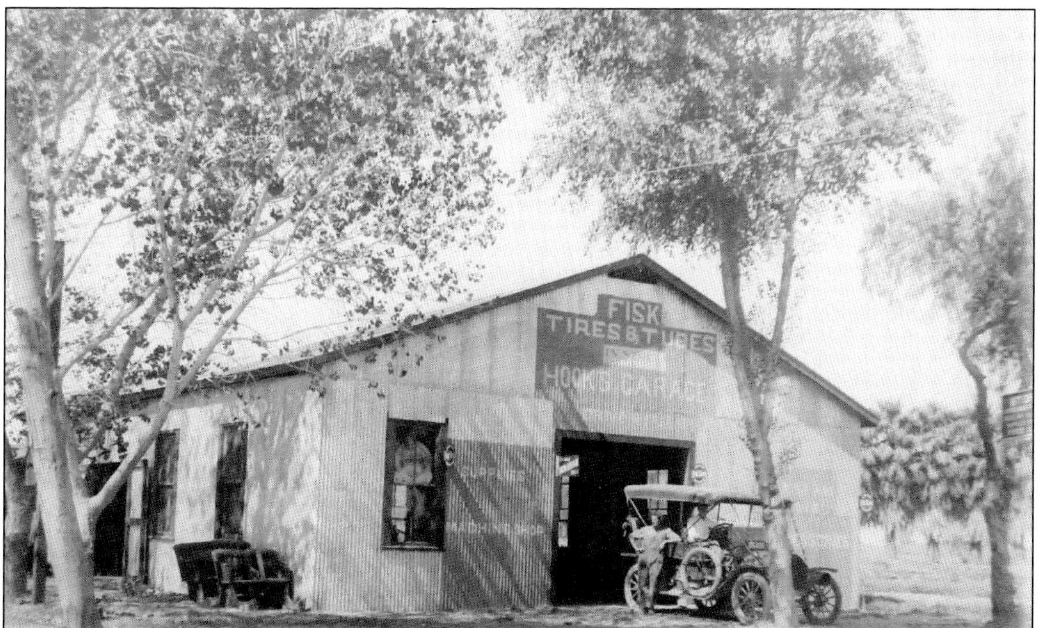

This photograph of Hook's garage was taken in 1914. Garage employees worked on tires and tubes and also repaired automobiles and machinery. Art Hook owned the garage and was the brother-in-law of Jack Halliday, who was a well driller. (Courtesy of the Coachella Valley History Museum.)

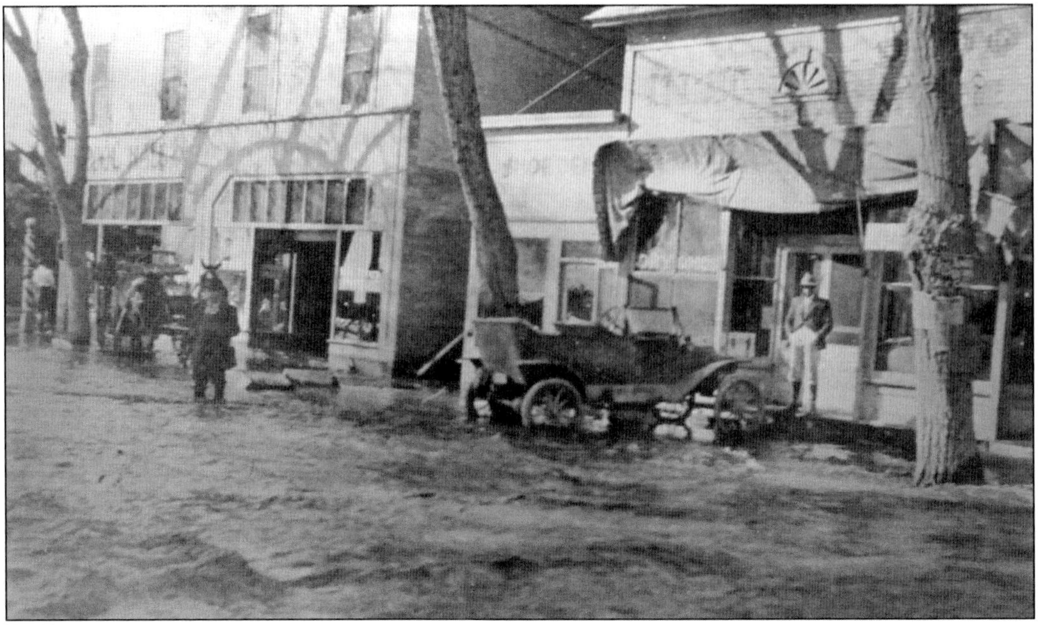

Flash floods are common in the Coachella Valley. The sandy desert soil cannot absorb large quantities of water quickly. During years of heavy rain, the people living in the Coachella Valley endured major floods. The 1916 flood affected both Indio, shown in this photograph of Miles Avenue and Fargo Street, and Coachella. (Courtesy of the Coachella Valley Water District.)

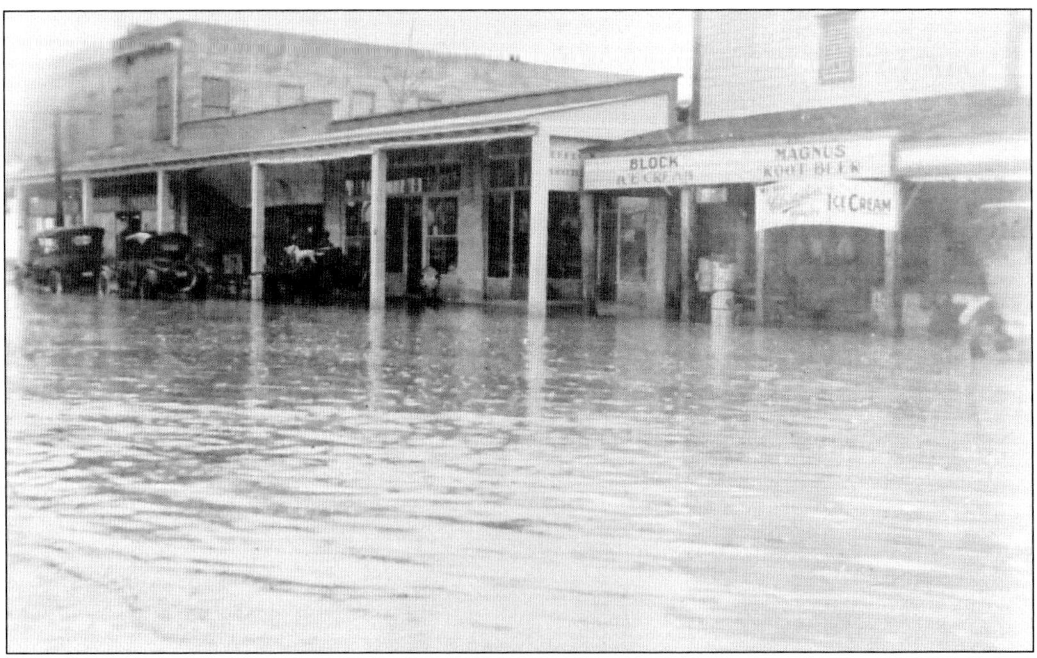

In February 1927, the people of Coachella experienced another major flood. The water rerouting systems of today were not in place yet. At that time, people anticipated having to deal with heavy flooding. The general height of the water can be seen in relation to the tires on the automobiles. (Courtesy of the Coachella Valley Water District.)

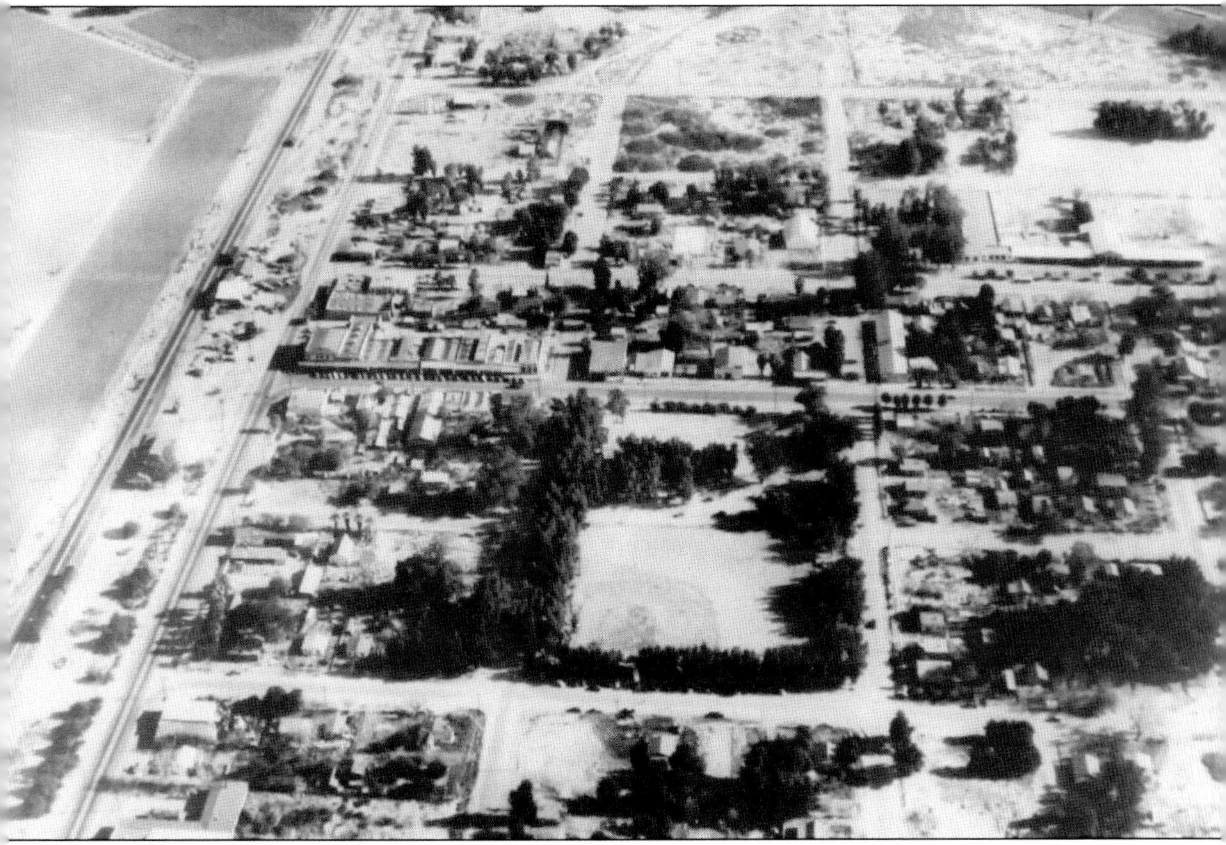

Growth is apparent in this 1930s aerial photograph. Also telling are the dramatic alterations of the landscape. The area has gone from an arid desert to an agricultural landscape. The ability to grow crops year-round continued to attract people once the Rector brothers had dug the artesian well. At center left, the railroad siding sits to the right of the train tracks. The siding is where much of the Coachella-grown crops were loaded onto railcars to be transported to other areas. Front Street runs from left to right at center. There is a lot of sand on some of the roads, as remains common today on roads with little development. (Courtesy of the Coachella Valley History Museum.)

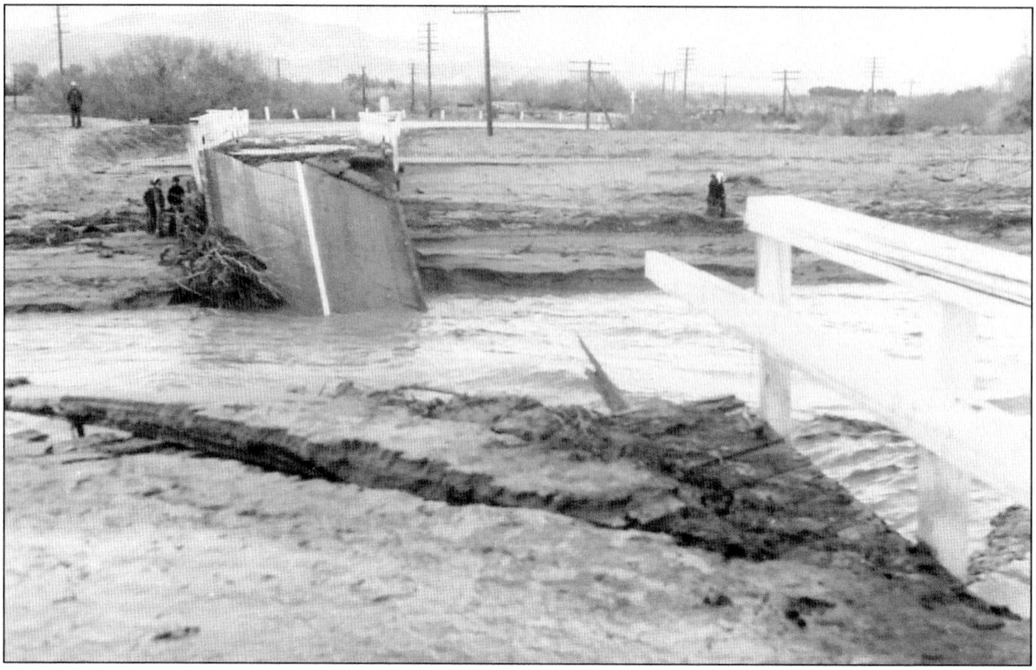

In September 1939, the valley flooded and washed out the bridge on Highway 60. The damaged bridge, shown here, would later be repaired. Washed out roads continue to be a part of life in the Coachella Valley desert. (Courtesy of the Coachella Valley History Museum.)

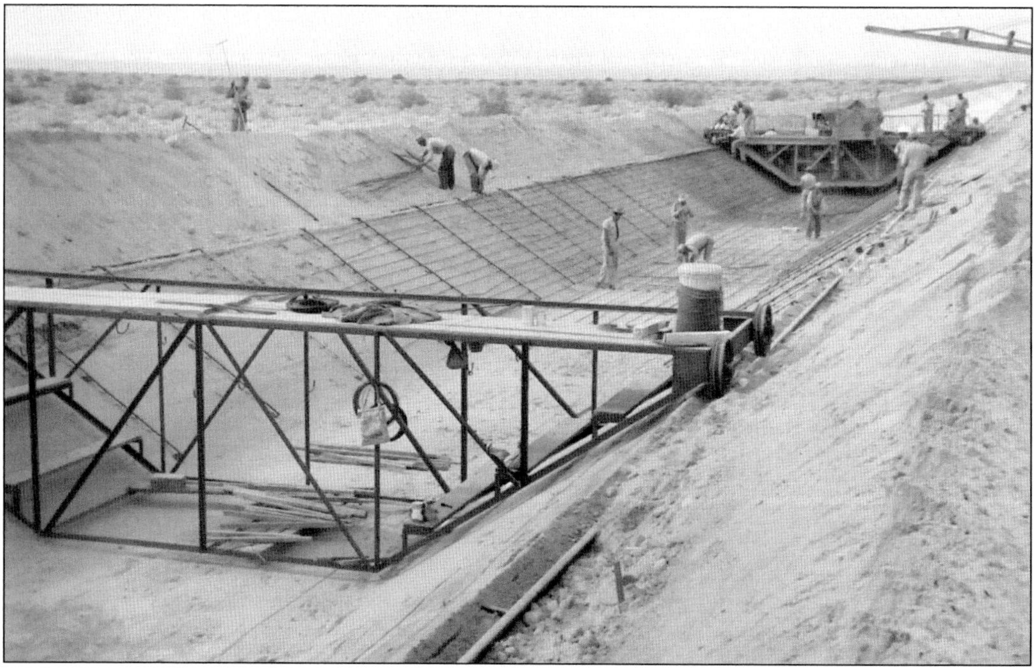

By 1938, construction of the All-American Canal had begun. The canal would divert water from the Colorado River to the Coachella Valley. This would provide much needed water for the growing agricultural industry. This June 1946 photograph shows work being done on a concrete spillway of the Coachella branch of the canal. (Courtesy of the US Bureau of Reclamation.)

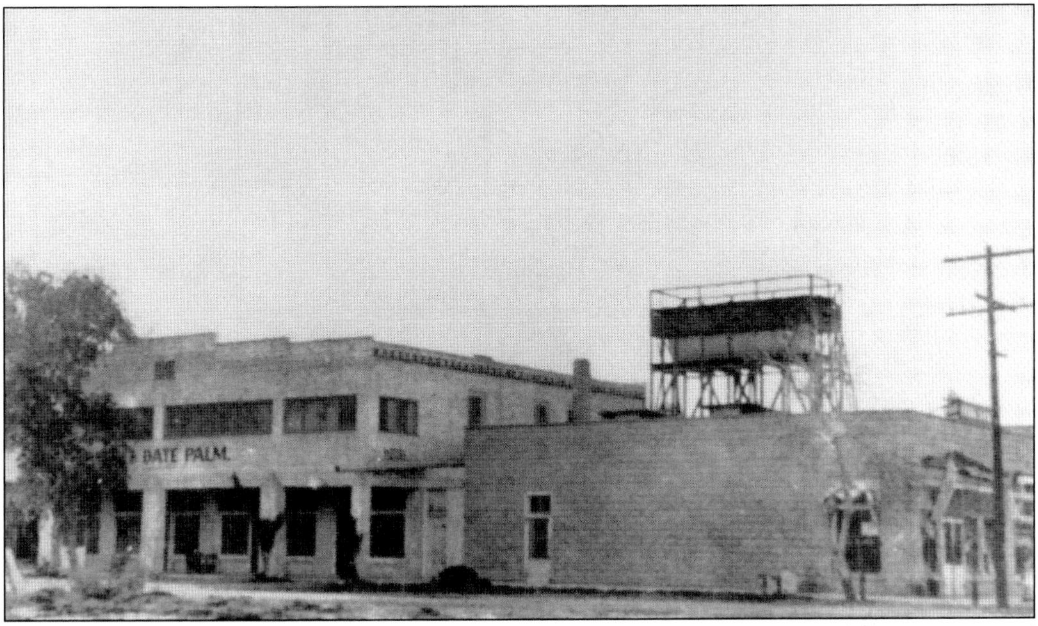

Here, the Date Palm Hotel is shown in 1920. The hotel was on the corner of Front Street and Broadway and was built in 1909 by a Mr. McDonald. The two-story building was constructed of cement blocks and included 12 guest rooms and a restaurant. Rooms were 25¢–50¢ per day, while meals were available for 25¢. (Courtesy of the Coachella Valley Water District.)

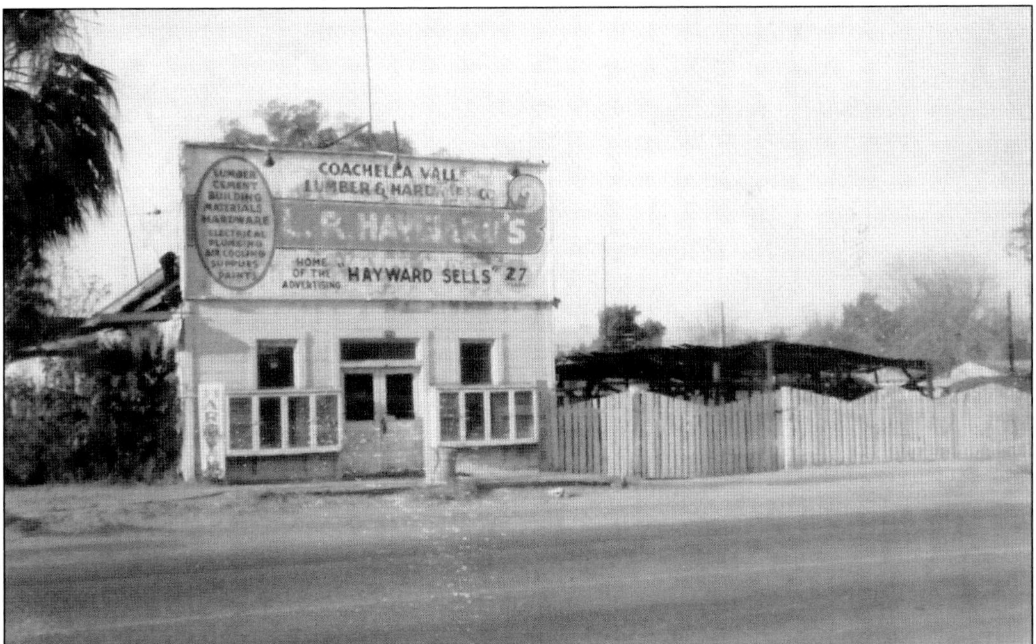

By the 1920s, the Hayward Hardware storefront had changed. The vegetation around the building had also significantly grown with the irrigation changes that were made. This building was located on what is now Grapefruit Boulevard. (*Coachella Valley Sun* photograph, courtesy of the Coachella Valley History Museum.)

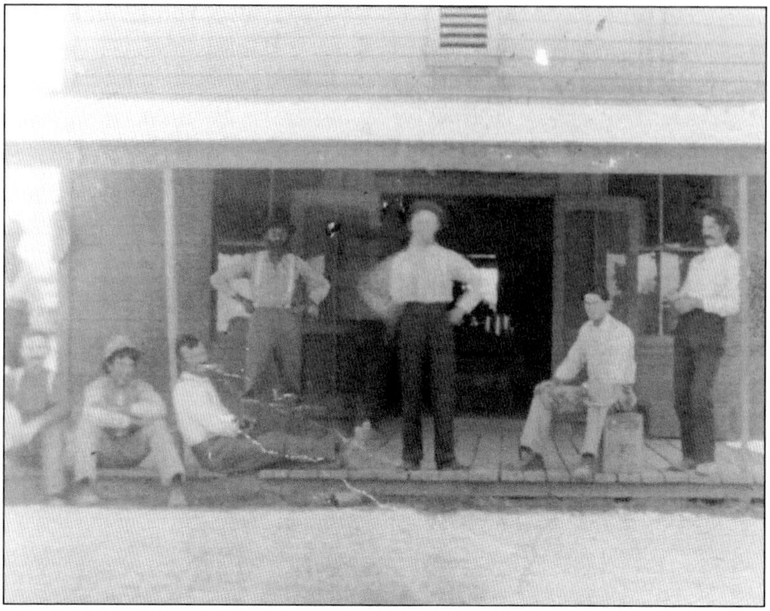

This 1905 photograph shows the first pool hall in Coachella. It provided entertainment for the residents, primarily the men, after their mostly labor-intensive jobs. Many of the residents during this time worked on farms and ranches, or for the railroad. The man in the center is blurred because he moved as the photograph was taken. (Courtesy of the Coachella Valley History Museum.)

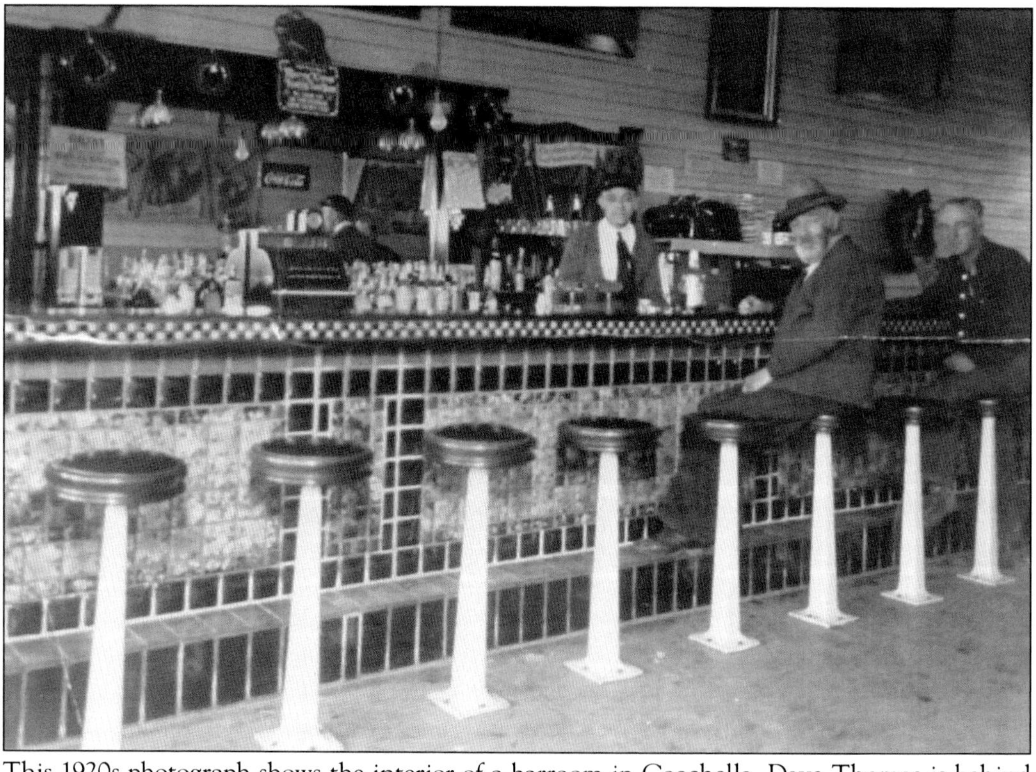

This 1920s photograph shows the interior of a barroom in Coachella. Dave Thomas is behind the bar, with two unidentified customers sitting in front. Along with the pool hall, the bar was another place for the people to get time away from their jobs and house duties. (Courtesy of the Coachella Valley History Museum.)

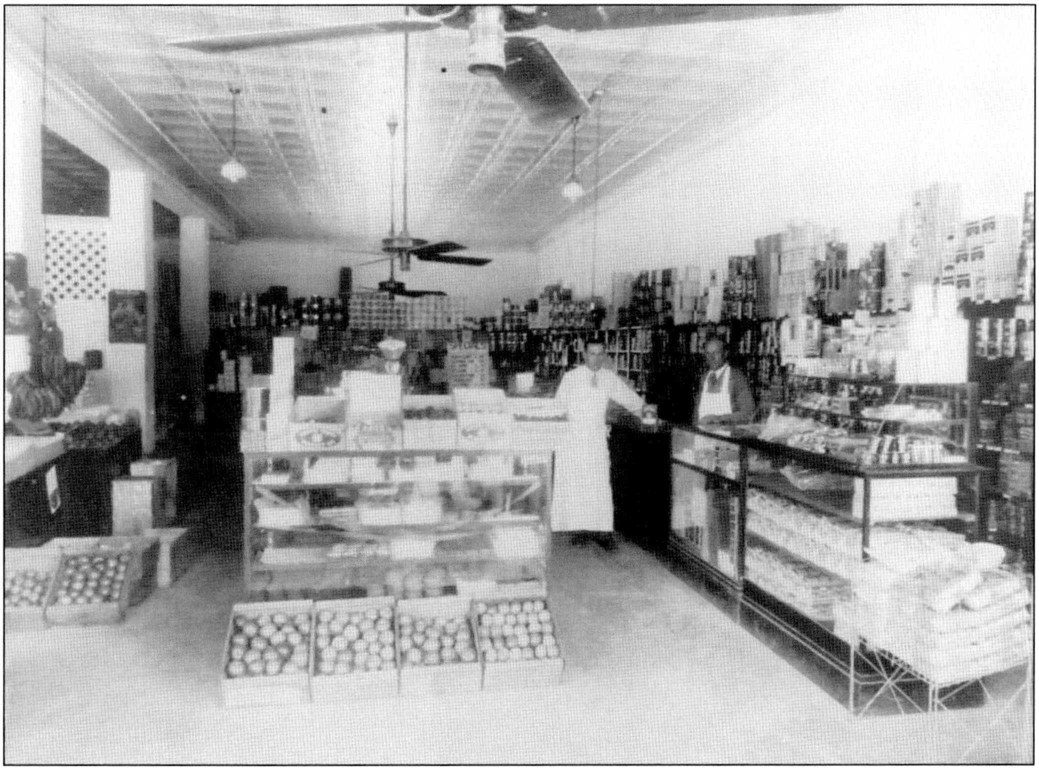

This photograph was taken inside a Coachella grocery store between 1926 and 1930. It is thought to be Pearson's grocery store. Much of the fruit and vegetables for sale would have been locally grown. (Courtesy of the Coachella Valley History Museum.)

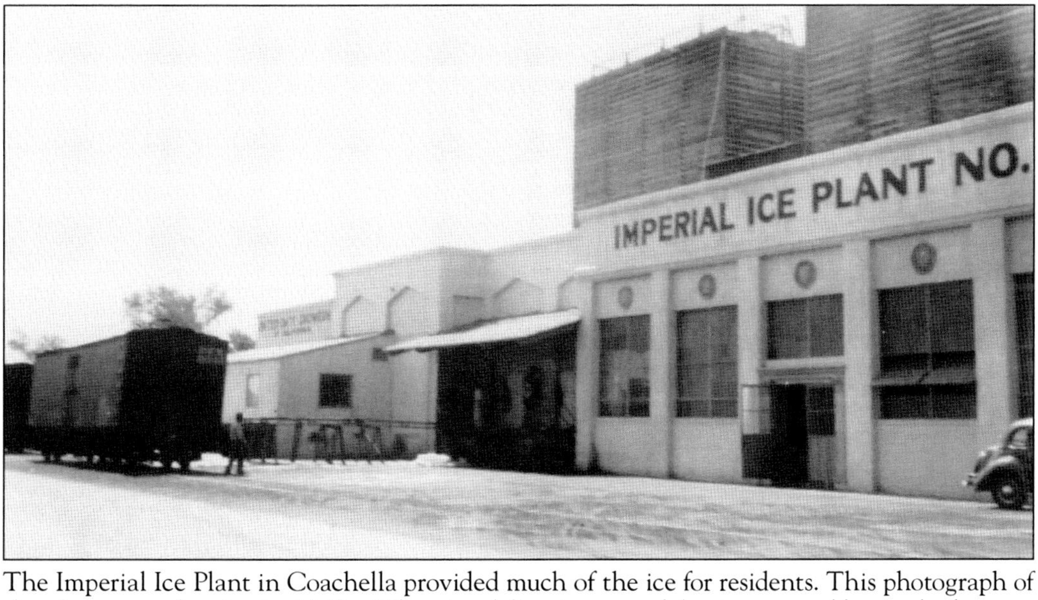

The Imperial Ice Plant in Coachella provided much of the ice for residents. This photograph of the plant was taken in the 1940s. When ice deliveries started, businesses and homes had square cards with preprinted numbers. The card with the number of pounds of ice desired was hung in the window. (Courtesy of the Coachella Valley History Museum.)

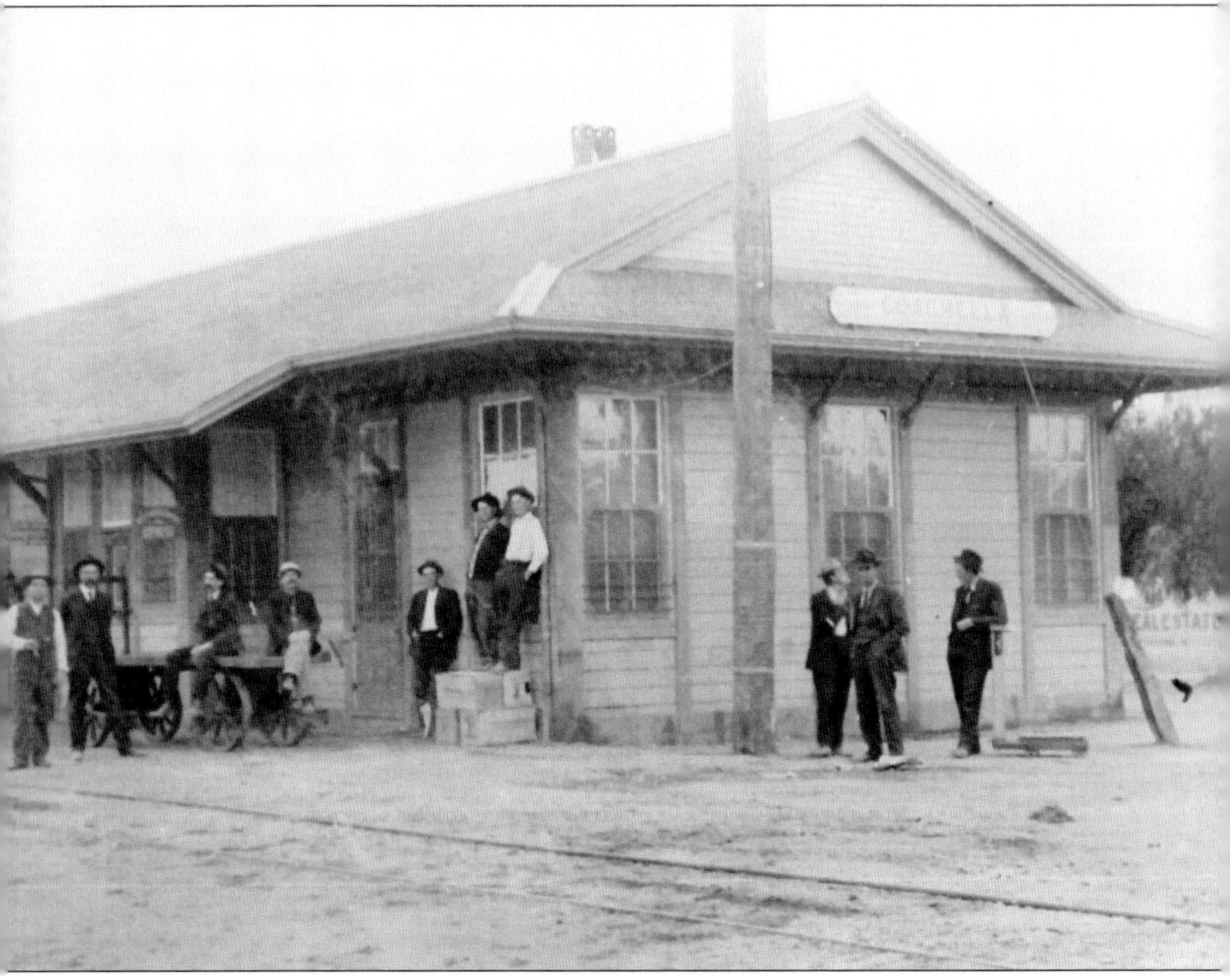

The Southern Pacific depot began as a railroad siding to load mesquite and greasewood. The depot expanded as the agricultural businesses grew. Many of the individuals in this early 1900s photograph are business owners and Coachella residents. They are, from left to right, John L. Smythe, J.L. Griffin, Dave Smythe, ? Freeman, Fred Santell, C.B. Jones, A.L. Pearson, ? Storey, and two unidentified. Dave Smythe was the railroad agent at the time. One of the biggest problems for the railroad was keeping the tracks clean of the blowing sand. Sandstorms were and still are very common in the valley, and a buildup of sand on the tracks can cause a train to derail. In the early development of the valley, train derailments were common. (Courtesy of the Coachella Valley History Museum.)

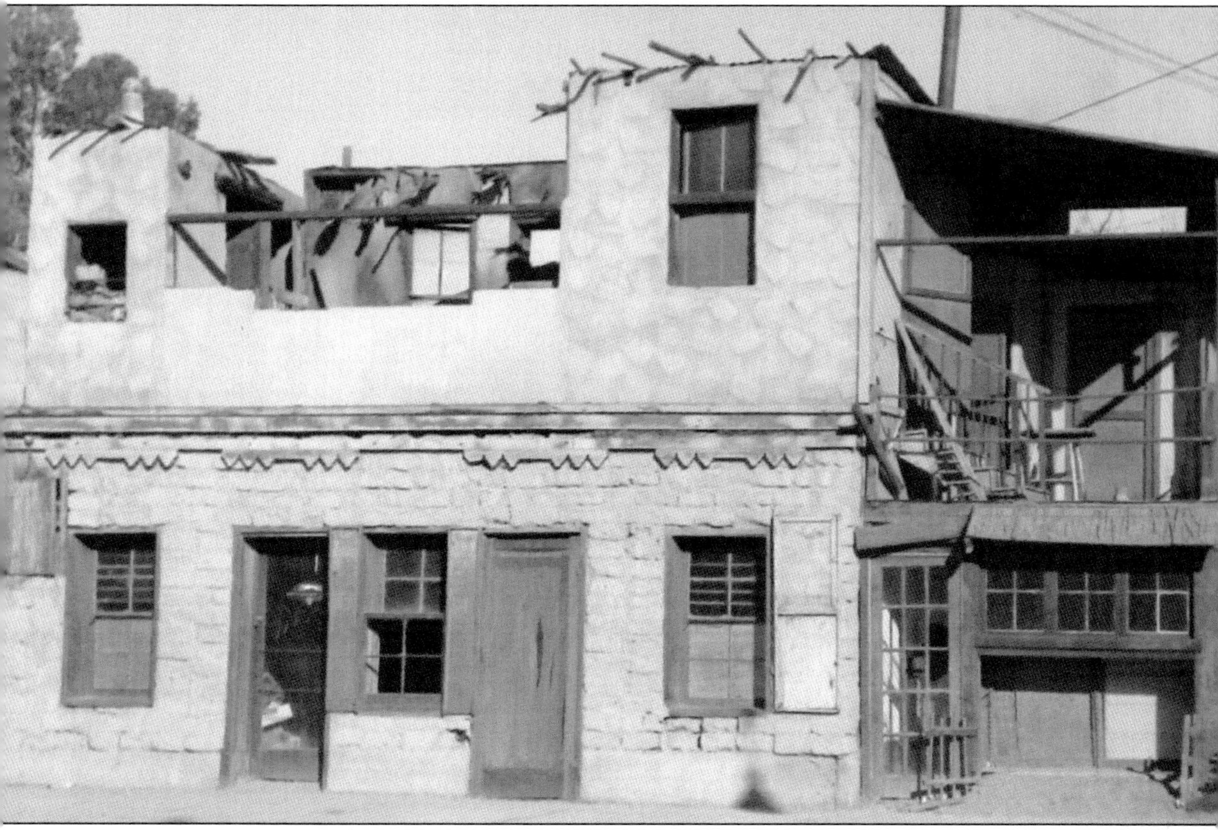

Lucy Smythe built and owned Lucy's Hopi House, which contained a small museum and a shop with Native American goods and bottling works available for purchase. In the area of Coachella, there are three Native American bands with reservations, the Cabazon Band of Mission Indians, Augustine Band of Cahuilla Indians, and the Twenty-Nine Palms Band of Mission Indians. The Cabazon Band and Augustine Band are both Cahuilla Indians, with the exception of a Chemehuevi family that is enrolled in the Cabazon Band. Both the Cabazon and Augustine Band reservations were established in 1865. The Twenty-Nine Palms Band is made up of Chemehuevi Indians rather than Cahuilla Indians. A Chemehuevi family migrated to the Coachella Valley in the early 1900s. It was not until the latter part of the 20th century that the reservation was established in the city of Coachella. (Roy J. Gilman photograph, courtesy of the Coachella Valley History Museum.)

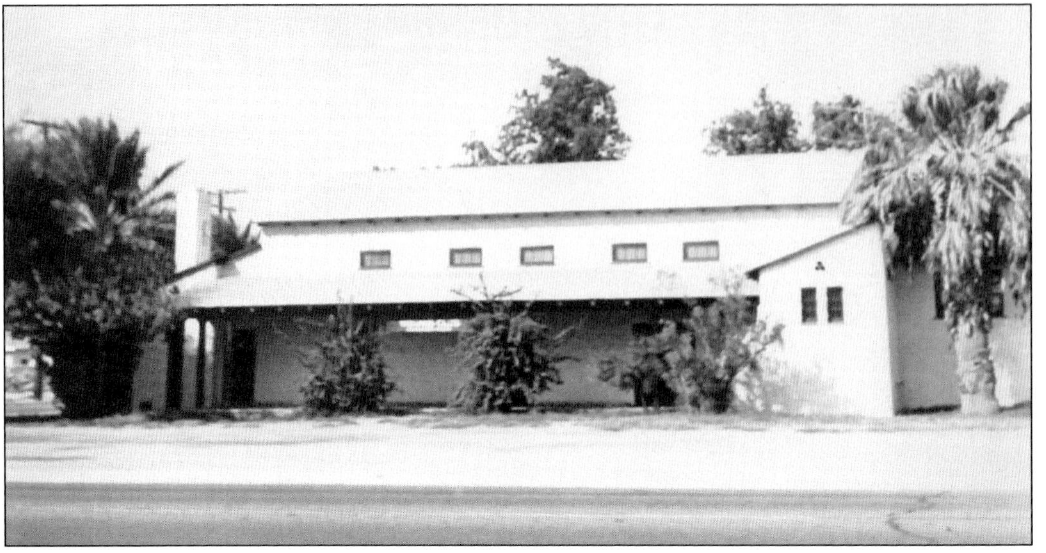

This 1920s photograph shows the Coachella Valley Women's Club. During this time, it was a social and philanthropic club for women. There is a sister club in Indio that still exists today. (Courtesy of the Coachella Valley History Museum.)

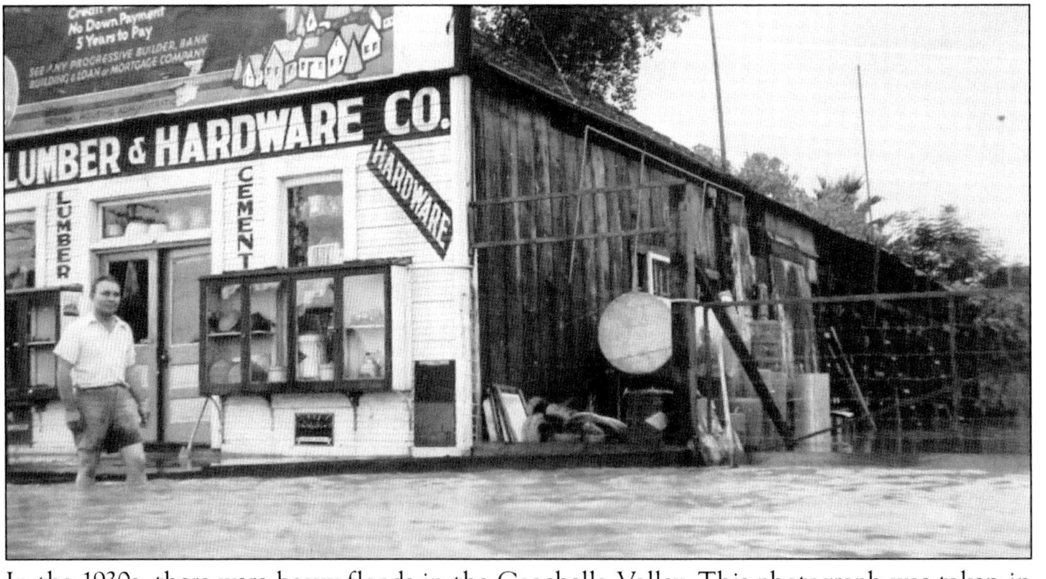

In the 1930s, there were heavy floods in the Coachella Valley. This photograph was taken in front of Hayward Lumber and Hardware Company as an unidentified man wades through the floodwaters. The waters lap onto the raised deck in front of the store. (Courtesy of the Coachella Valley History Museum.)

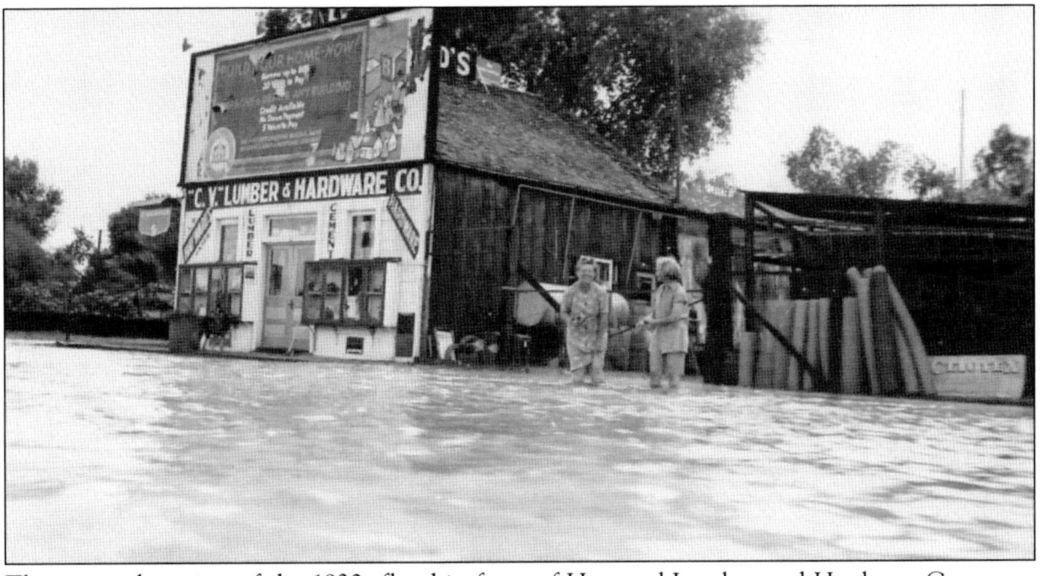

This is another view of the 1930s flood in front of Hayward Lumber and Hardware Company. The water is just below the knees of these unidentified women. (Courtesy of the Coachella Valley History Museum.)

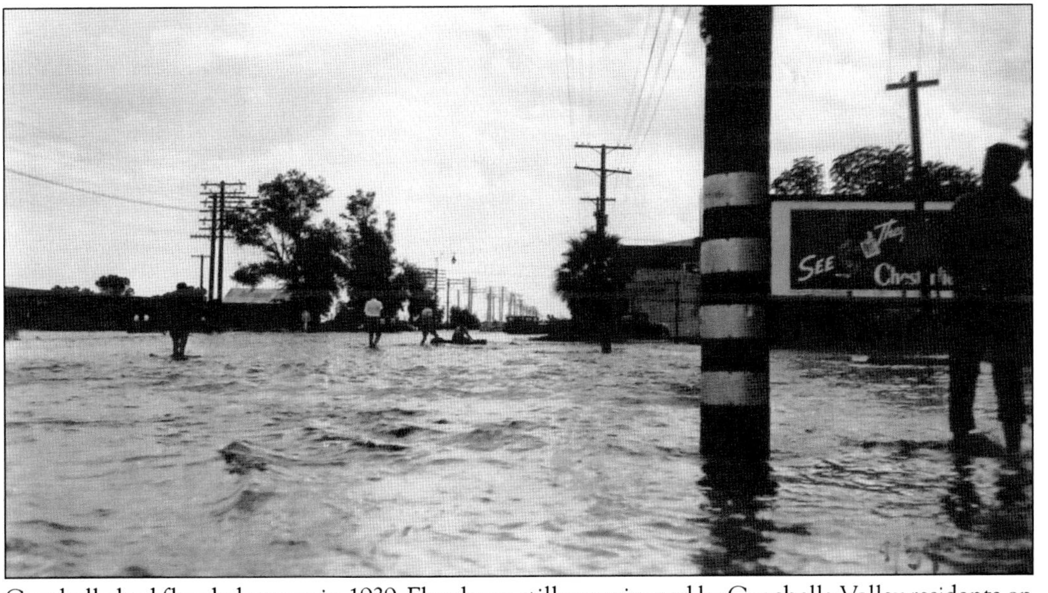

Coachella had flooded streets in 1939. Floods are still experienced by Coachella Valley residents on an annual basis; however, where and how much it floods have dramatically changed. Improvements to water diversion methods, such as cement washes, have helped with flooding. (Courtesy of the Coachella Valley History Museum.)

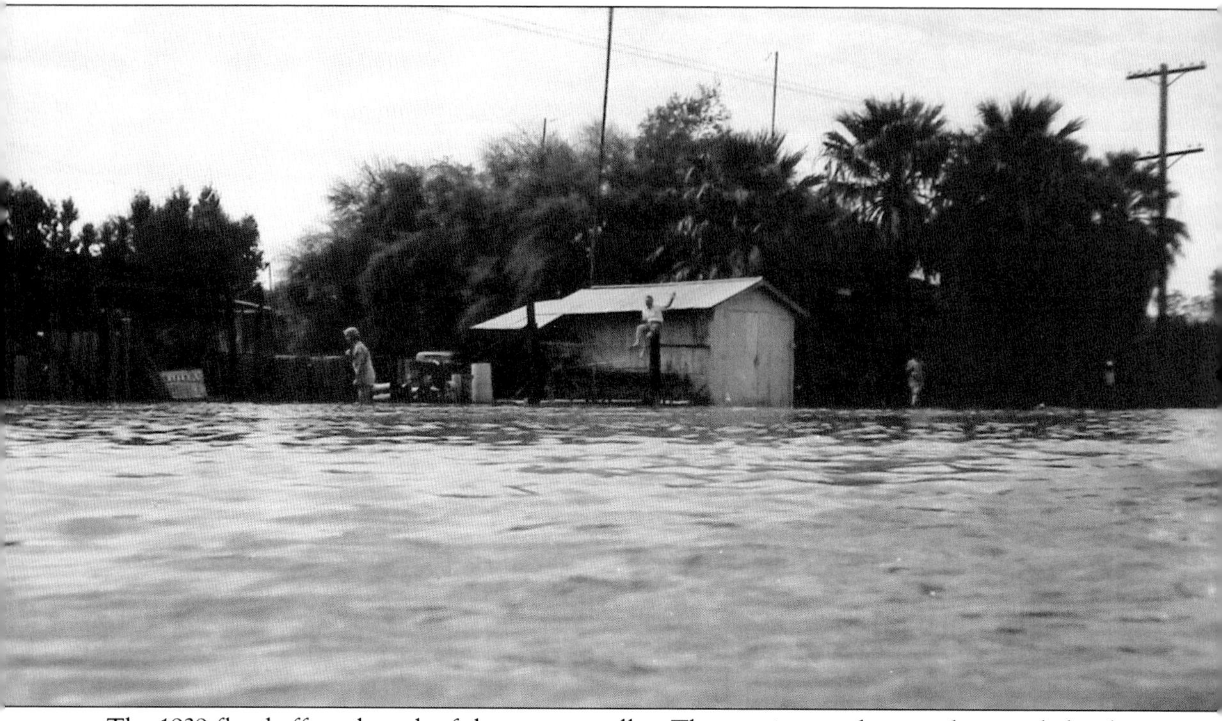

The 1939 flood affected much of the eastern valley. The continuous damage that needed to be repaired and funded could take a toll on a family or business. This photograph of the flooding shows an unidentified woman wading through the floodwaters and surveying the damage. To her right is a boy sitting on top of a fence post. Another woman is walking from the tree line toward the boy. Much as children today find snow days a welcome change to their normal routine, it is likely that most children found the flooding a welcome change to their routines. Today, flooding normally remains in the wash areas; however, at times it does breach these areas. Most of the flooding is caused by a mixture of heavy rains and runoff from the surrounding mountains. (Courtesy of the Coachella Valley History Museum.)

Three

Establishing Home

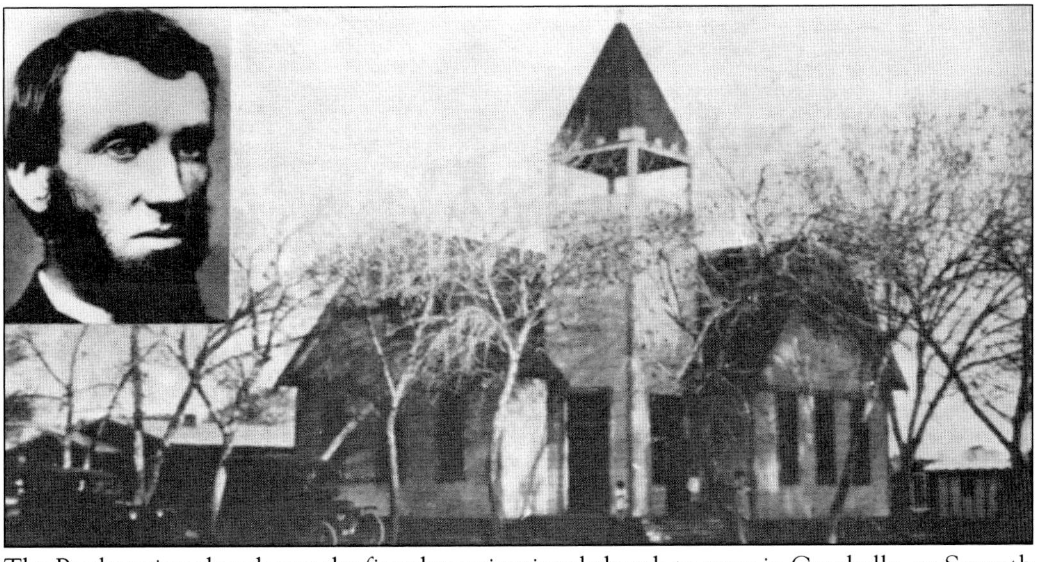

The Presbyterian church was the first denominational church to open in Coachella, on Seventh Street and Orchard Avenue; Rev. Albert Dilworth, pictured in the inset, led the church. The congregation first organized in October 1902 and began by meeting in their homes until the church, pictured here, was built. (*Coachella Valley Submarine* photograph, courtesy of the Coachella Valley Water District.)

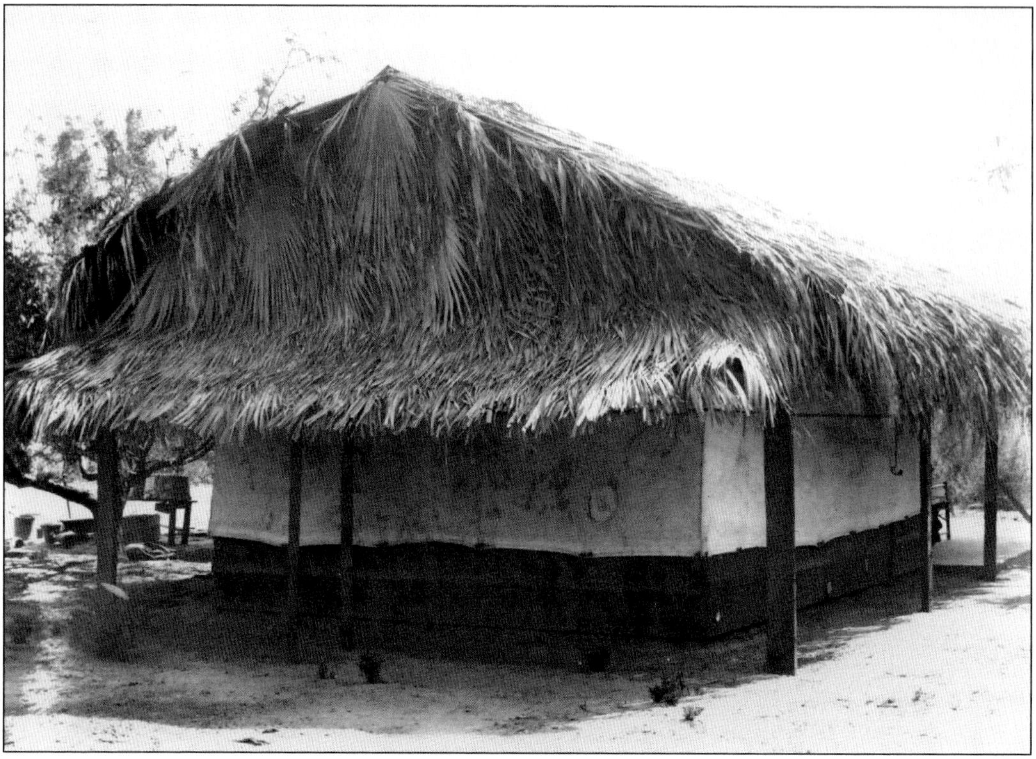

The 1912 tent house pictured above was one of the early types of housing for residents. This house belonged to Otho Moore and his wife, who were members of a prominent Indio family. The tent houses provided shade and allowed a breeze to circulate the air inside. Pictured below is the early home of Pat Gale of the Southern Pacific Railroad. (Both, courtesy of the Coachella Valley Water District.)

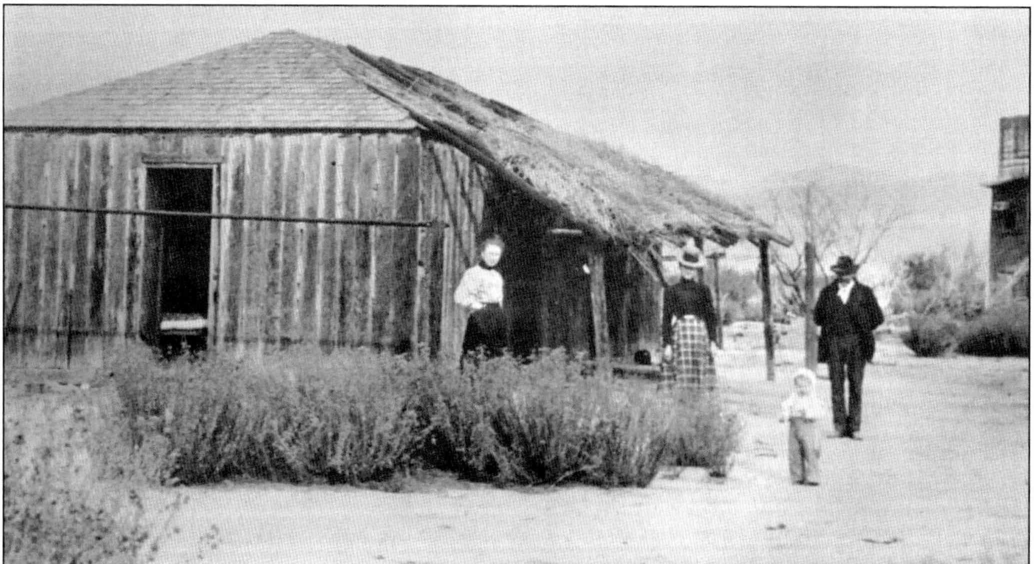

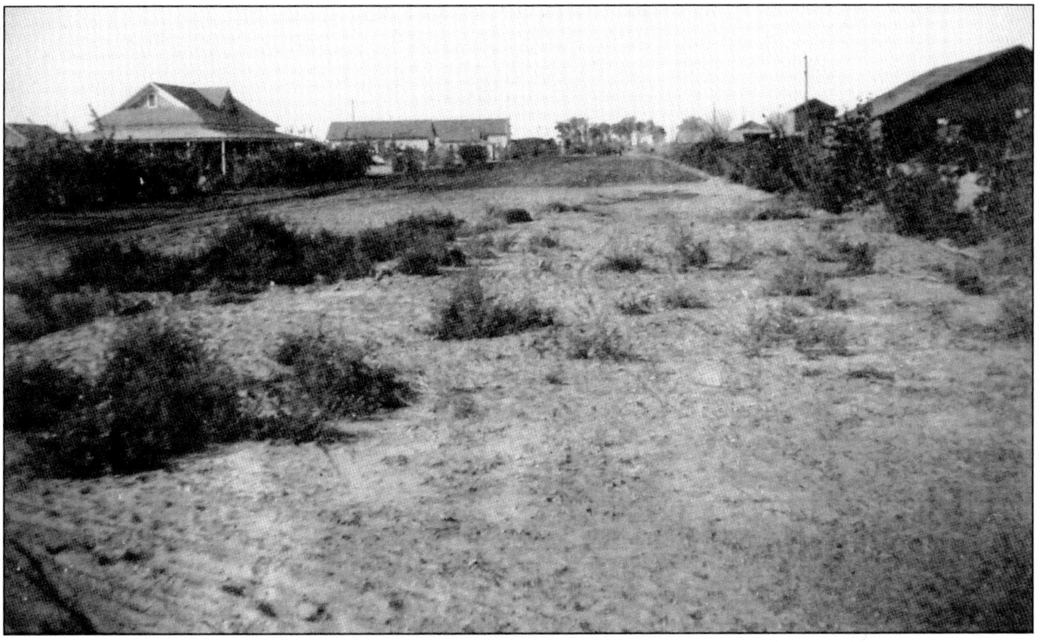

Despite the growth of Coachella by the 1920s, when the above photograph was taken, Main Street still remained untamed. Throughout the next several decades, residents would go from living in a town in the middle of nowhere to a thriving, busy city. The 1920s photograph below was taken looking north. The area between the cities of Indio and Coachella remained essentially empty desert. Today, there are patches of land between the two cities that remain empty, but for the most part, development has encompassed both. (Both, Otho Moore photographs, courtesy of the Coachella Valley History Museum.)

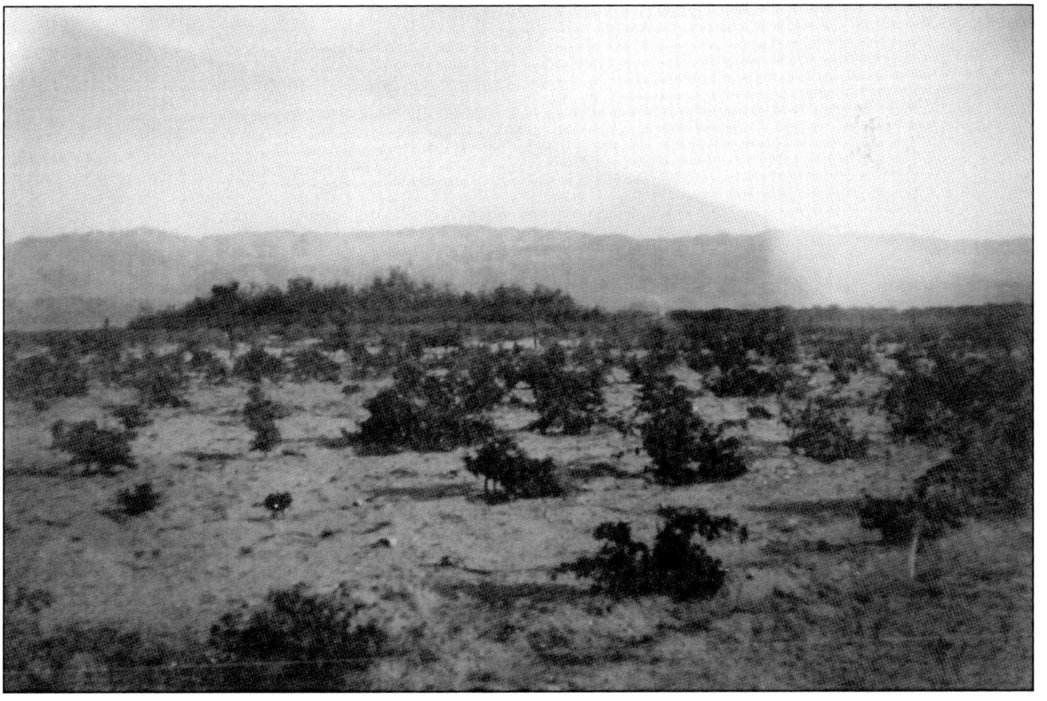

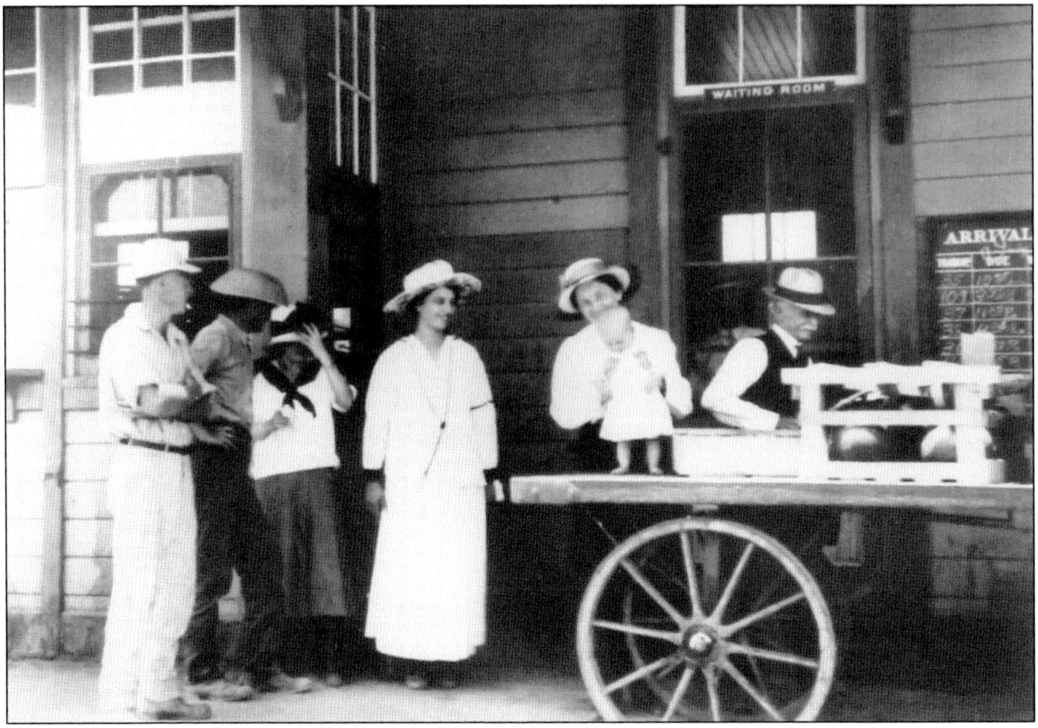

This 1917 photograph shows the Southern Pacific depot. From left to right are Hugh Proctor, Claude Hyde, Julia Proctor, Grace Proctor, Alberta Hyde, and Albert Proctor; the baby is Margaret Proctor. (Courtesy of the Coachella Valley History Museum.)

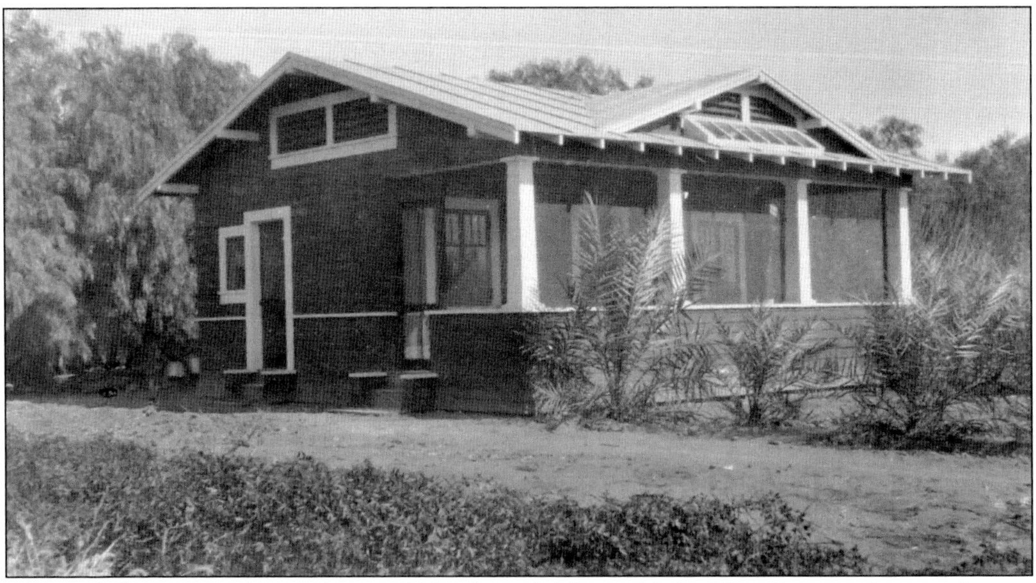

This early house was the residence of Claude and Alberta Hyde. The photograph was taken in 1915. Often, desert residents would build porches and enclose them with screens. During the hot summers, they would sleep in the screened-off areas to stay as cool as possible. (Courtesy of the Coachella Valley History Museum.)

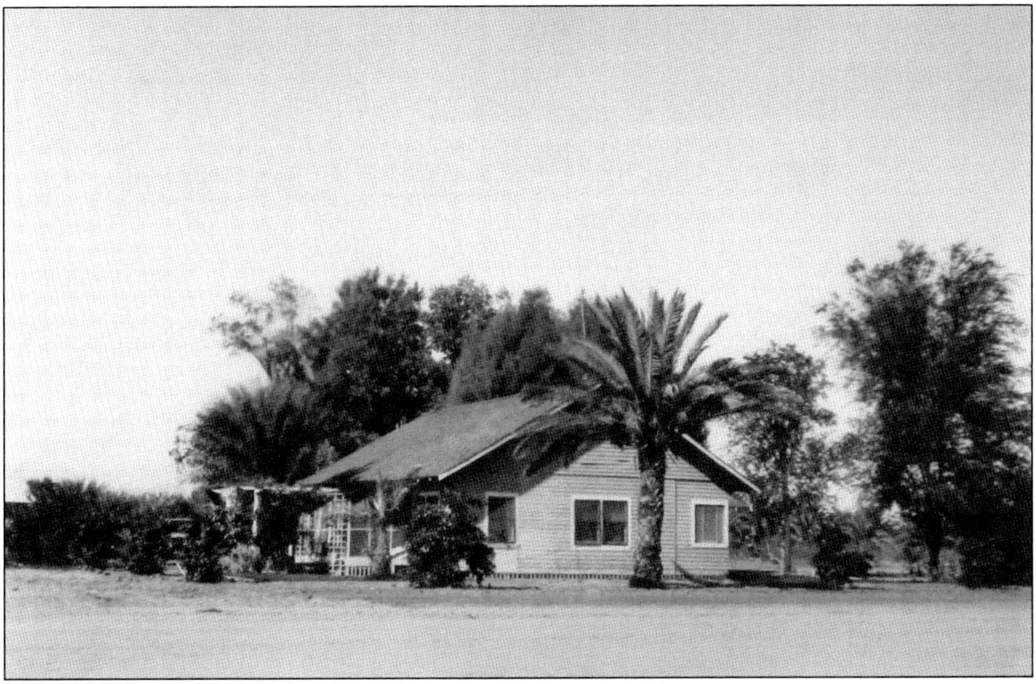

These 1927 photographs show the Proctors' ranch house. Non–Native American residents of the Coachella Valley often collected Native American goods and products. Otho Moore and his wife were major collectors of baskets woven by the Desert Cahuilla Indians, especially those living locally. The Desert Cahuilla Indians' basketry skills are well known, and their baskets are appreciated for their tightly woven, intricate designs. The Moore basket collection is currently on display at the Coachella Valley History Museum. (Both, courtesy of the Coachella Valley History Museum.)

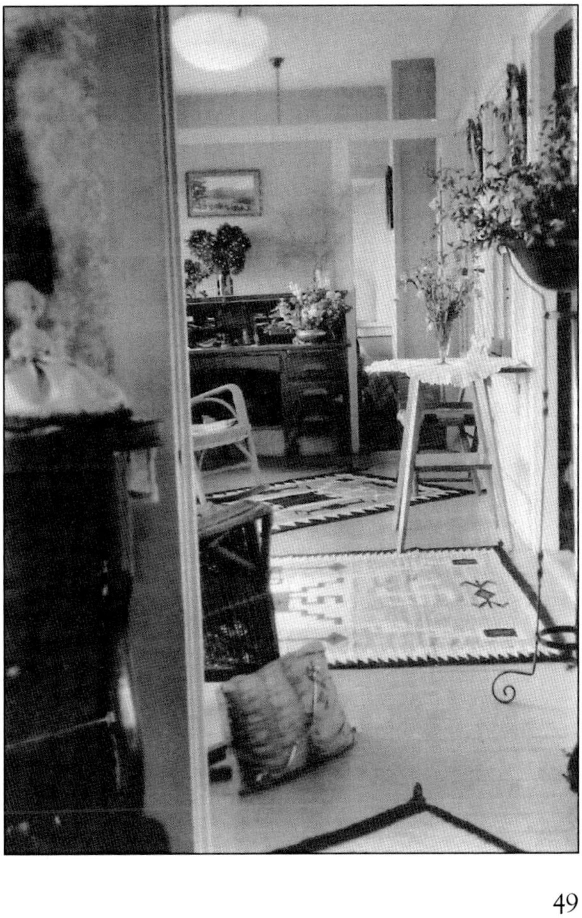

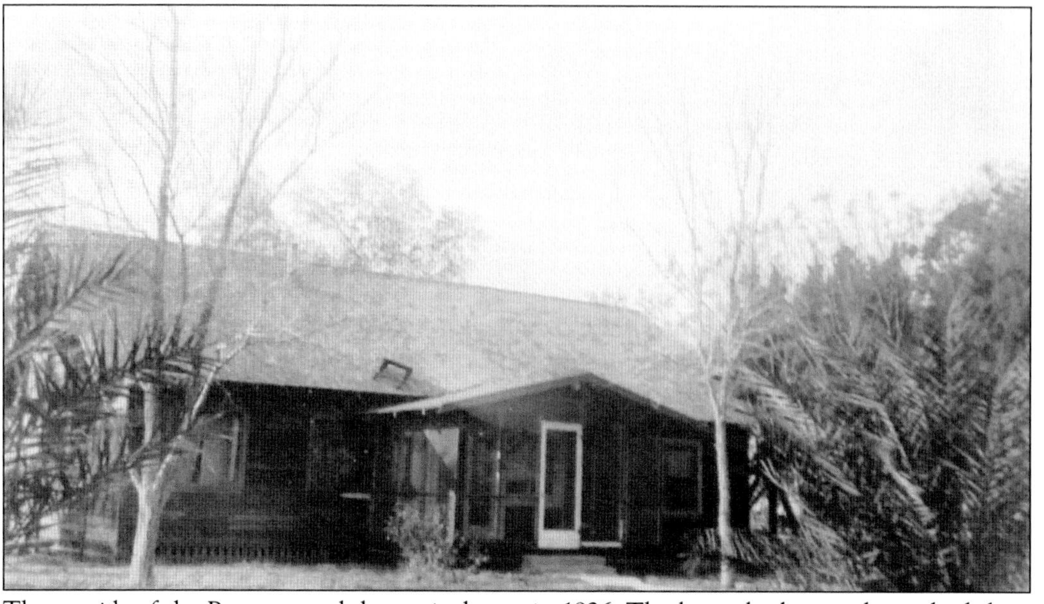

The outside of the Proctor ranch house is shown in 1926. The large shade trees have shed their leaves during the cooler winter months. (Courtesy of the Coachella Valley History Museum.)

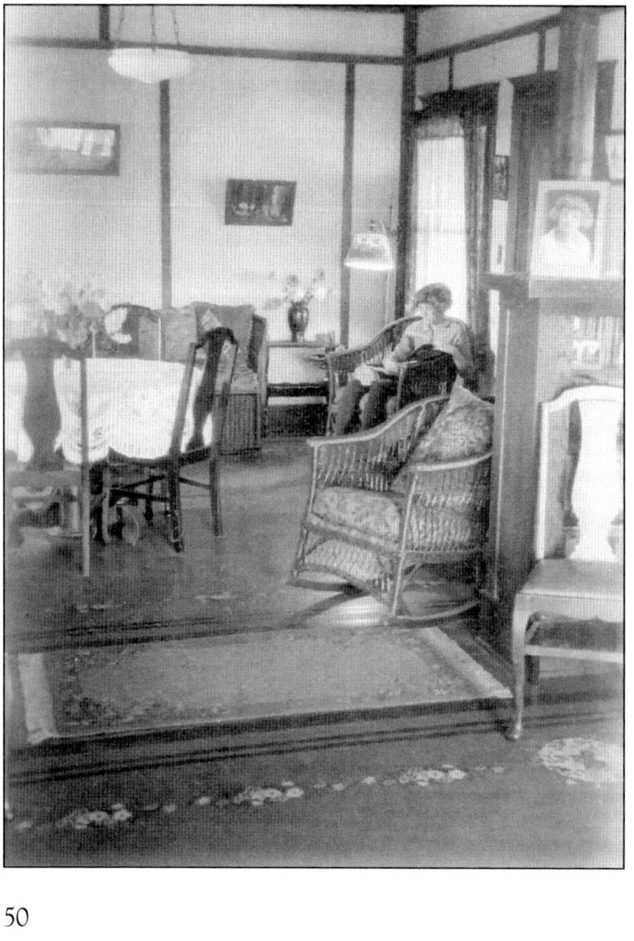

This c. 1927 photograph of Margaret Proctor was taken as she was reading in the dining room of the Proctor ranch house. A photograph of Margaret sits on the built-in bookcase, an architectural feature commonly found in homes of this era. (Courtesy of the Coachella Valley History Museum.)

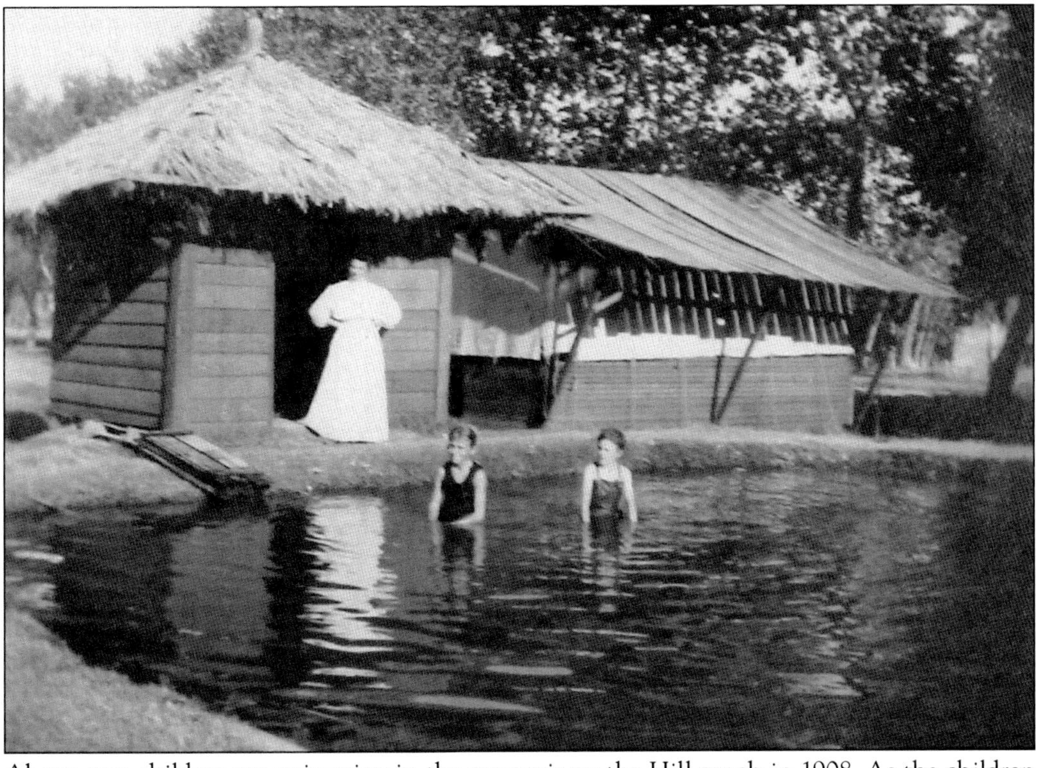

Above, two children are swimming in the reservoir on the Hill ranch in 1908. As the children play and cool down, a woman watches over them. Swimming was one of several ways residents cooled down in the intense desert heat. After the arrival of electricity, residents purchased blocks of ice and set them in front of a fan to create cool breezes in homes. In the c. 1910 photograph below, Ben and Katherine Teagle pose while riding their horses. (Both, courtesy of the Coachella Valley History Museum.)

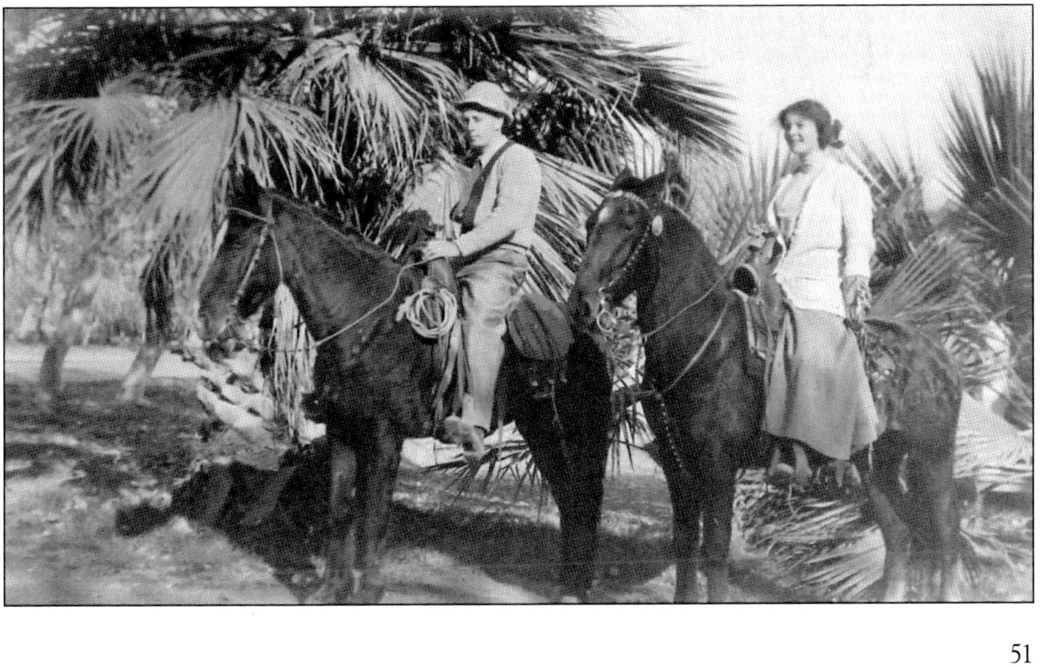

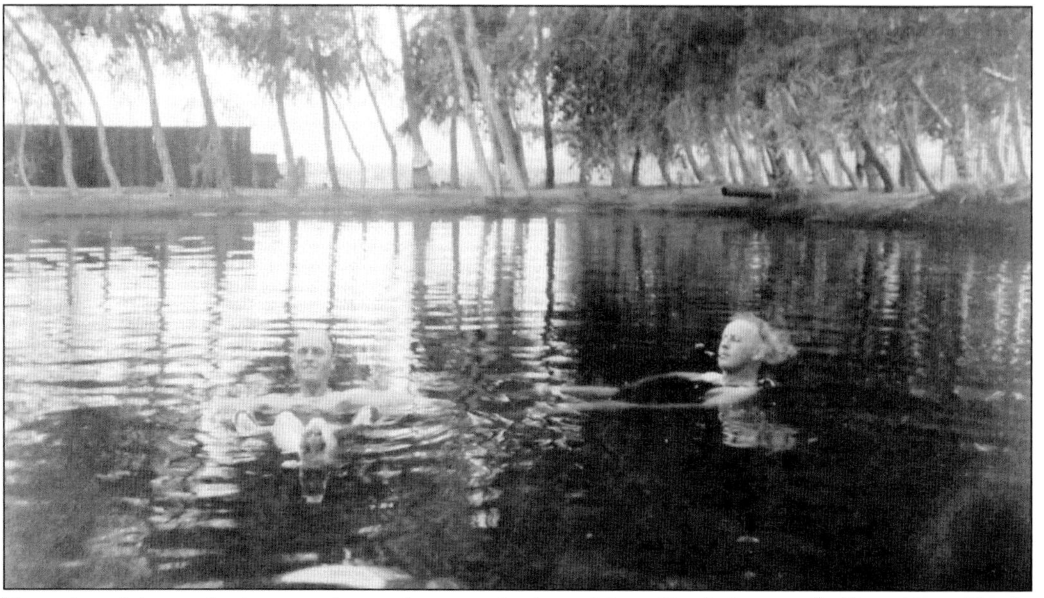

Even the adults made time to relax and escape the heat. Here, Hugh Proctor (left) and Ben Teagle are seen floating in a reservoir on the Proctors' ranch in 1920. (Courtesy of the Coachella Valley History Museum.)

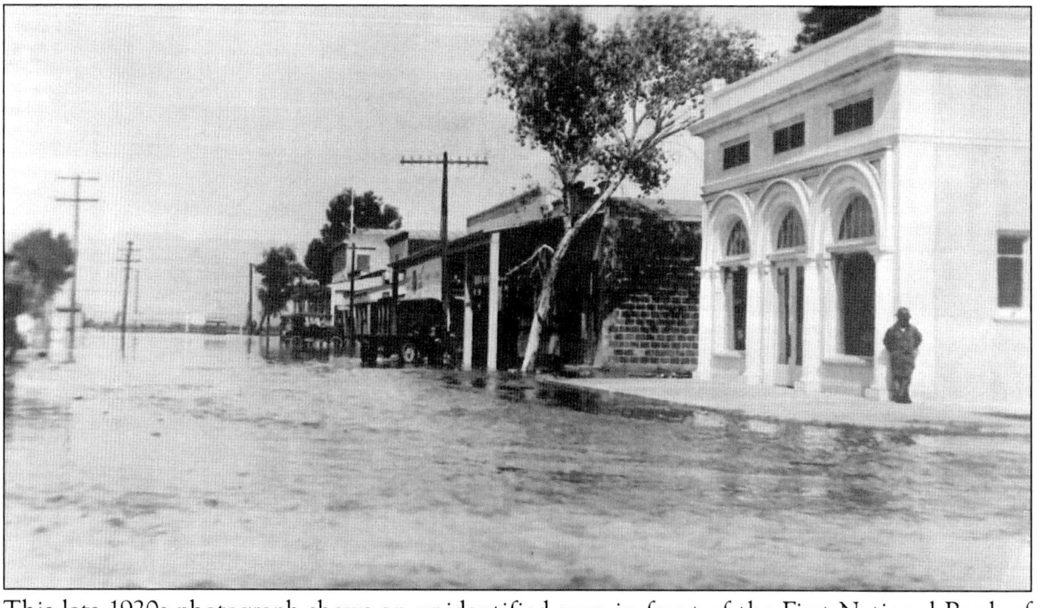

This late 1920s photograph shows an unidentified man in front of the First National Bank of Coachella. The floodwaters reached the edge of the curb. (Courtesy of the Coachella Valley Water District.)

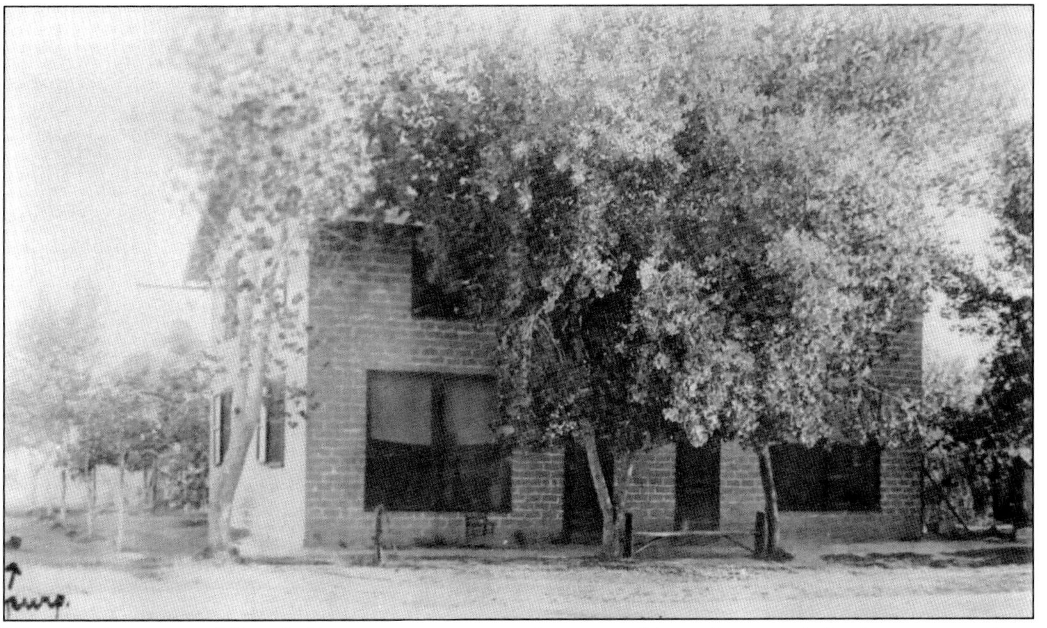

The development of Coachella came as more settlers moved into the area, bringing new services and businesses like the bakery shown here in 1910. By making fresh baked goods such as bread available for purchase, families could focus on running their own farms, ranches, or businesses instead of baking. (Courtesy of the Coachella Valley History Museum.)

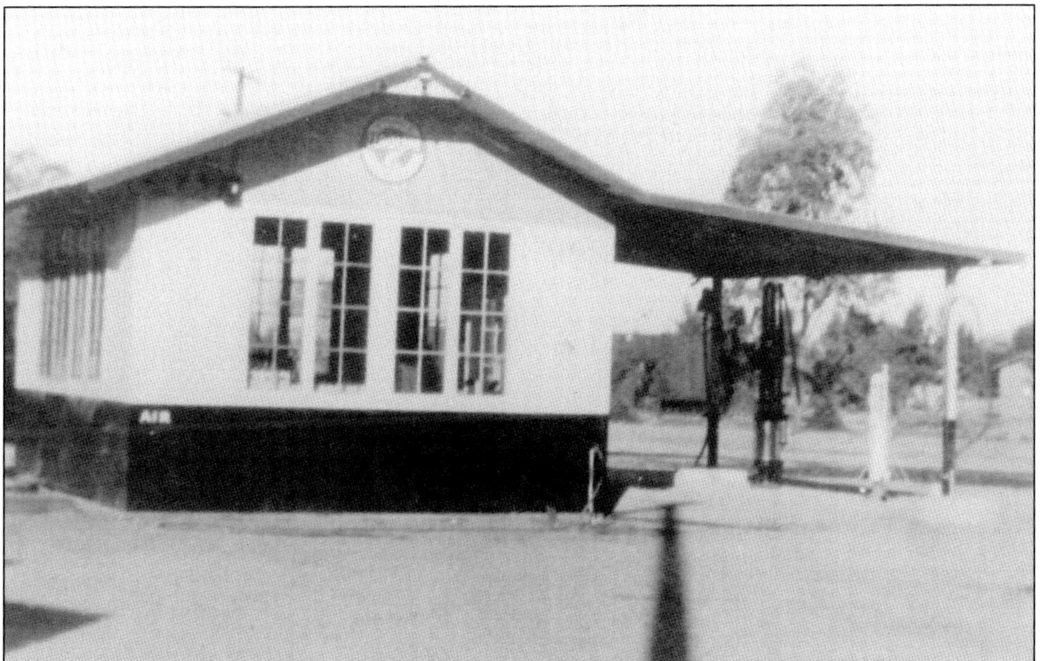

This is a gas station in the Coachella Valley in 1925, believed to be in Coachella. The popularity of automobiles immediately caused the development of new service businesses. The need for gas stations, tire shops, and garages to maintain and repair automobiles drove many people into this type of work. (Courtesy of the Coachella Valley History Museum.)

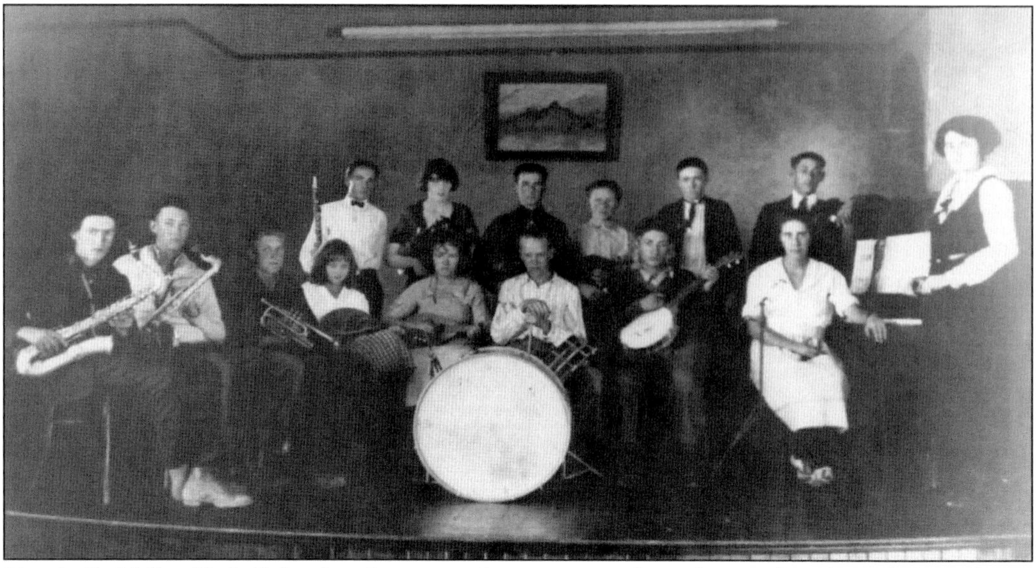

Coachella Valley High School orchestra students are seen here during the 1922–1923 academic year. Two of the students have been identified. The fifth person from the left is clarinet player Nelson Dometrius, and sitting at the piano is Sabra Kirk Kelly. High school students in Coachella, Indio, and Thermal all attended the Coachella Valley High School, founded in 1910, until Indio High School was built in 1958. (Courtesy of the Coachella Valley History Museum.)

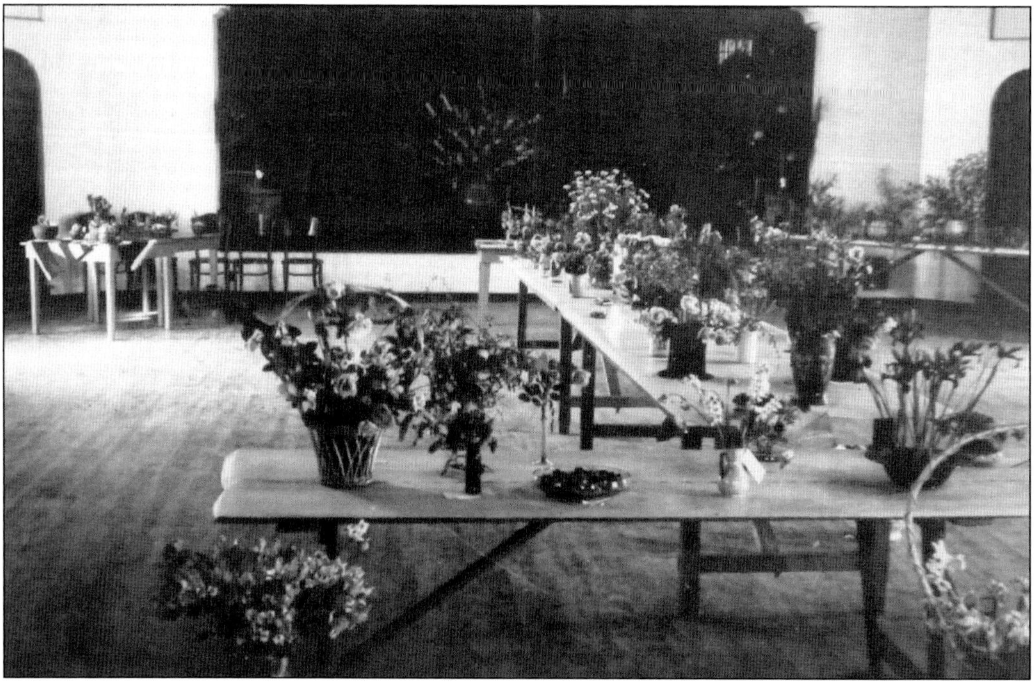

In the 1920s, the Coachella Valley Women's Club held a flower show. Women's clubs started nationwide as women looked for ways to participate in community social, philanthropic, and political activities. The flower shows held by this club and its sister club in Indio were used to raise money for local charitable causes. (Courtesy of the Coachella Valley History Museum.)

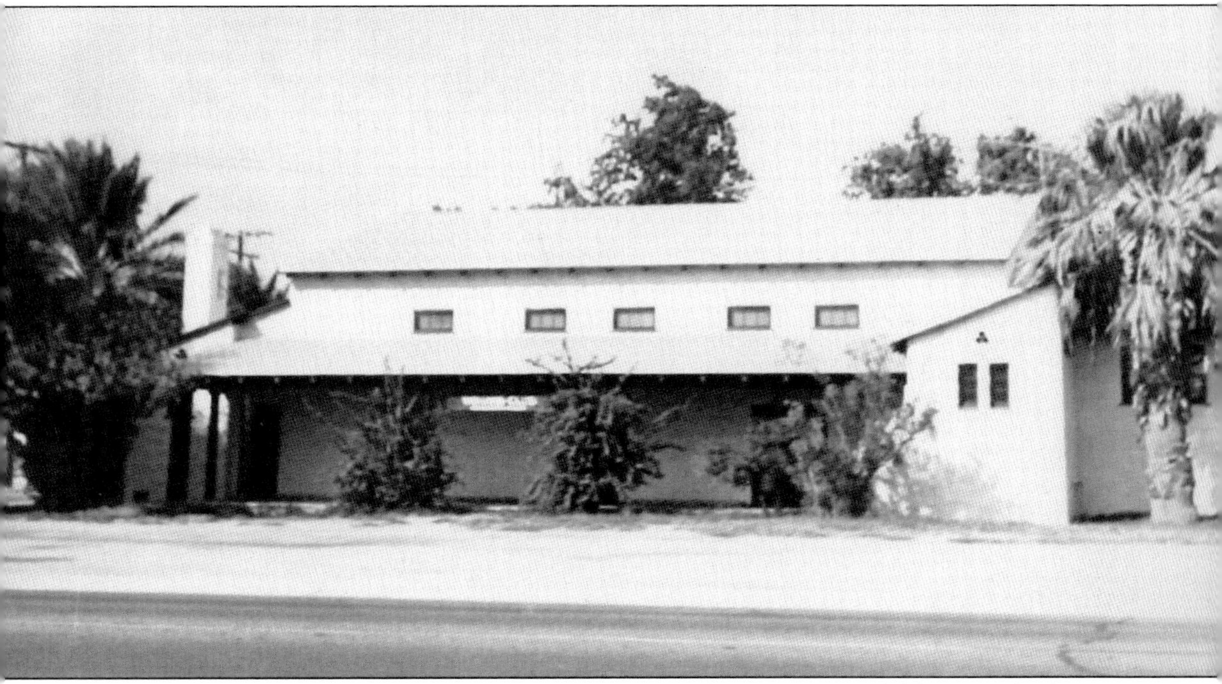

Pictured in this 1930s photograph is the Coachella Valley Women's Clubhouse, which was built in 1930 at 51-893 Highway 86. The club began October 13, 1924, at Eva Pearson's house. The first president was Zelba Yant. Many of the women's clubs during this time were started to provide women with a reprieve from the often-isolating life of a farmer's or rancher's wife. Before telephones, computers, cars, and great city development, many women were kept busy on the farms and ranches. Women's clubs, like this one, provided women a time to socialize with others in the community and a place to exercise their other skills and talents, such as music and literature. The Coachella Valley Women's Club was dissolved in April 2000. (Courtesy of the Coachella Valley History Museum.)

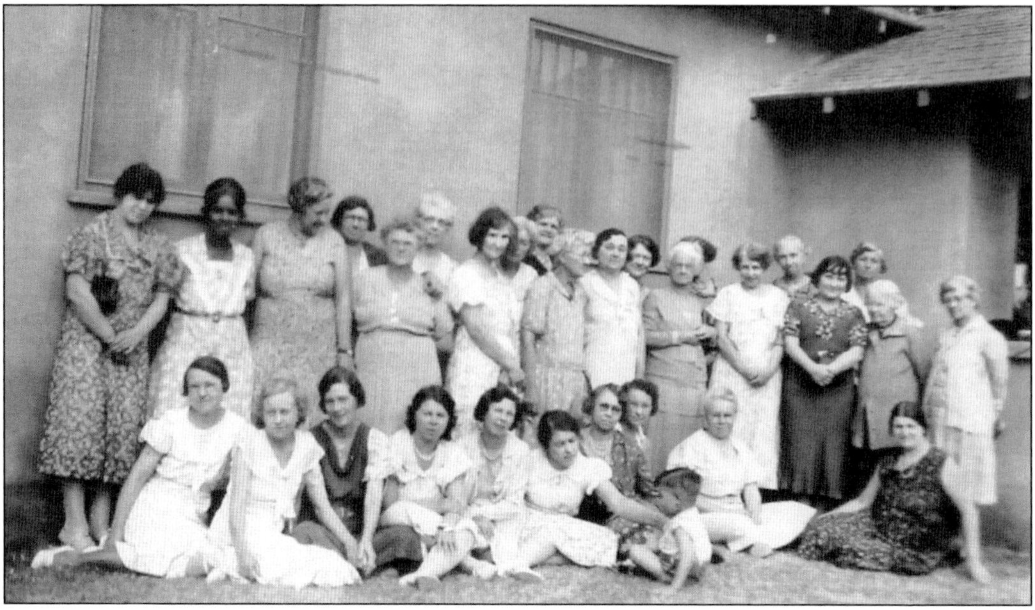

During the 1930s, the Coachella Ladies Aid Society met at various members' houses. Often, they brought their young children, who played as their mothers talked and focused on their charitable projects. Pictured below are, from left to right, (first row) Alvina Zabler, Priscilla Faries, Emma Howell, Elsie Westerfield, and two unidentified; (second row) Alice C. McClelland, Mabel Baker, unidentified, Frances Allen, Mrs. Fathergill, Gladys R. Johnson, Mrs. Burkhardt, and unidentified. Sitting in front are, from left to right, Mary Johnson and Mary Westerfield. (Both, courtesy of the Coachella Valley History Museum.)

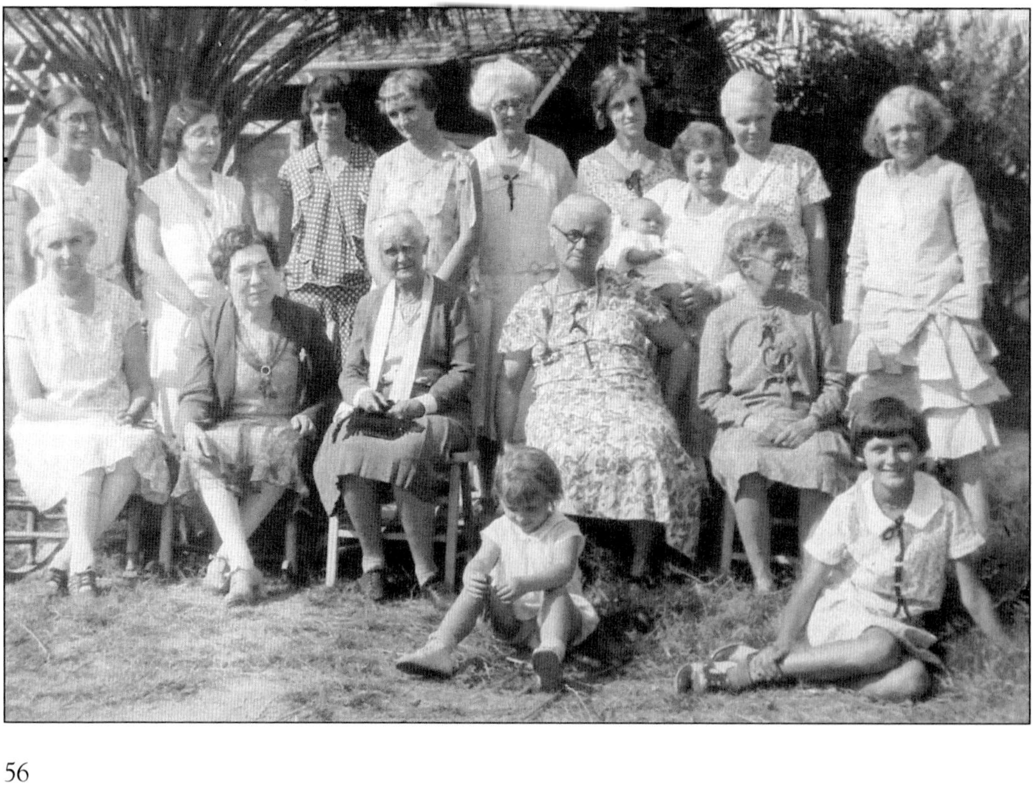

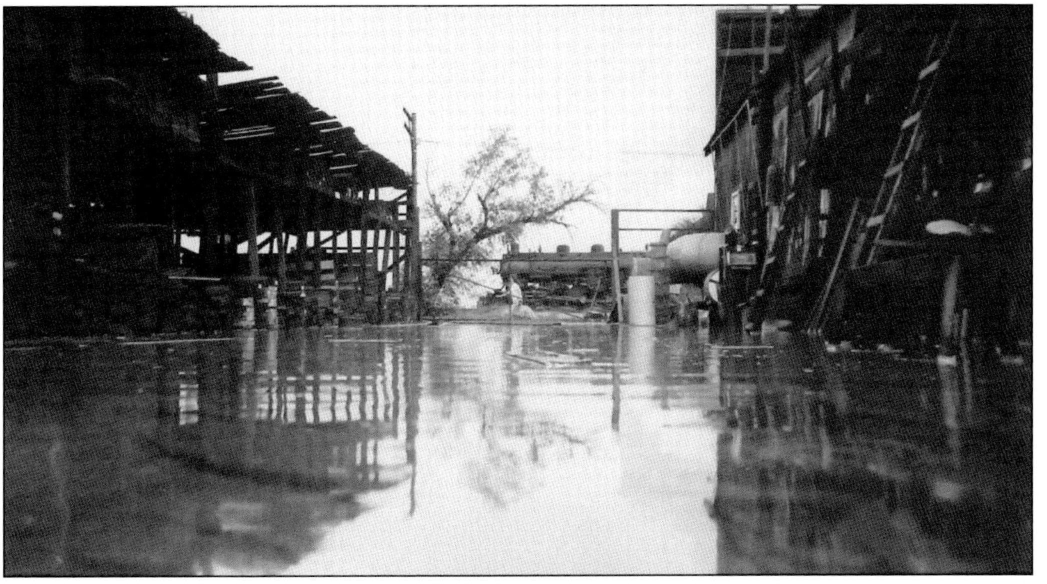

This 1930s photograph was taken at Hayward's Lumber. Note the unidentified man in the background trudging through the floodwater next to the steam engine stopped on the tracks behind the store. (Courtesy of the Coachella Valley History Museum.)

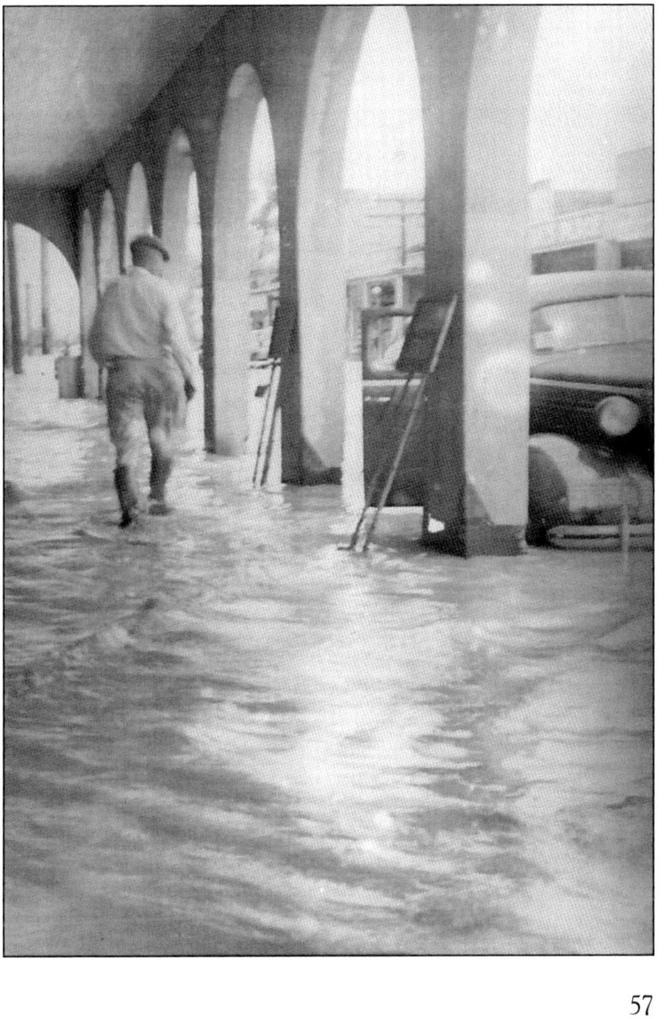

During the 1939 flooding in downtown Coachella, residents went about their regular daily routine the best they could. The irony of needing knee-high rain boots in the middle of a hot desert is still apparent to those who live through the flash floods and annual flooding in the Coachella Valley. (Courtesy of the Coachella Valley History Museum.)

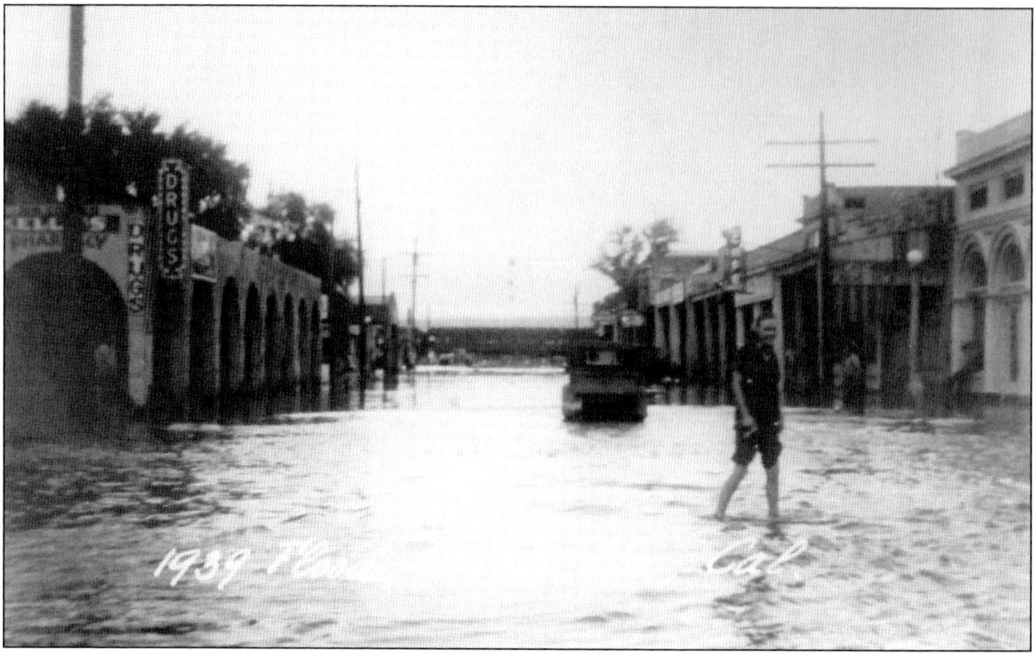

Here, an unidentified woman wades through the 1939 floodwaters. On the right is the First National Bank of Coachella, and on the left is Kelly Pharmacy. It was just another flood season in the Coachella Valley. (Courtesy of the Coachella Valley History Museum.)

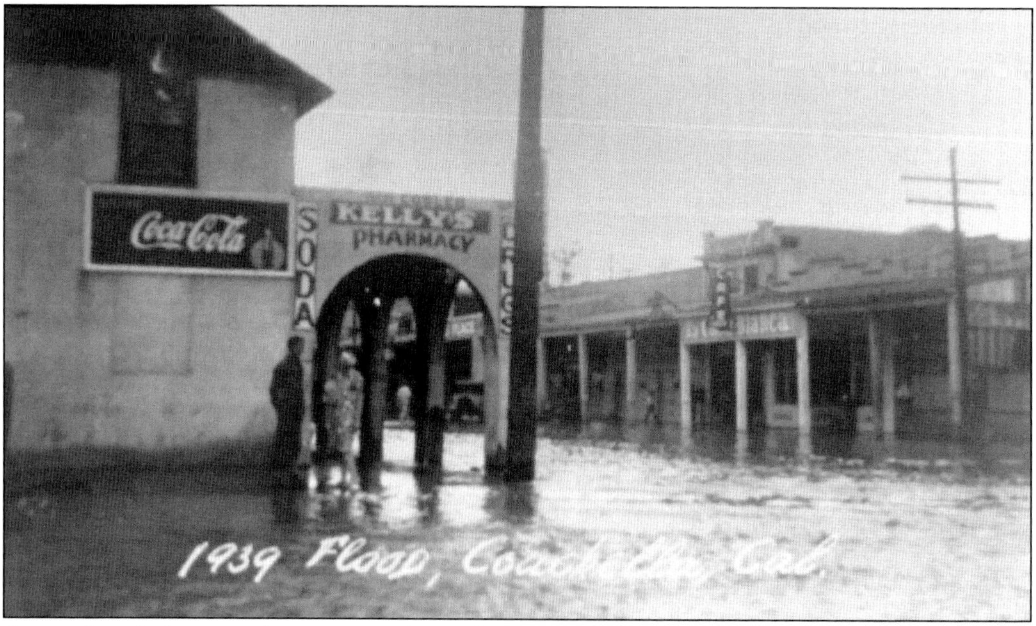

An unidentified man and woman stand outside Kelly's Pharmacy conversing while the floodwaters from 1939 surround the building. The curbs in Coachella and entryways were and are still often built higher than average to accommodate the annual flooding. These people are not standing in the floodwaters but on a raised walkway that the waters have not reached. (Courtesy of the Coachella Valley Water District.)

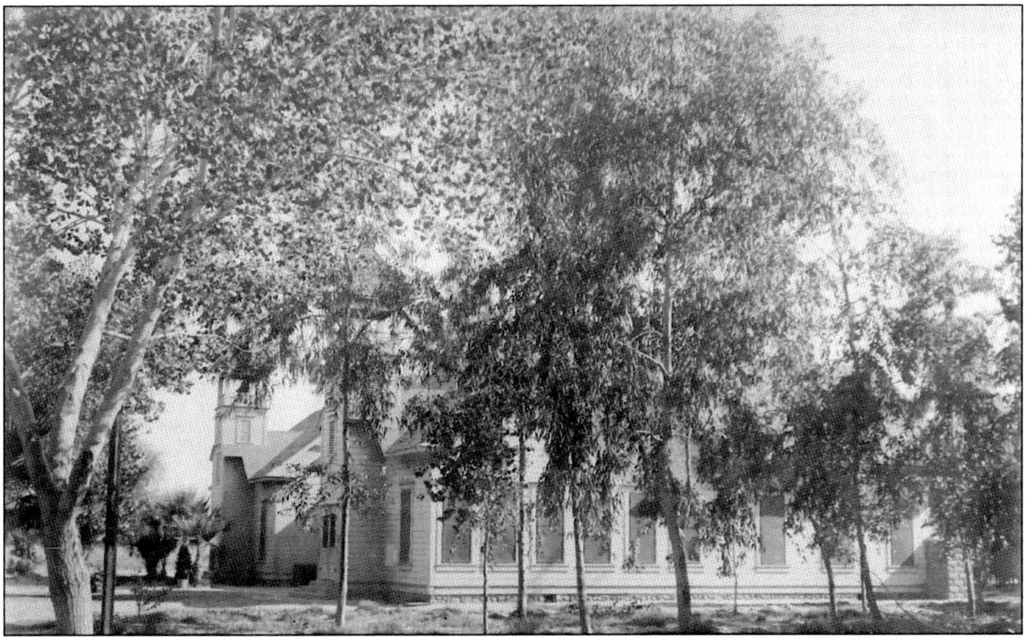

Pictured is the Coachella Grammar School on Seventh Street, seen through the trees in this 1914 photograph. Students of different grade levels were taught in the same room. Teachers were usually unmarried women, who would often stop teaching when they got married. (Courtesy of the Coachella Valley History Museum.)

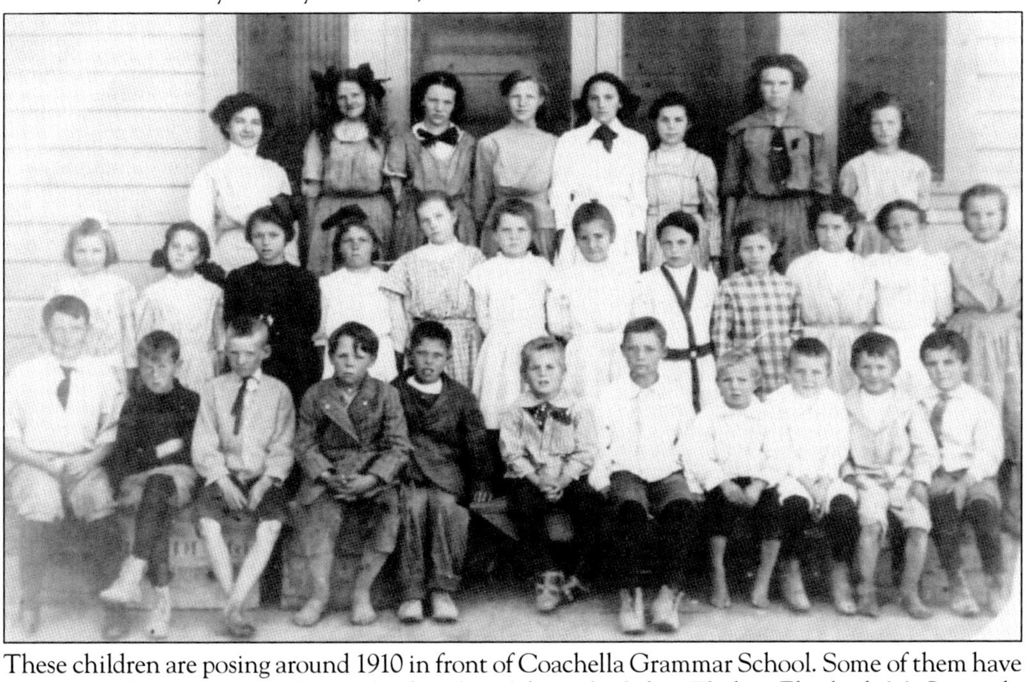

These children are posing around 1910 in front of Coachella Grammar School. Some of them have been identified. In the third row, the fourth girl from the left is Thelma Elizabeth McCormick, and eighth from the left is Mary Ann McCormick. The third girl from the left in the second row is Alice Makosky. In the first row, the seventh boy from the left is Howard McCormick, and eighth from the left is Rick McCormick. (Courtesy of the Coachella Valley History Museum.)

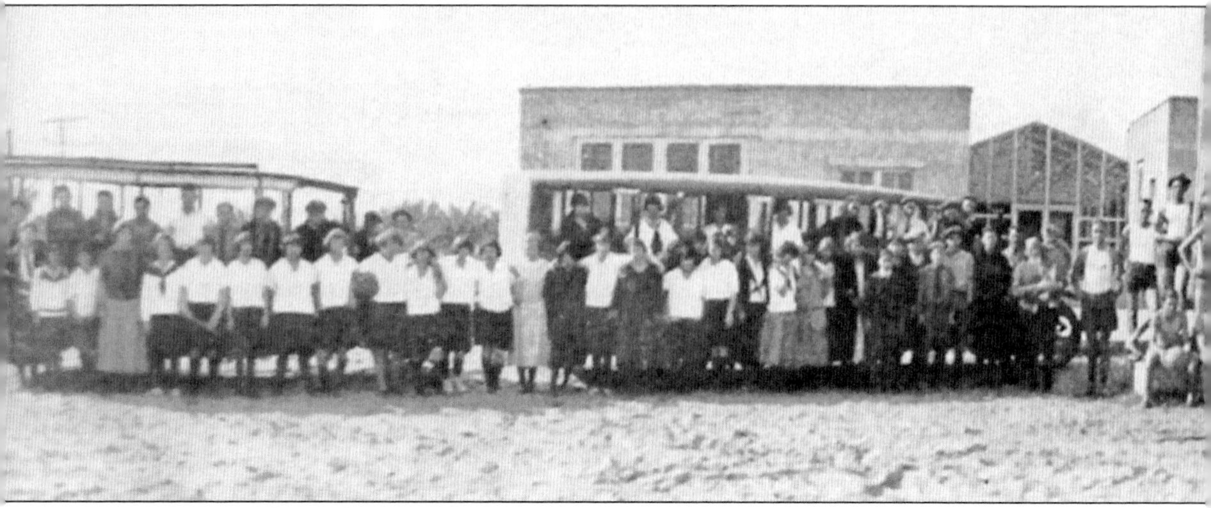

In 1922–1923, the student body of the Coachella Valley High School posed outside their school for this photograph in front of the school buses. Coachella Valley High School was founded in 1910. The school's mascot, the Arab, was chosen in 1930. Residents decided to use the Arab as a way to honor the contributions of people in the Middle East toward the establishment and

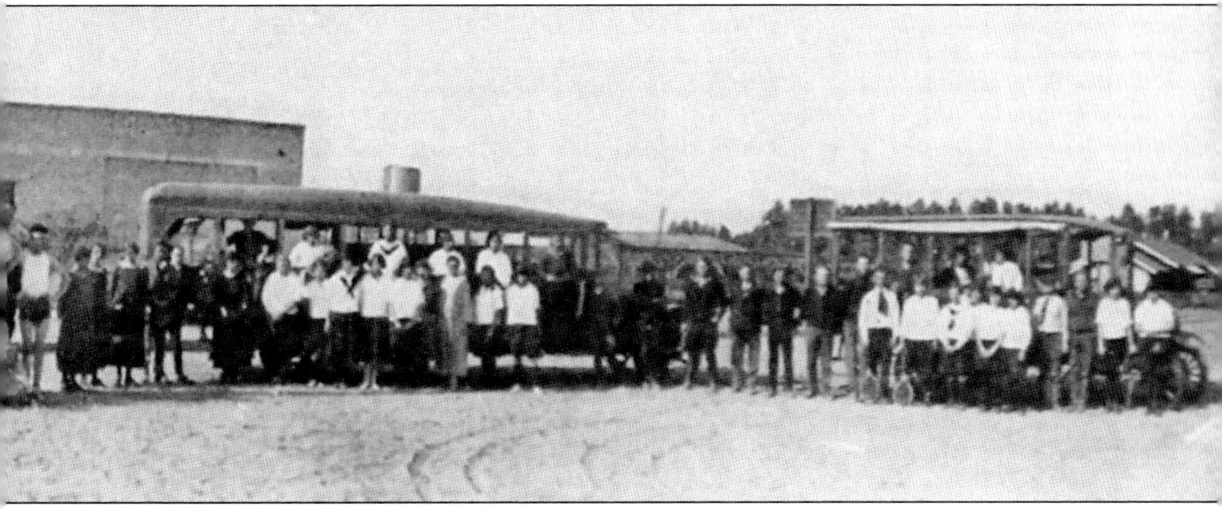

development of the date industry in the Coachella Valley. In 2013, there was some controversy over the use of the mascot between the intention of the mascot and the disrespect felt by Arabic people. (Courtesy of the Coachella Valley History Museum.)

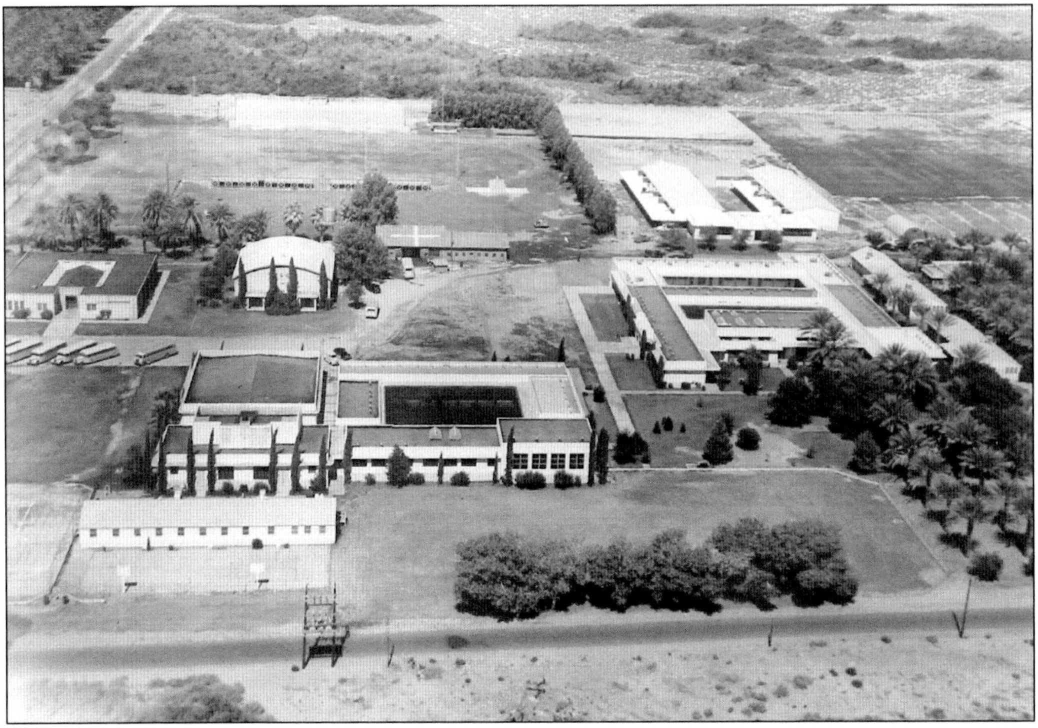

This aerial view of the Coachella Valley High School is from the 1940s. A donation of 10 acres of land was used to build the school; it was equidistant from Coachella and Indio and is located in Thermal. (Courtesy of the Coachella Valley History Museum.)

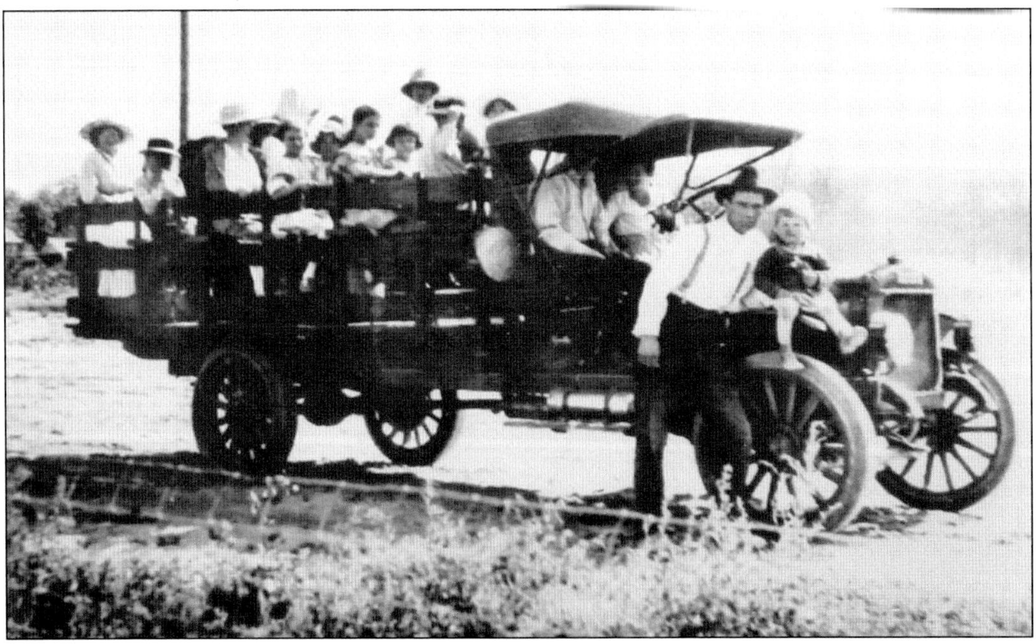

This 1920s photograph shows Coachella children riding an early school bus, a stake bed truck. It was not until the late 1930s that American schools began to use yellow school buses. (Courtesy of the Coachella Valley History Museum.)

This photograph was taken in the early 1920s in the Hurkey Creek area of the San Jacinto Mountains. The men are working on expanding a developed road. In the early 1900s, a lot of the basic infrastructure for the valley was developed as more settlers came to the Coachella Valley. (Courtesy of the Coachella Valley Water District.)

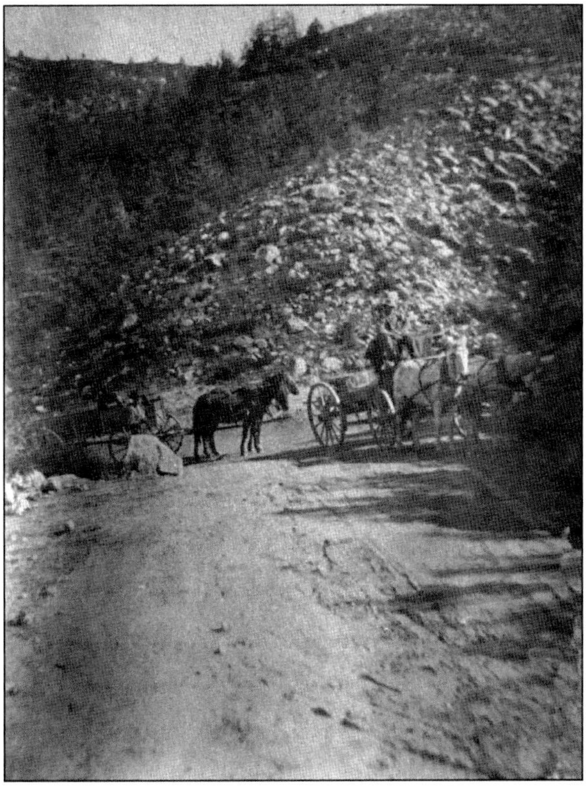

These unidentified homesteaders are pictured in the early 1900s. Many of the new residents created farms, or date ranches once dates were established. Both required the development of irrigation systems as people took advantage of the ability to grow year-round crops. (Courtesy of the Coachella Valley Water District.)

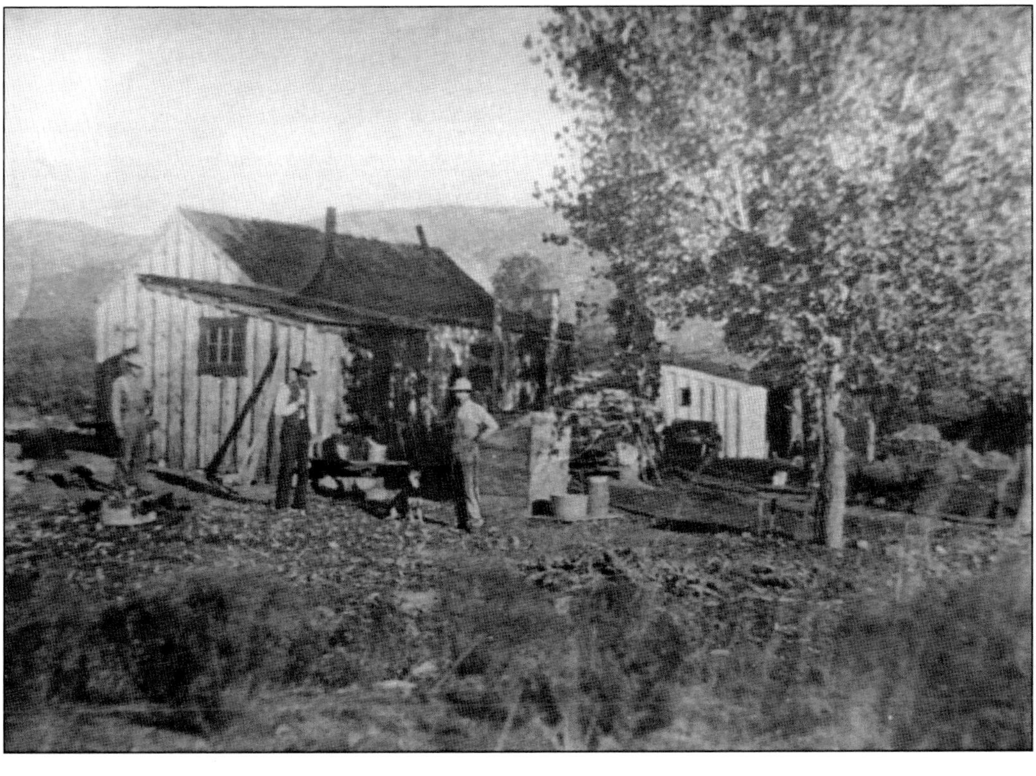

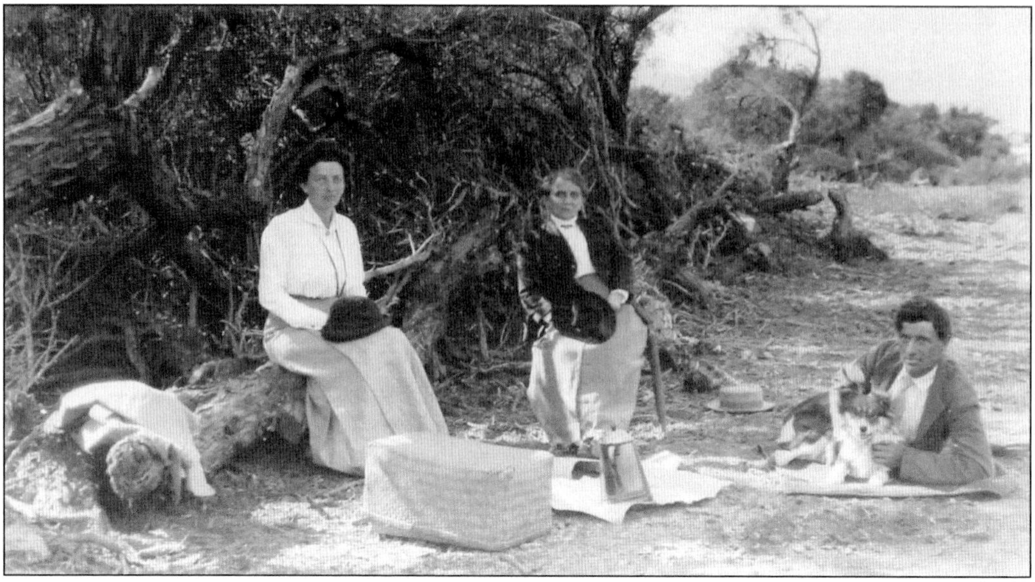

Creating an agricultural life in an arid desert was difficult; however, people still found ways to relax, socialize, and enjoy the desert beauty. The above c. 1915 photograph shows a picnic near Coachella. From left to right, Alberta Hyde, unidentified, and Claude W. Hyde enjoy the day with good company and food. In the 1914 photograph below, Grace Proctor (left) and Katherine Teagle pose amongst flowers in Coachella. (Both, courtesy of the Coachella Valley History Museum.)

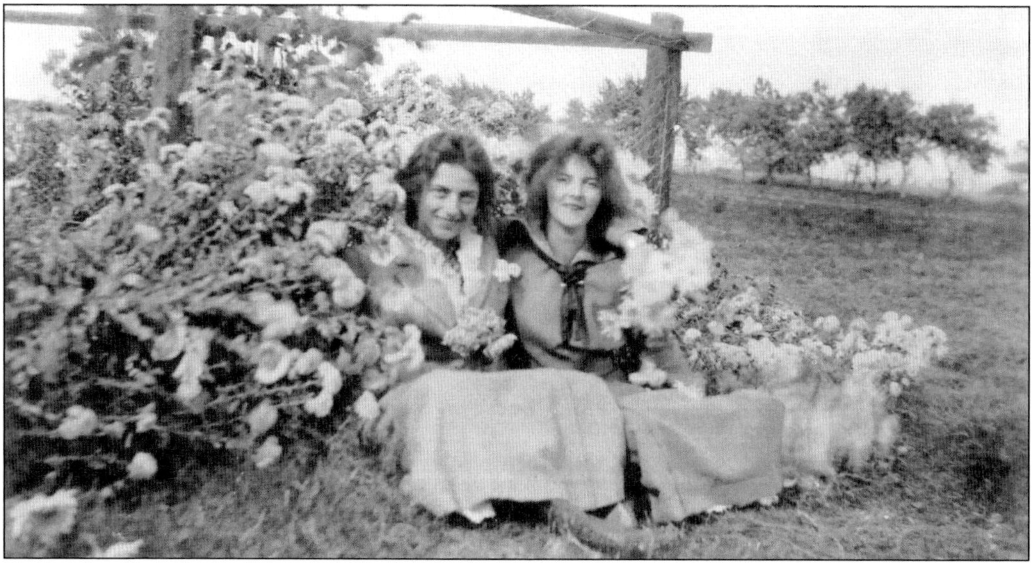

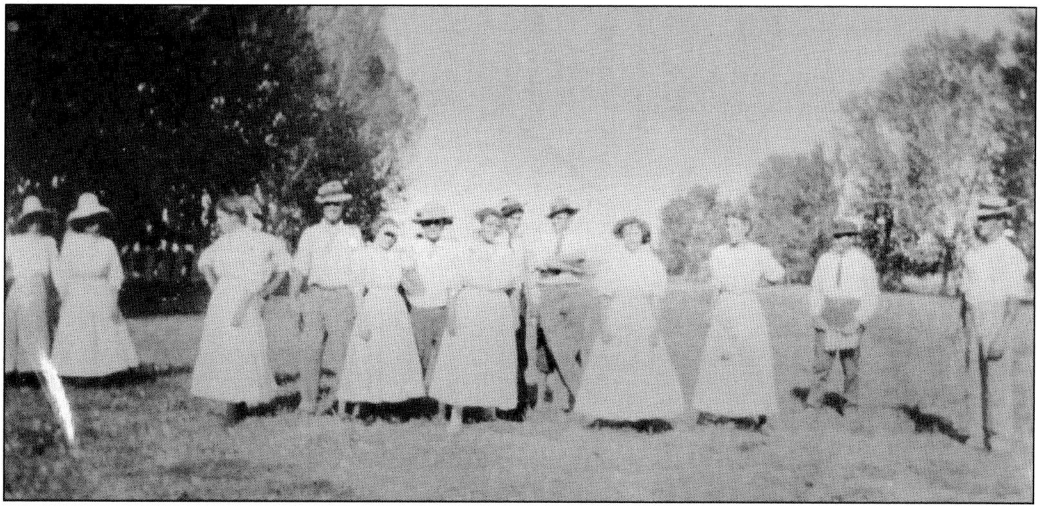

Coachella residents sometimes hosted garden parties in their leisure time. Three of the individuals at this 1909 garden party have been identified as Grace (Makisky) Proctor (second from left), Lenore (Peterson) Koehler (fourth from right), and Eva (Thomas) Pearson (third from right). (Courtesy of Coachella Valley History Museum.)

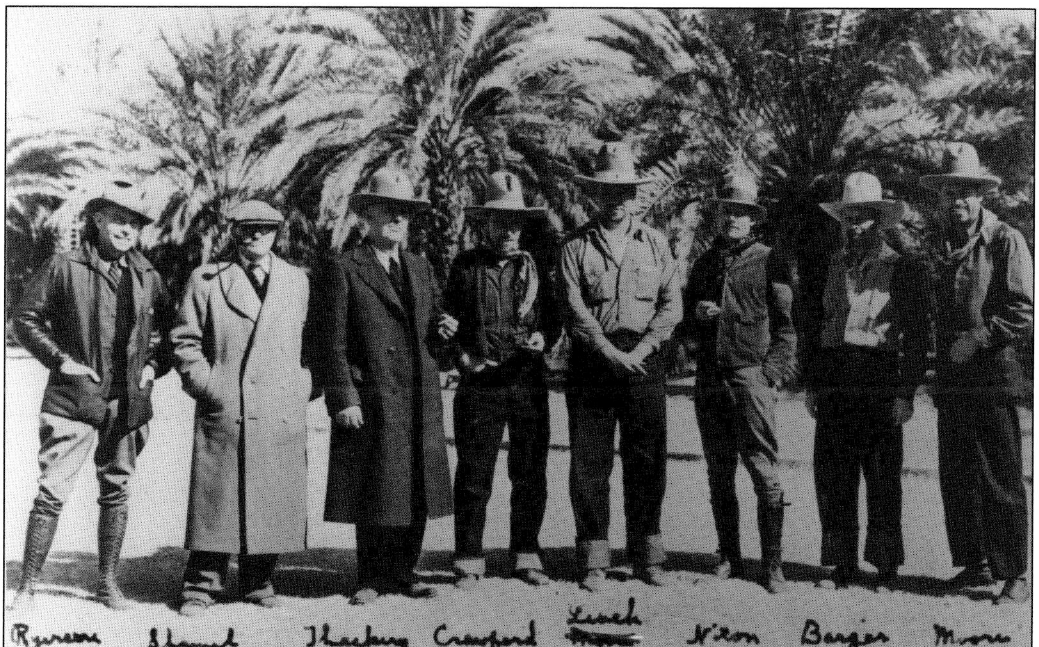

Residents also held rodeos and other community gatherings. This 1937 photograph was taken of the US Department of Agriculture (USDA) Date and Citrus Experiment Station's staff. They were dressed in their best clothing to attend Indio Rodeo days. (Courtesy of the Coachella Valley Water District.)

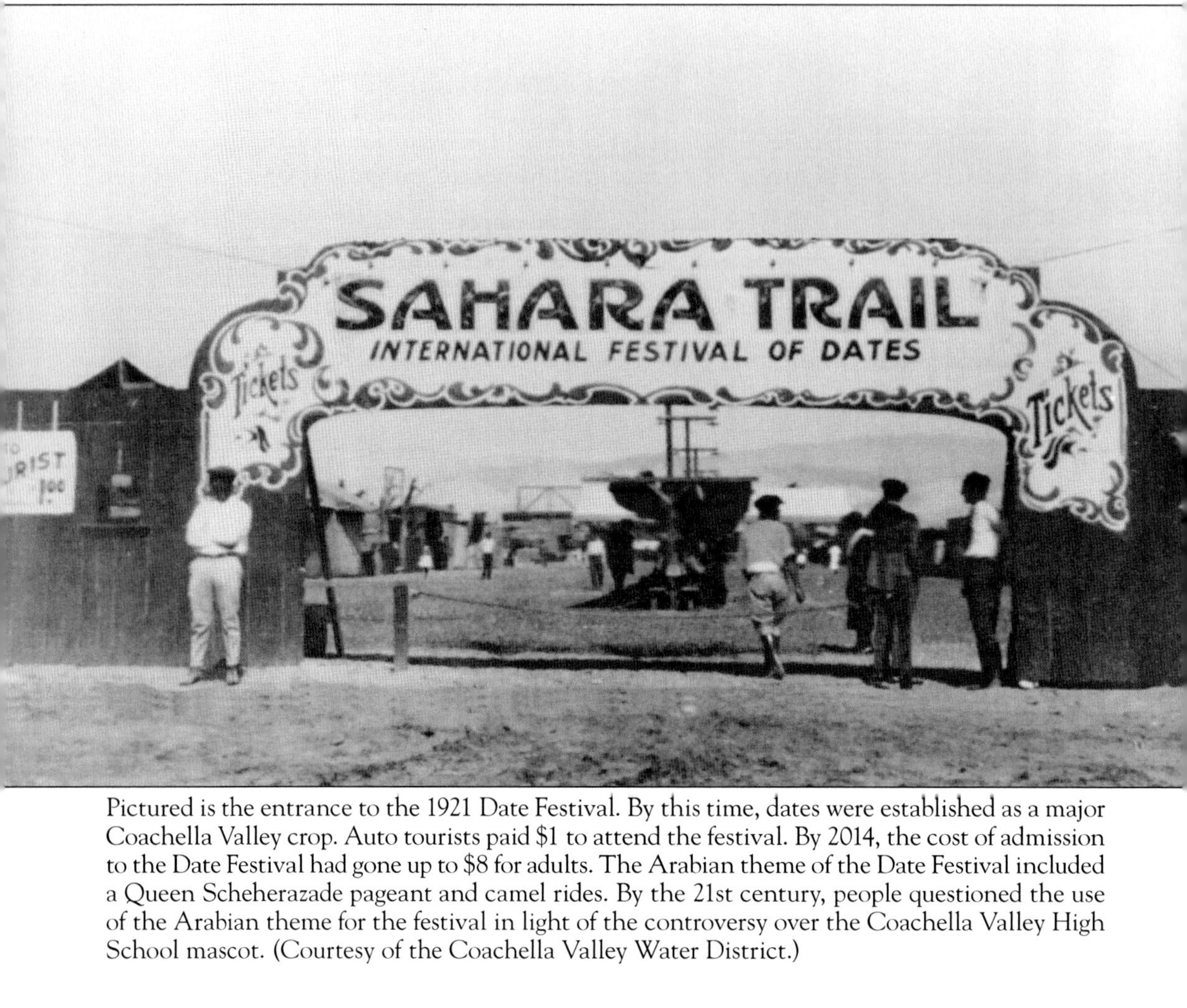

Pictured is the entrance to the 1921 Date Festival. By this time, dates were established as a major Coachella Valley crop. Auto tourists paid $1 to attend the festival. By 2014, the cost of admission to the Date Festival had gone up to $8 for adults. The Arabian theme of the Date Festival included a Queen Scheherazade pageant and camel rides. By the 21st century, people questioned the use of the Arabian theme for the festival in light of the controversy over the Coachella Valley High School mascot. (Courtesy of the Coachella Valley Water District.)

The first school in the neighboring town of Indio is seen at right during the 1900–1901 school year. The teacher was Miss Quinn. This photograph of Miss Quinn is one of a few of the early Coachella Valley schoolteachers. Schoolteachers in the early 1900s often taught grades first through eighth in a one-room building. These teachers taught arithmetic, English, reading, history, and other subjects for the varying levels of students. The photograph below shows three unidentified school-age boys around 1907. (Both, courtesy of the Coachella Valley Water District.)

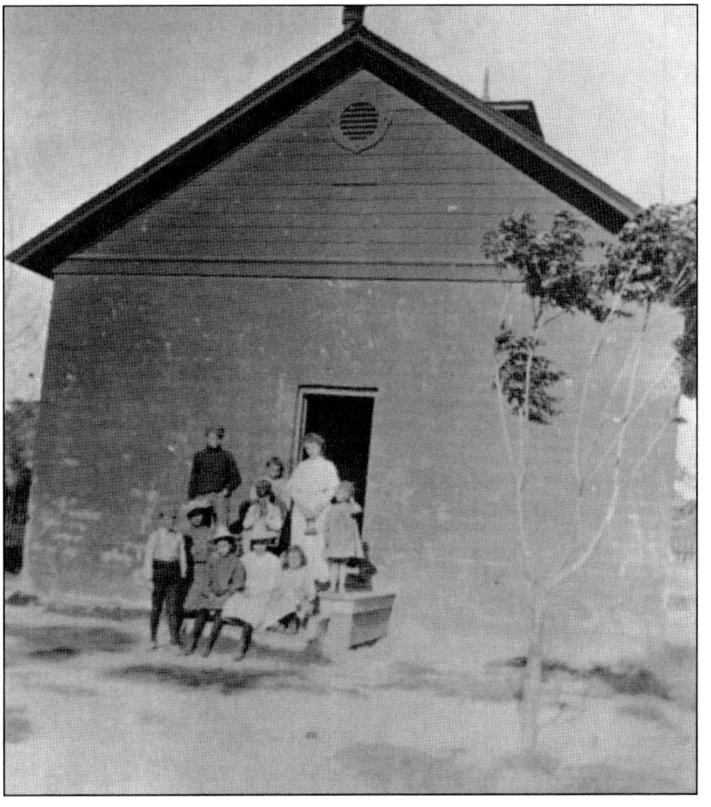

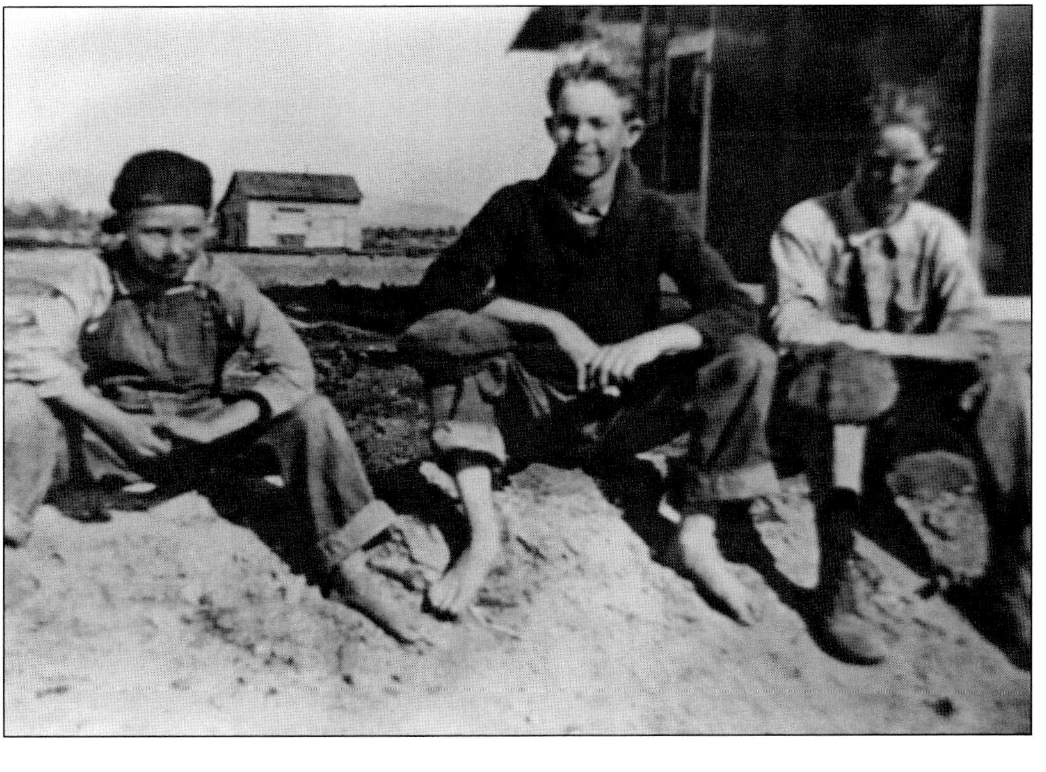

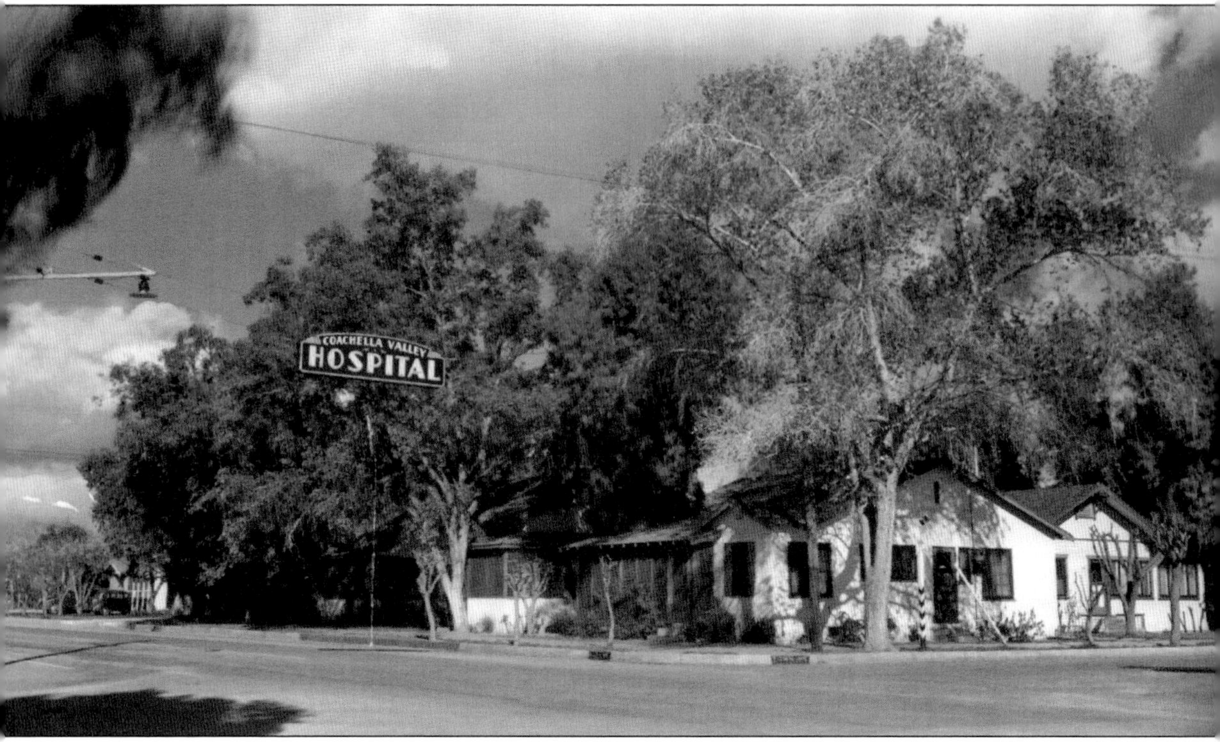

In 1928, Dr. Russell Gray opened the valley's first hospital, pictured here. His wife served as nurse and cook. The hospital consisted of several small homes that were remodeled and joined together to make treatment rooms and patient rooms. It was located on the northeast corner of Towne and Miles Avenues and later became known as Coachella Valley Hospital. Dr. B. Gene Morris built the second valley hospital, Casita Hospital, in the 1940s. Casita Hospital was later converted into a mental health facility. In 1966, the Indio Community Hospital was erected by several physicians, including Dr. Reynaldo Carreon, on land donated by Dr. Reynaldo Carreon on the corner of Monroe Avenue and Dr. Carreon Boulevard. The hospital's name was changed to John F. Kennedy Memorial Hospital after the assassination of President Kennedy. (Courtesy of the Coachella Valley Water District.)

Four

STRENGTHENING THE COMMUNITY

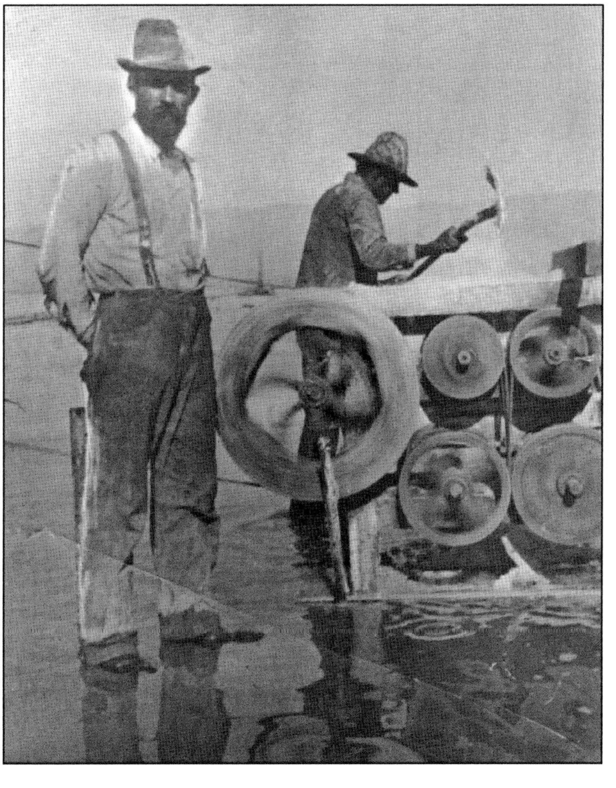

This photograph of two unidentified men working in the fields was taken around 1900. Converting the arid desert of the Coachella Valley took determination and technology to divert water to sustain the agriculture industry. The diversion of water from the Colorado River enabled the Coachella Valley to take advantage of the perpetual growing season in this area. (Courtesy of the Coachella Valley Water District.)

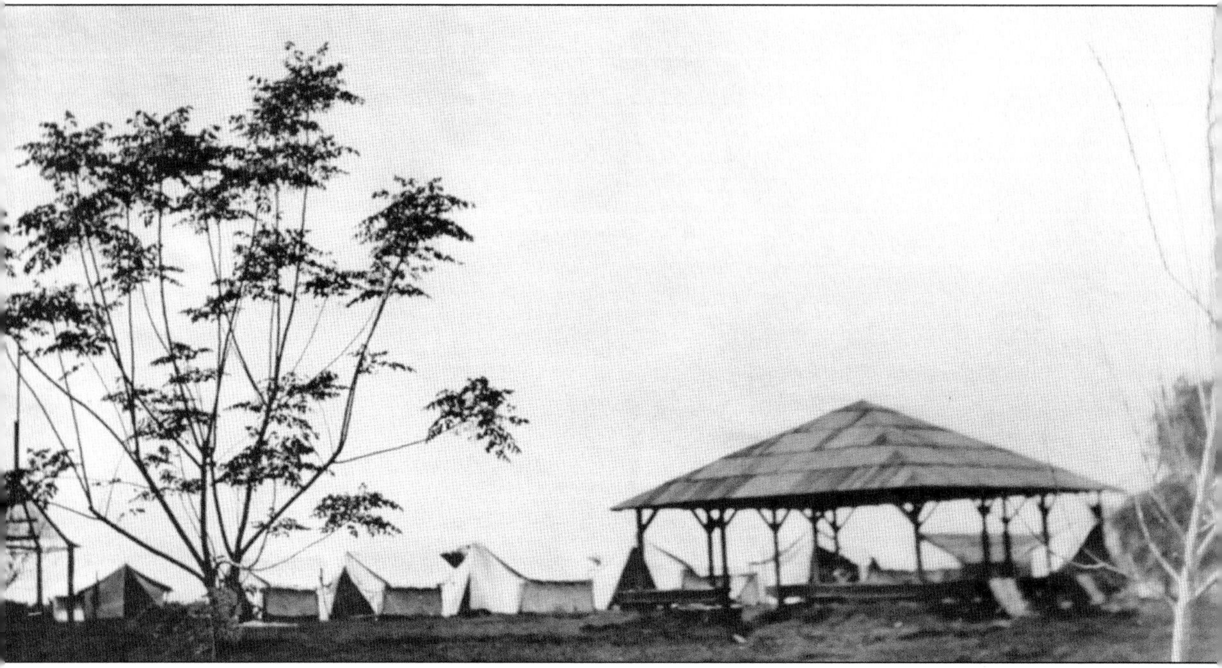

This early 1900s photograph shows the Indio Health Camp, located north of the railroad tracks between Jackson Avenue and Market Street. The camp provided services for those with tuberculosis seeking the benefit of the arid heat provided by the Coachella Valley. Dr. June Robertson (McCarroll) arrived in the valley in 1904 with her husband, John Robertson, who was ill with tuberculosis. He died in 1914, but she remained in the valley and practiced medicine as one of the early physicians. She remarried in 1916 to Southern Pacific Railroad station manager Frank McCarroll. McCarroll is well known for advocating the use of a white paint line dividing opposing traffic on roads as a preventative measure against head-on collisions. The California Highway Commission adopted the use of the white lines in 1924 after McCarroll led a successful statewide letter campaign for the paint lines with the help of the Woman's Club of Indio and other social organizations. (Courtesy of the Coachella Valley Water District.)

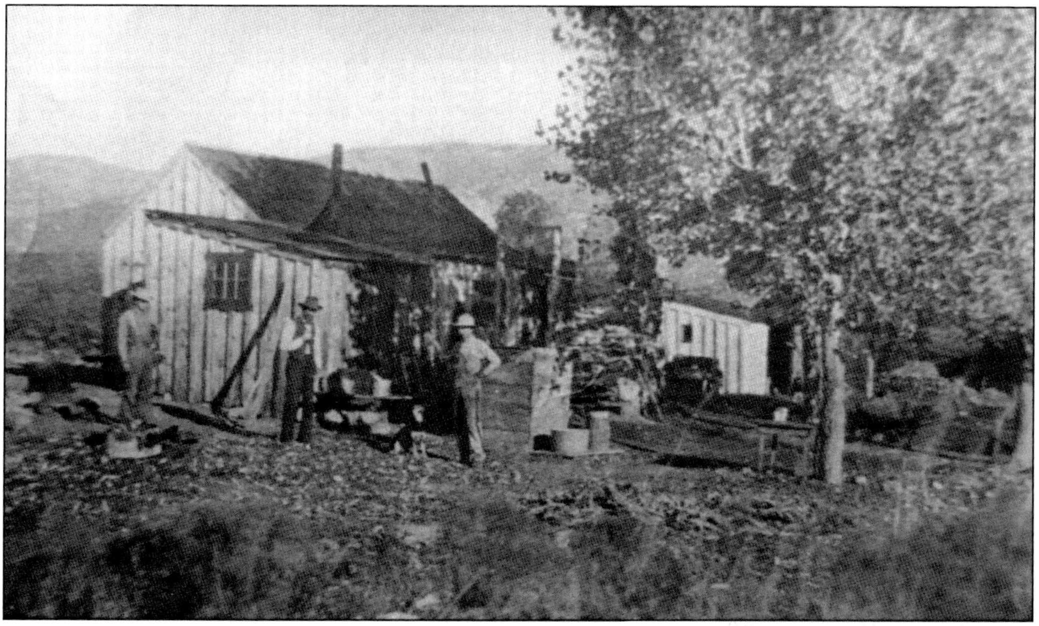

The photograph above of a Coachella homestead is part of the Elizabeth Moore Collection. The Coachella Valley Water District (CVWD) houses the Moore collection and many more photograph collections. During the early development of the Coachella Valley, CVWD photographers recorded the evolving and changing lives of the people and landscape in the Coachella Valley. These images will continue to be invaluable to researchers. This early 1900s picture of a homestead shows three unidentified men. The photograph below features an unidentified woman feeding chickens in front of a Coachella tent house in 1907. (Above, courtesy of the Coachella Valley Water District; below, courtesy of the Coachella Valley History Museum.)

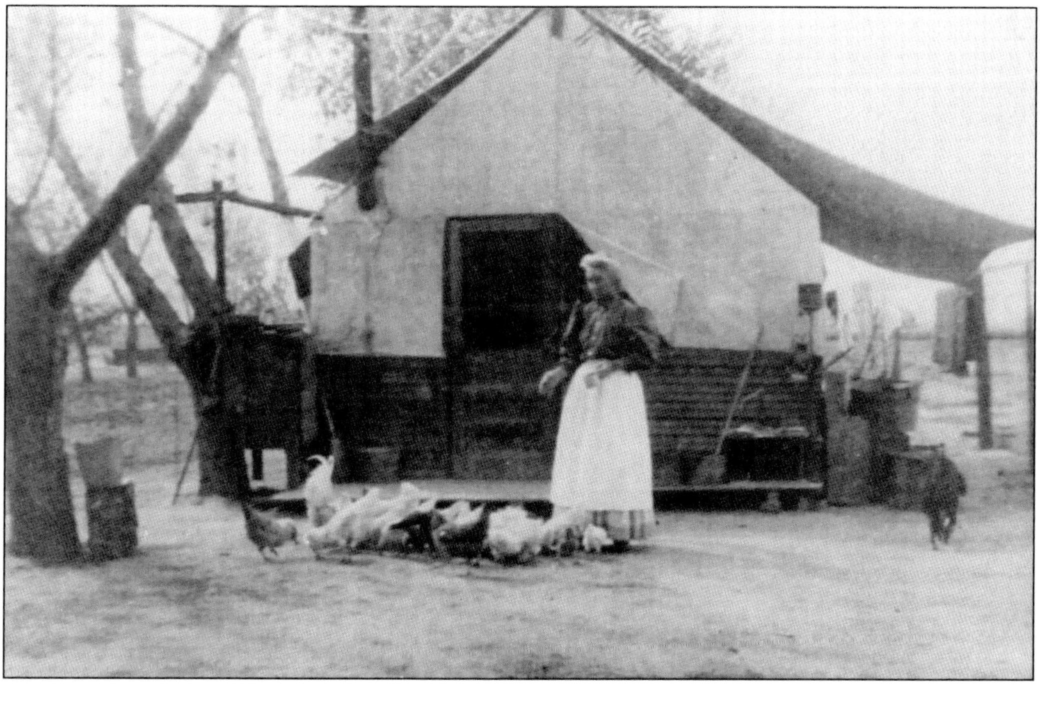

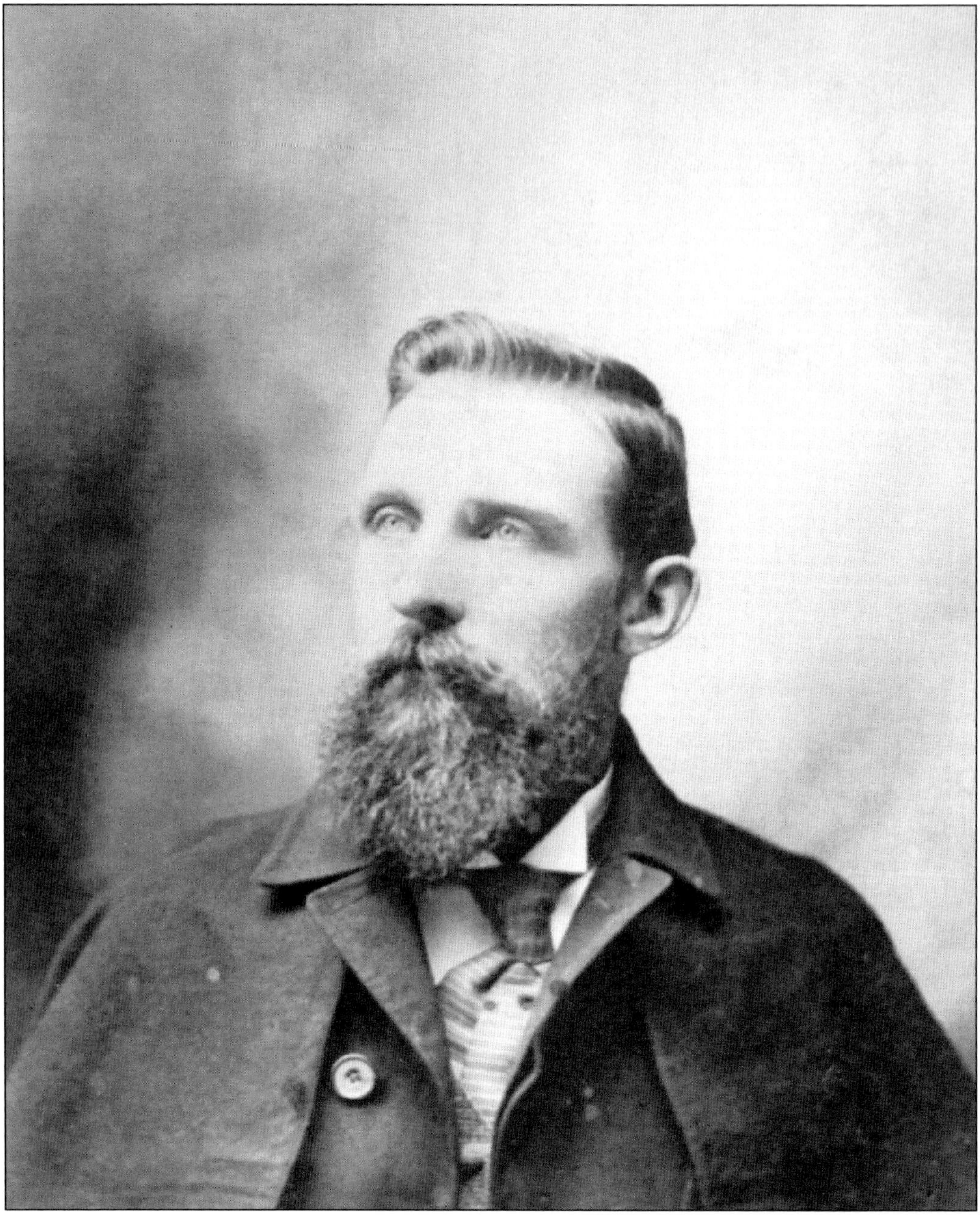

Henry Williamson McKay operated the New Liverpool Salt Company in the Salton Sink. Owner George Durbrow established the saltworks on January 15, 1885, after learning about the significant amount of salt in the Salton Sink southeast of Coachella. The purity of Salton Sink's salt eliminated some of the steps required in most salt processing. Durbrow built the saltworks processing plant and hired McKay to oversee the operation. McKay hired local Cahuilla Indians and Japanese immigrants. The salt was processed and then loaded into railcars at a Southern Pacific siding near the company. The Desert Cahuilla Indian workers were from the Salton Sink area and were part of the Torres Martinez Indian reservation, which was established in 1876 in the Coachella and Imperial Valleys. (Courtesy of the Coachella Valley Water District.)

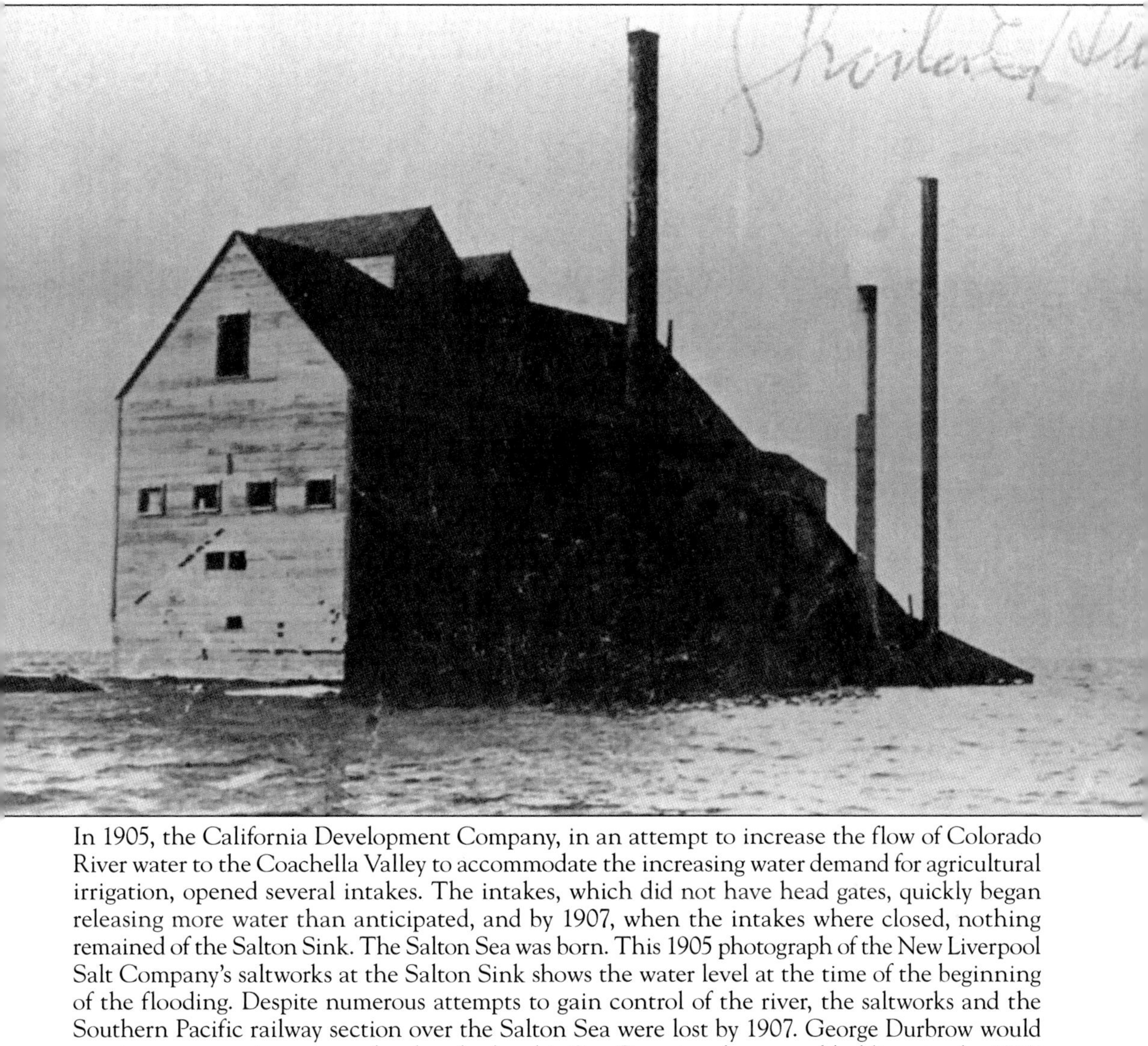

In 1905, the California Development Company, in an attempt to increase the flow of Colorado River water to the Coachella Valley to accommodate the increasing water demand for agricultural irrigation, opened several intakes. The intakes, which did not have head gates, quickly began releasing more water than anticipated, and by 1907, when the intakes where closed, nothing remained of the Salton Sink. The Salton Sea was born. This 1905 photograph of the New Liverpool Salt Company's saltworks at the Salton Sink shows the water level at the time of the beginning of the flooding. Despite numerous attempts to gain control of the river, the saltworks and the Southern Pacific railway section over the Salton Sea were lost by 1907. George Durbrow would continue to experience tragedy when he lost his San Francisco home and holdings in the 1906 San Francisco earthquake and fire. (Courtesy of the Coachella Valley Water District.)

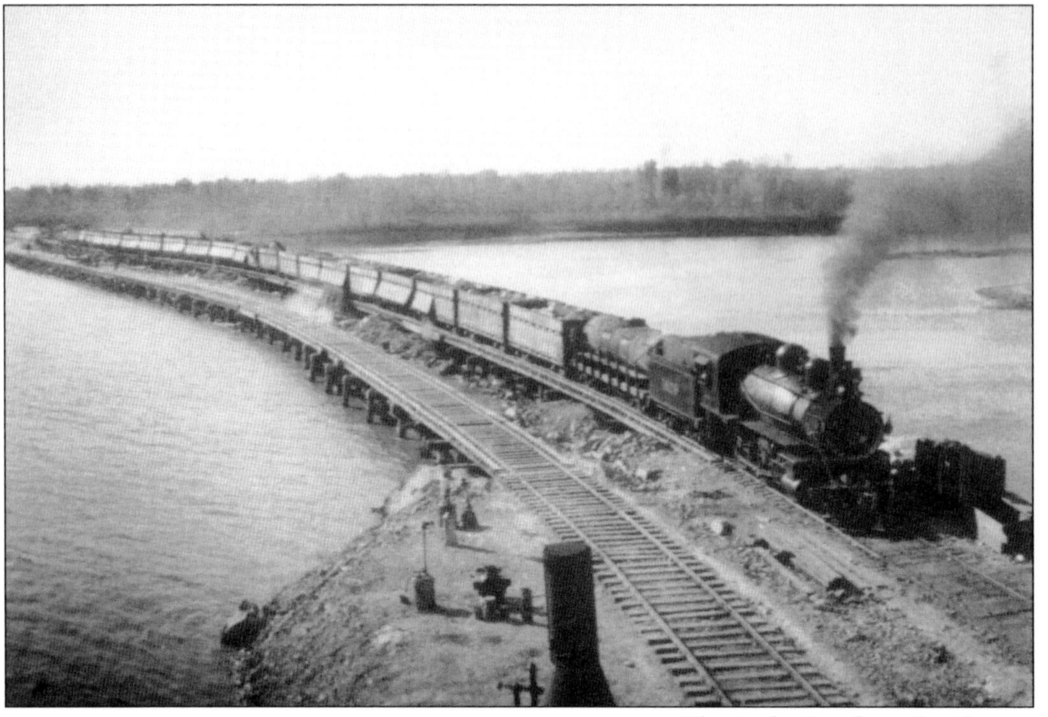

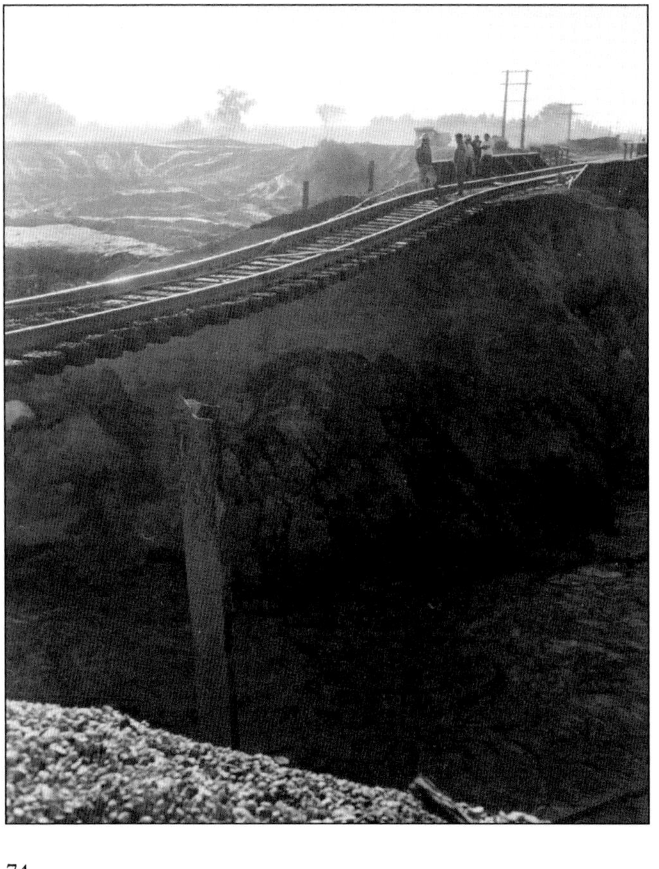

This is the Southern Pacific Railroad track section built over the Salton Sink. The picture was taken prior to 1907 when flooding caused the creation of the Salton Sea covering the railway tracks and local buildings, like the New Liverpool Salt Company's saltworks. (Courtesy of the Coachella Valley Water District.)

This early 1900s photograph shows a Southern Pacific Railroad bridge that was built in the Coachella Valley. This section of the tracks was built over a chasm. (Courtesy of the Coachella Valley Water District.)

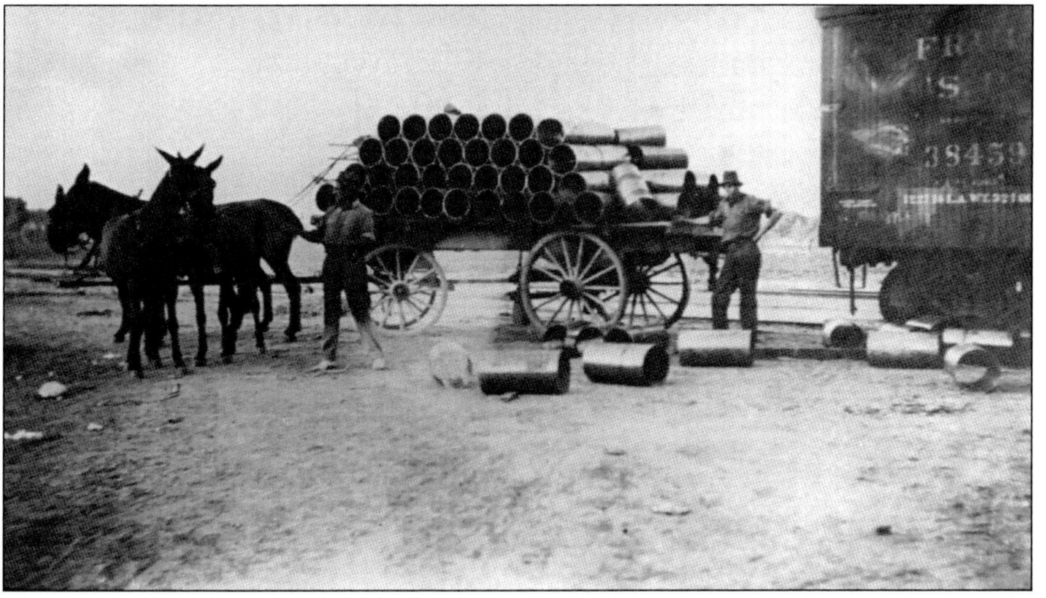

This 1915 photograph shows E.N.T. Burnett, on the left, as he tries to soothe his mules at the Coachella siding. An unidentified man is at the back of the wagon. Burnett explained to the Coachella Valley Water District photographer that the passing train had frightened his mules. (Courtesy of the Coachella Valley Water District.)

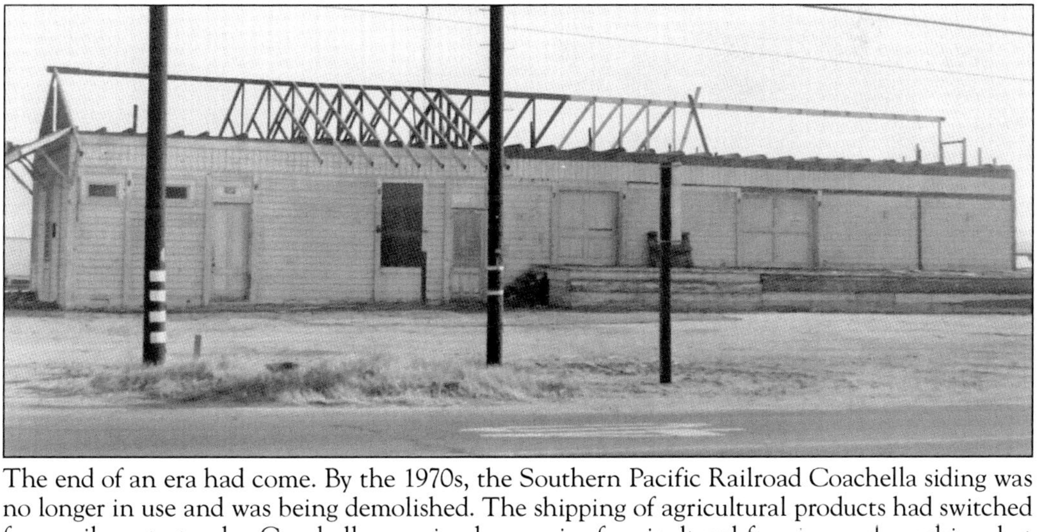

The end of an era had come. By the 1970s, the Southern Pacific Railroad Coachella siding was no longer in use and was being demolished. The shipping of agricultural products had switched from railcars to trucks. Coachella remained an oasis of agricultural farming and ranching, but without a tie to the railroad. (Courtesy of the Coachella Valley History Museum.)

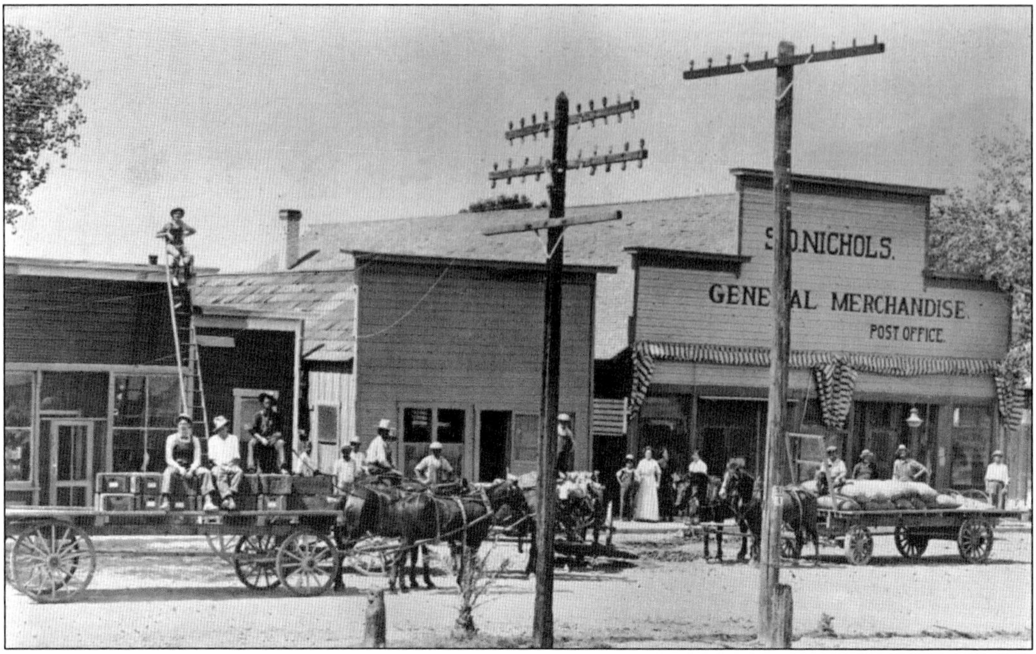

Other areas surrounding the town of Coachella also flourished. The above early 1900s photograph features the Nichols store in Thermal. Thermal would remain an unincorporated area well into the 21st century while other towns grew and expanded into urban city areas. The area of Thermal developed into a rural agricultural landscape, while nearby areas like Coachella developed a city center. The below photograph was taken in 1936 in the town of Indio. Development on Miles Avenue included several hotels, including the Hotel Potter shown here. A 1991 fire destroyed this hotel. (Both, courtesy of the Coachella Valley Water District.)

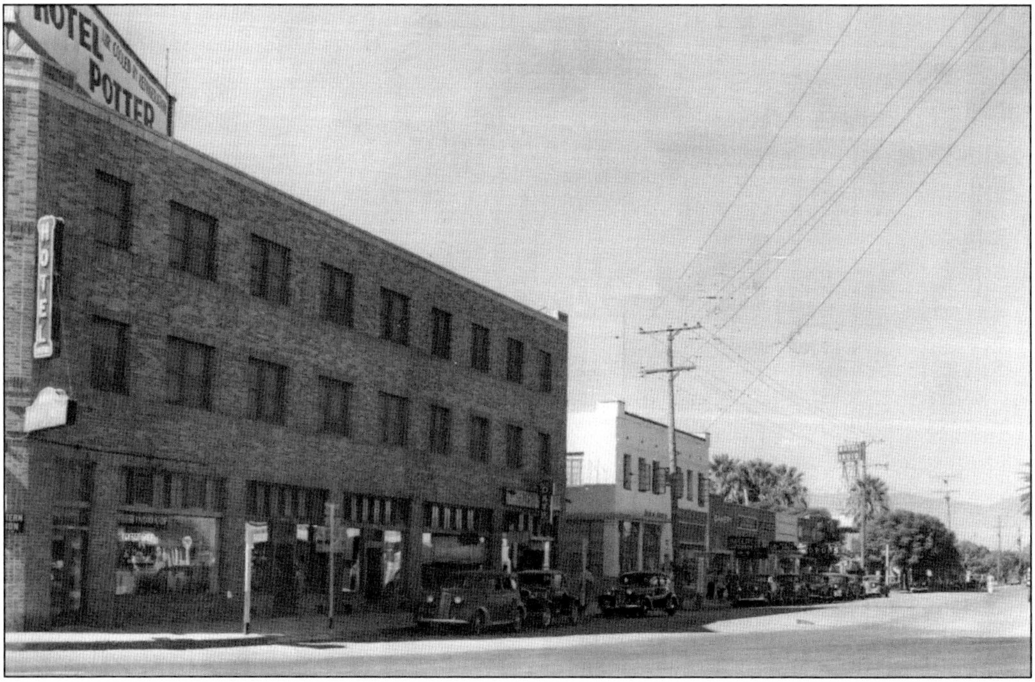

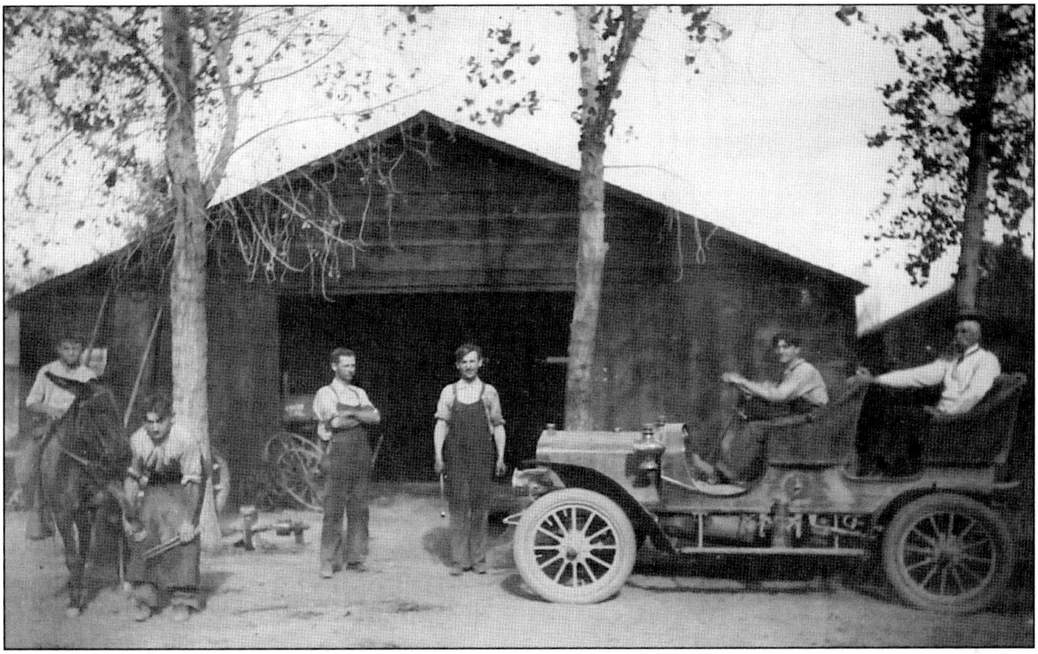

The stark difference between the mule and automobile can be seen in this 1911 photograph of the Kelly and Rouff Blacksmith Shop at 1637 Seventh Street in Coachella. A man on the left is shoeing the mule while the rider waits atop. At the same time, two men sit in the automobile at right. (Courtesy of the Coachella Valley Water District.)

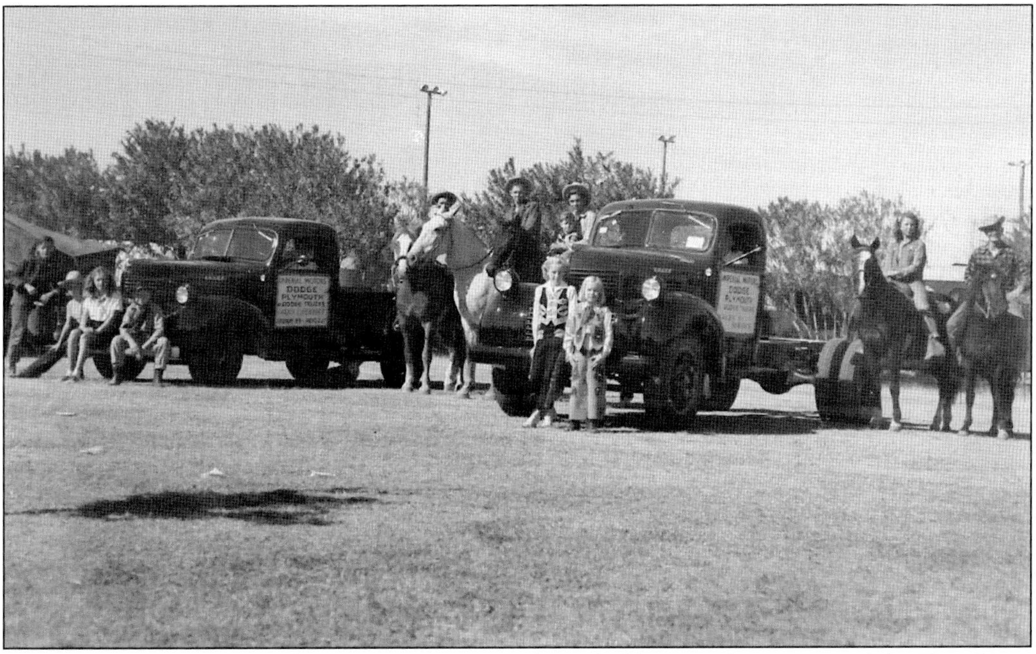

By 1951, when this photograph was taken, most households owned one automobile. Kay Olsen of Imperial Motors posed two Dodge trucks with several people either riding horses or standing. Imperial Motors was located on Highway 99 in the city of Indio. (Courtesy of the Coachella Valley History Museum.)

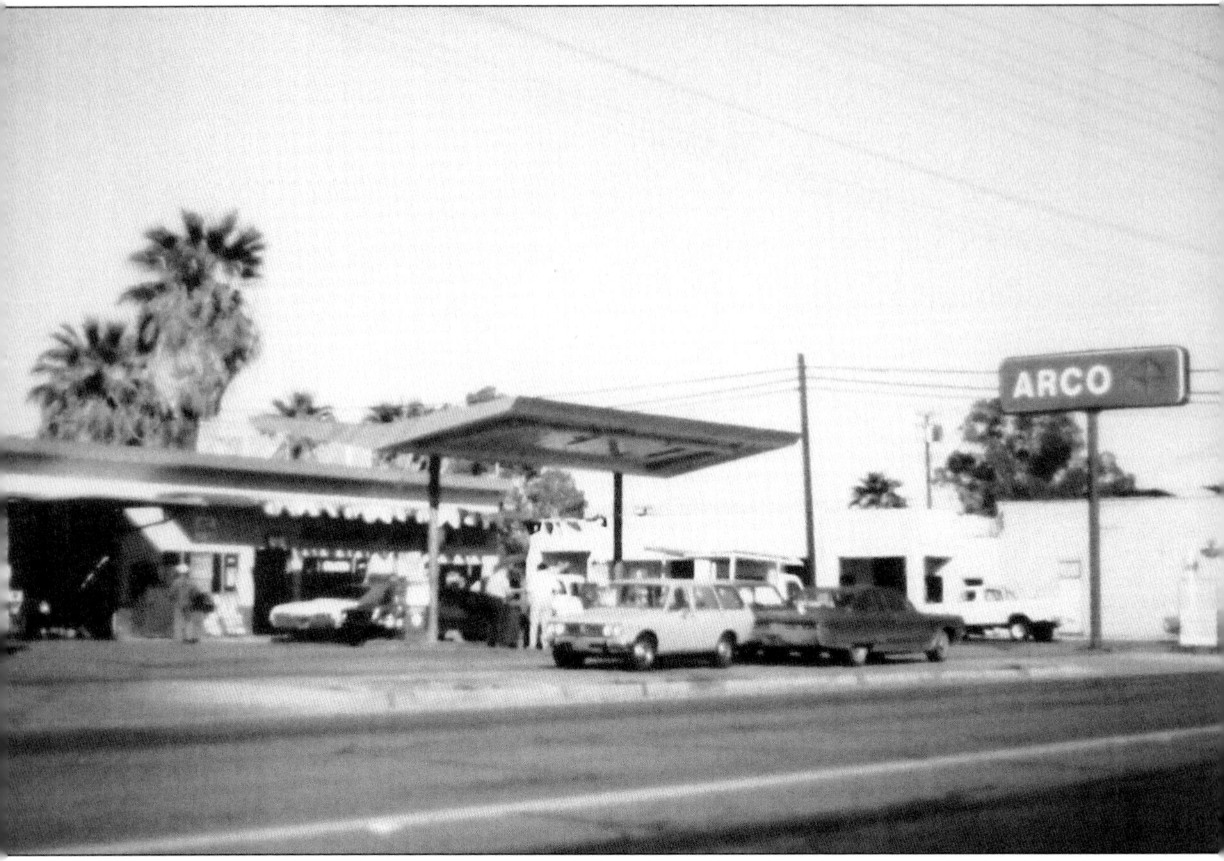

The advancement of the automobile industry drove the expansion and development of the interstate highways, gas stations, auto mechanics, and more. The Arco gas station, pictured here in 1991, was located on Highway 111 in Coachella. Gas stations evolved over time, starting with full-service stations and leading to the predominantly self-service gas pumps with convenience stores. The gas pumps went from offering one gas product to the option of three different types. The development of the highways and other paved roads made areas of the Coachella Valley more accessible and influenced further development of the surrounding desert land. By the late 20th century, a growing concern to protect the environment and living beings forced many to consider whether or not fully developing the Coachella Valley was the right choice. (Courtesy of the Coachella Valley History Museum.)

The 1920s photograph at right shows four men next to a biplane. There were two airports in Indio at this time. One was for the post office's mail deliveries, and the other was for public use. The second Indio airport was where Jacqueline Cochran would often fly into, since it was located near her Coachran-Odlum ranch in Indio. There was also an airport in Thermal, which changed its name to the Jacqueline Cochran Airport in Thermal. Pictured below is the La Quinta airstrip, which was located off of Washington Avenue and Eisenhower Drive in 1938. (Right, courtesy of the Coachella Valley History Museum; below, courtesy of the Coachella Valley Water District.)

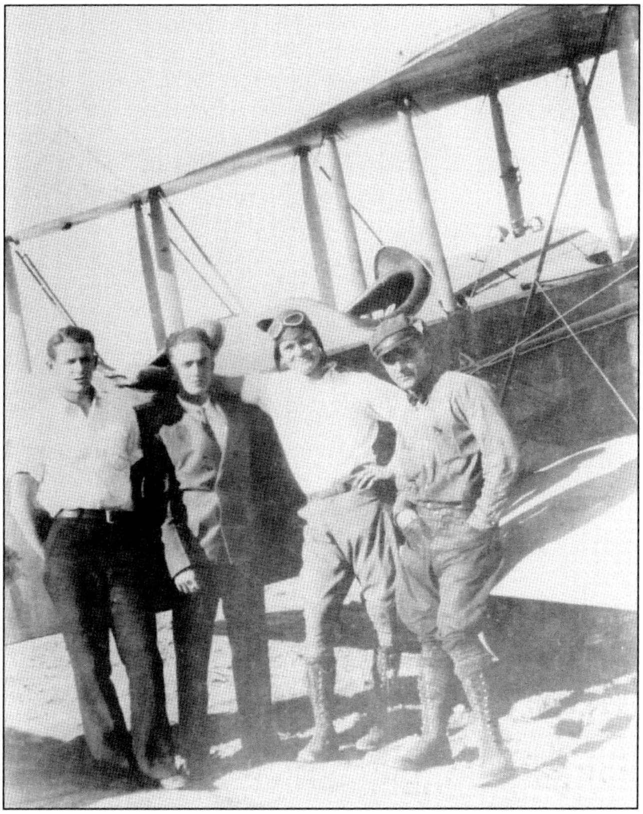

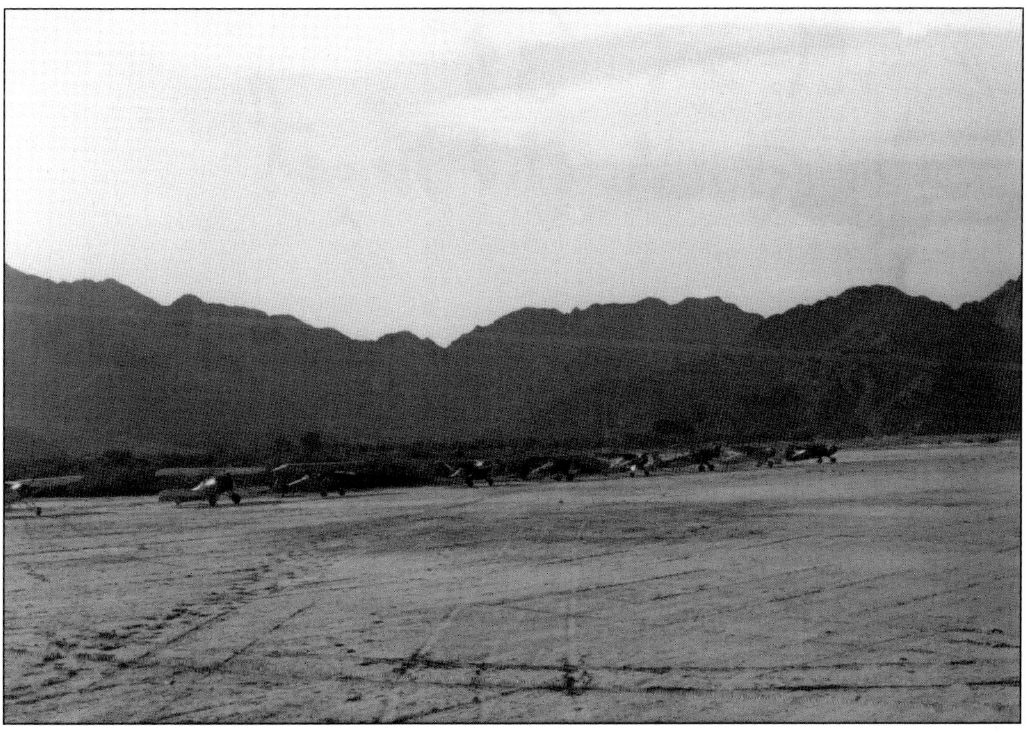

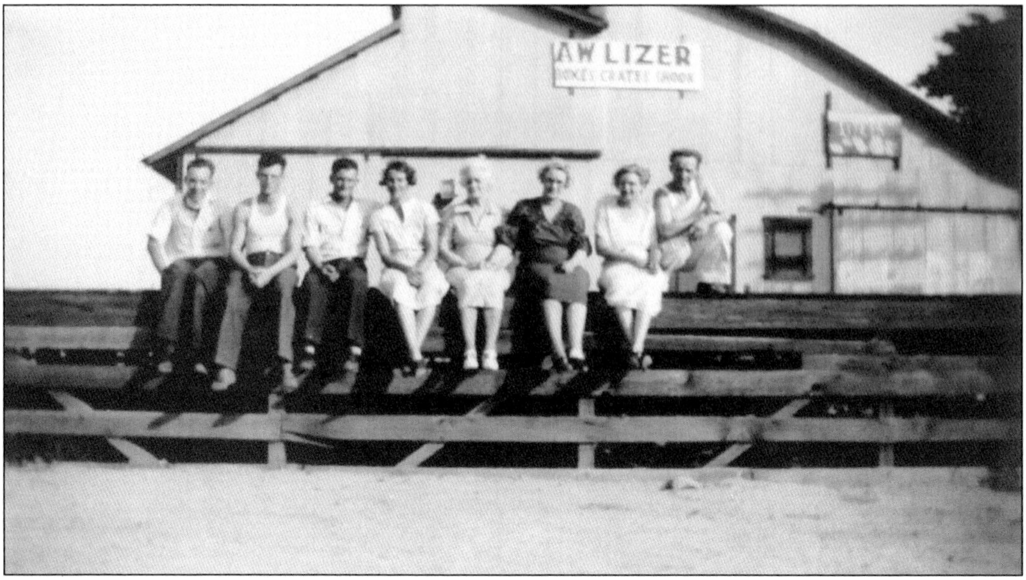

Family-owned businesses were common in Coachella during the 1930s, when this photograph was taken of the A.W. Lizer box company. Pictured are, from left to right, Jack Lizer, Arthur Lizer Jr., Bill George, Elva George, unidentified, Mollie Spencer, Clara Lizer, and Arthur Lizer Sr. (Courtesy of the Coachella Valley History Museum.)

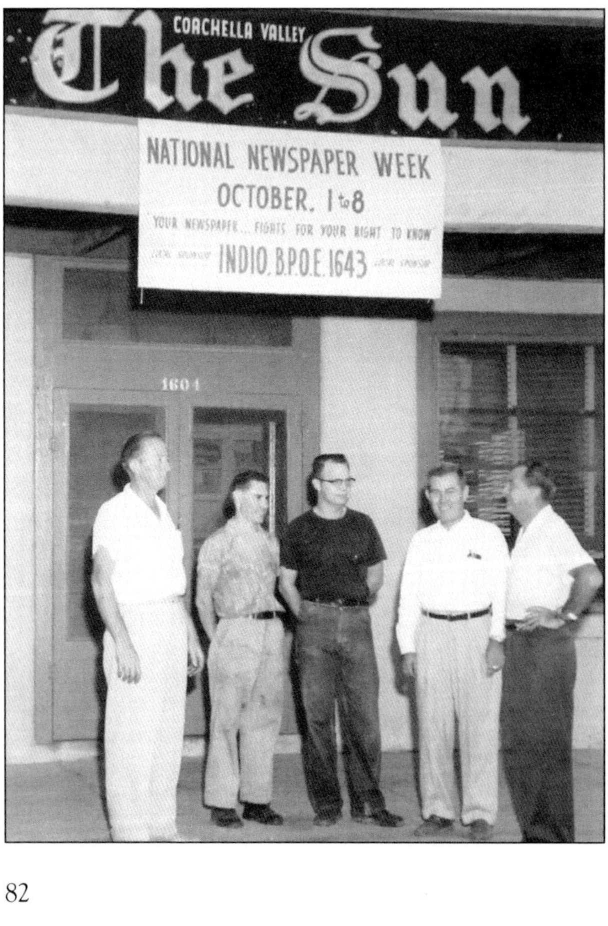

News often found its way to the Coachella Valley via the local newspapers. Some of the papers available to locals were the *Daily News* and the *Desert Rancher*. This 1945 photograph shows the *Coachella Valley Sun* in Coachella. From left to right are John Lafayette, Mike Council, unidentified, George O'Tool, and Ward Grant. (Courtesy of the Coachella Valley History Museum.)

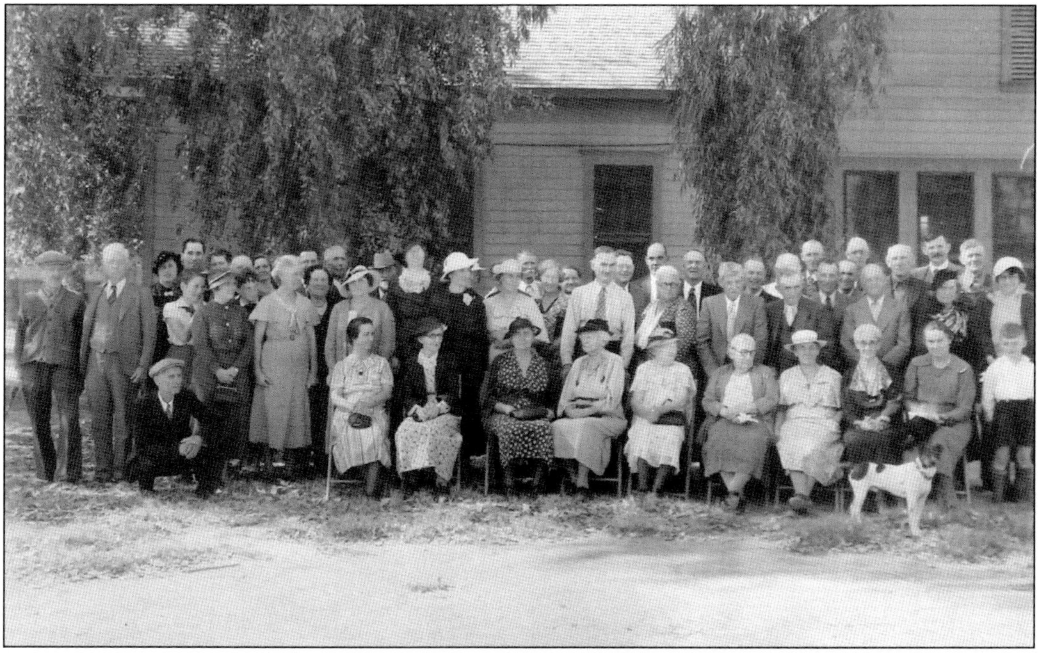

Social organizations played important roles in the development of different valley towns. The organization focused on the preservation of the history of the Coachella Valley was the Coachella Valley Pioneer's Society. Pictured above is a society meeting in the 1930s, and below is a 1940s gathering. Several photo albums compiled and preserved by this organization were inherited by its successor, the Coachella Valley Historical Society, and are now stored at the Coachella Valley History Museum's Archives. (Both, courtesy of the Coachella Valley History Museum.)

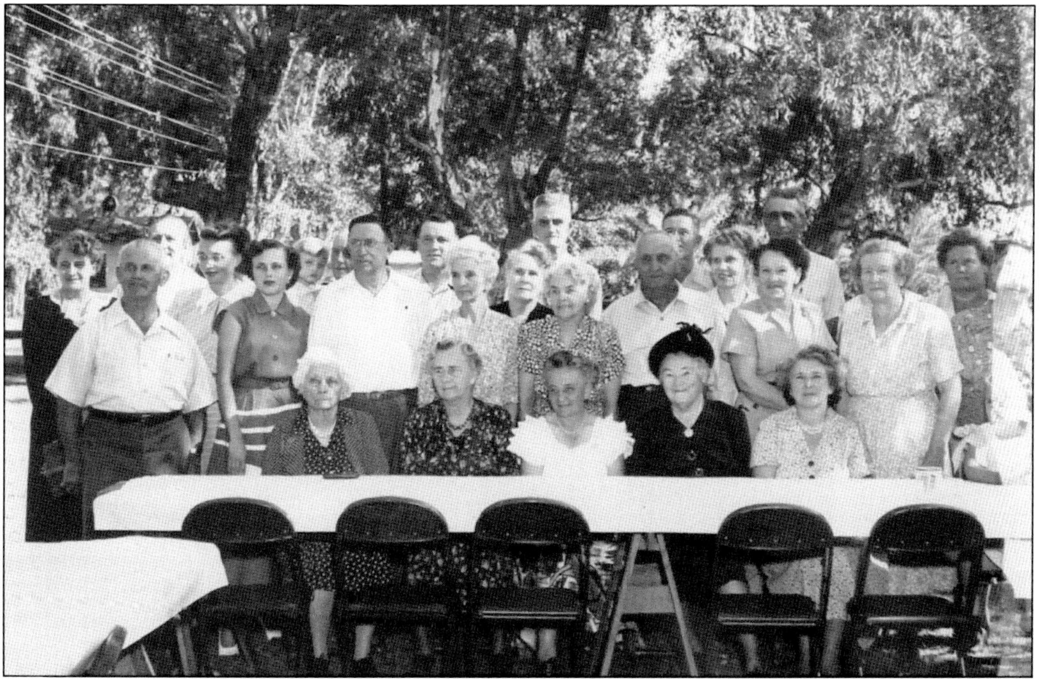

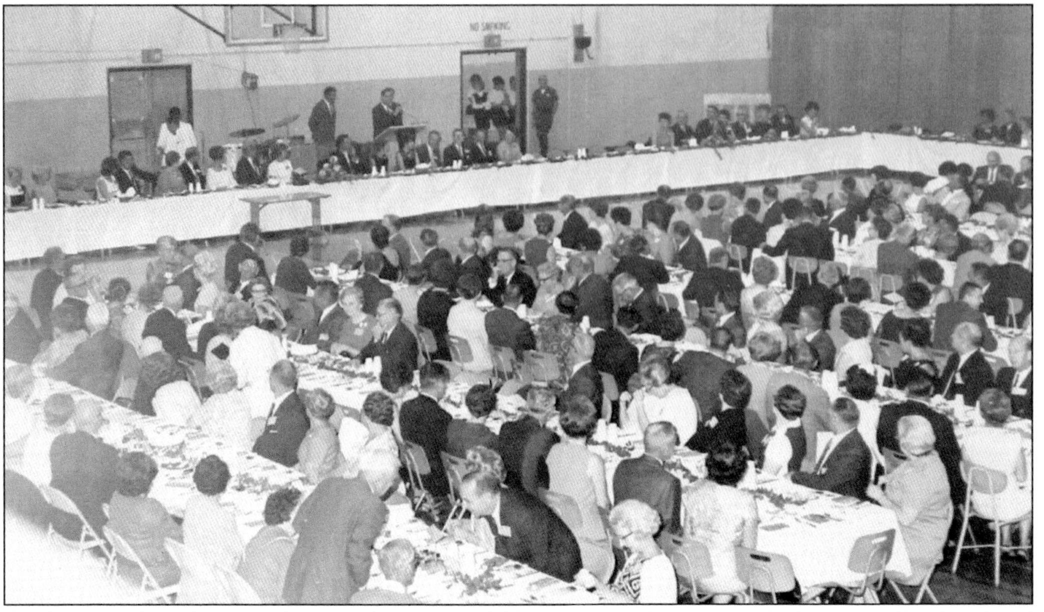

By the time this photograph was taken in the 1960s, the number of Coachella Valley High School alumni had grown tremendously. Social functions, such as this reunion, provided a continued connection between graduates and their peers. The alumni also award scholarships to newly graduated students who go on to college. (Courtesy of the Coachella Valley History Museum.)

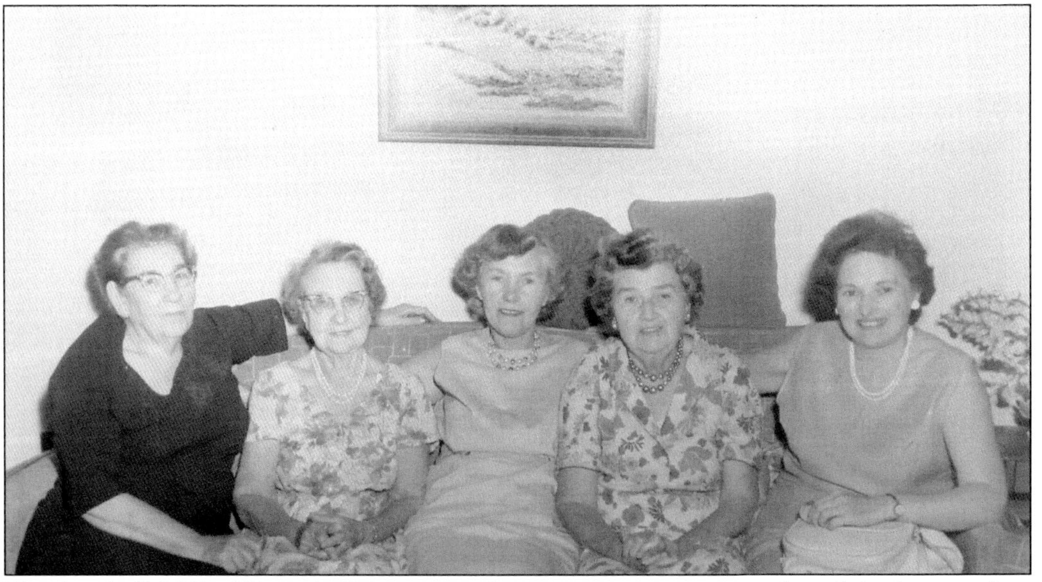

The Coachella Valley Women's Club gave members an opportunity to socialize while also providing assistance to various causes, like the American Red Cross. From left to right are members Eva Pearson, Mildred Wheeler, unidentified, Rozena Schmid, and unidentified. (Courtesy of the Coachella Valley History Museum.)

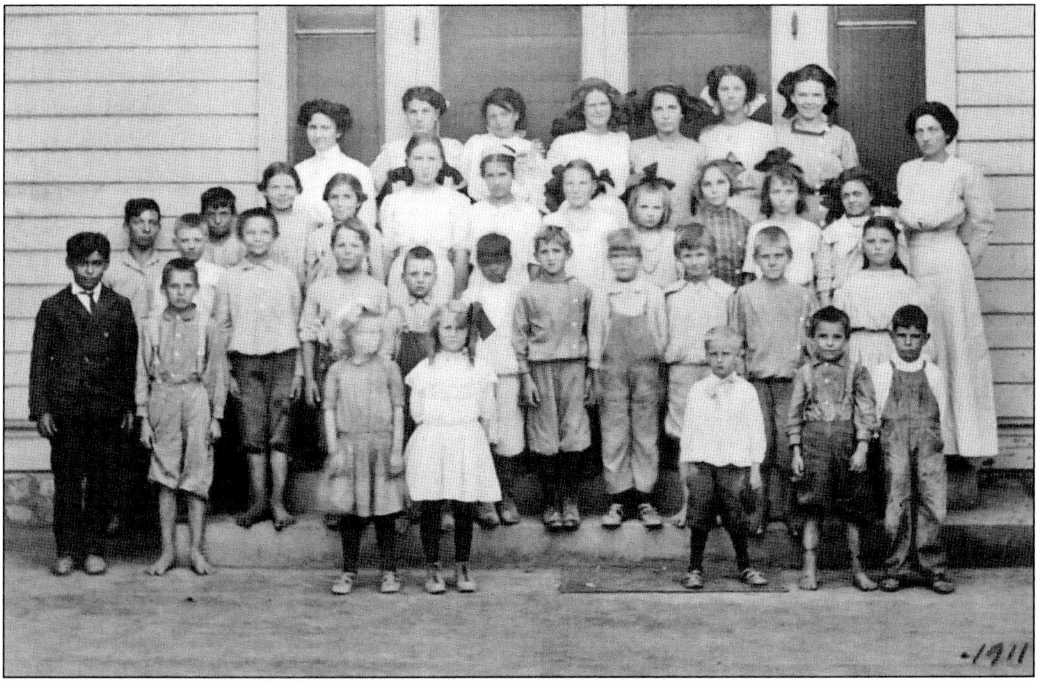

The Coachella Grammar School class of 1911 posed with teachers for this photograph in front of the school. Most of the children were dressed in their best clothes. Note that several boys in front are not wearing shoes. The teacher on the right is Alberta Proctor, and the student to her left is Julia Proctor. (Courtesy of Louise Saunders.)

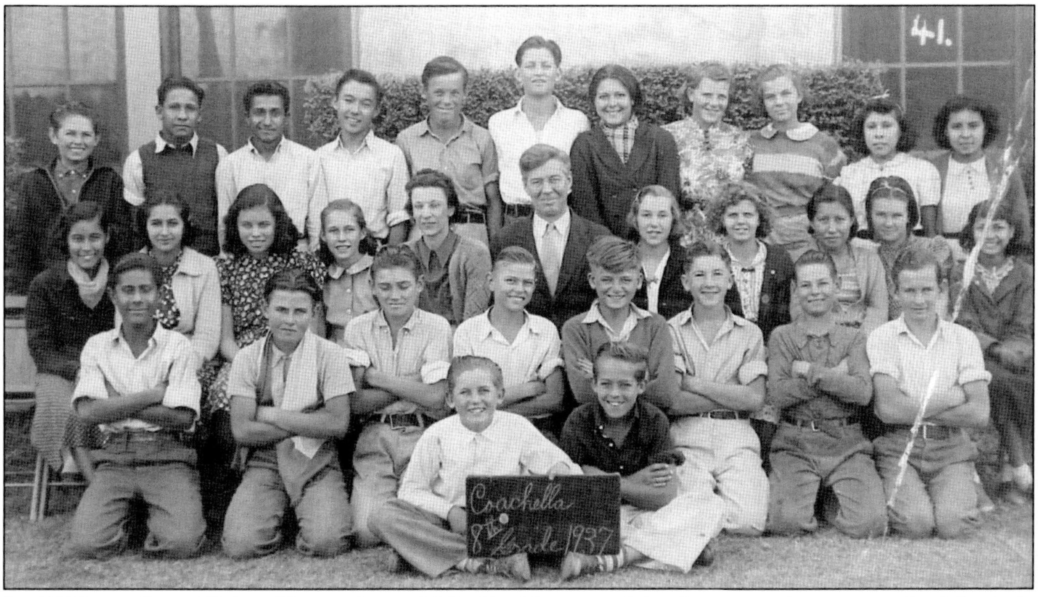

In 1937, teachers Elaine Buttrude and Mr. Smith, seated in the second row, posed with their eighth-grade class from the Coachella Grammar School. Students enjoyed the time outdoors and away from their studies. (Courtesy of the Coachella Valley History Museum.)

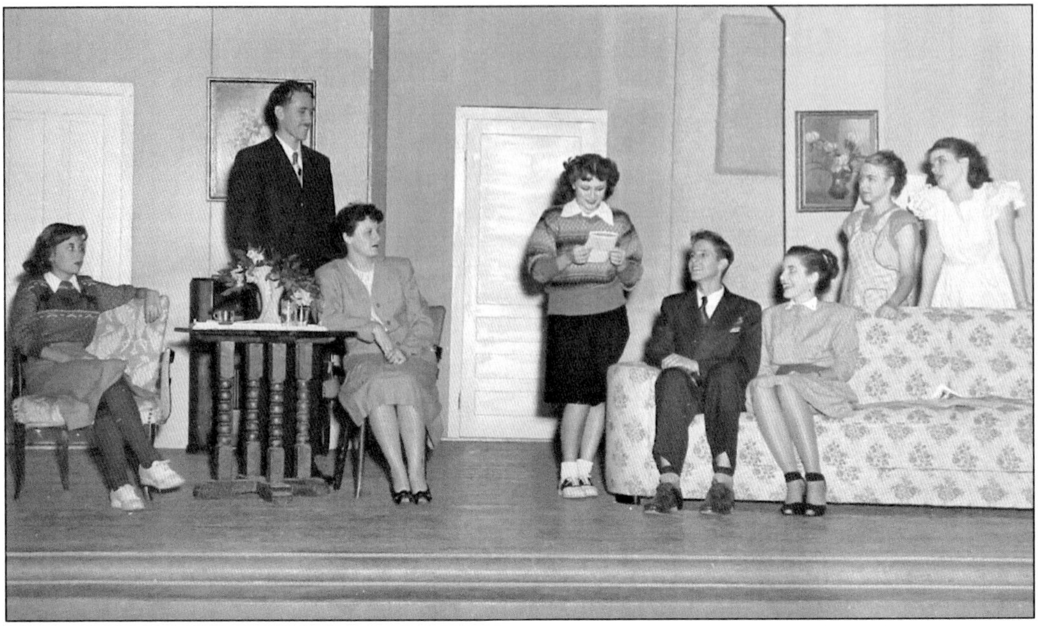

The Coachella Valley High School gave students the opportunity to explore their dramatic side during school plays. This 1948 photograph is of the play *Junior Miss* put on by the class of 1949. From left to right are Marie Sparks, Lloyd Dearmore, Veramae Spencer, Johanna Nelson, Jerry Freeman, Mary Pollaro, Ruth Dugan, and Beth Clifford. (Courtesy of the Coachella Valley History Museum.)

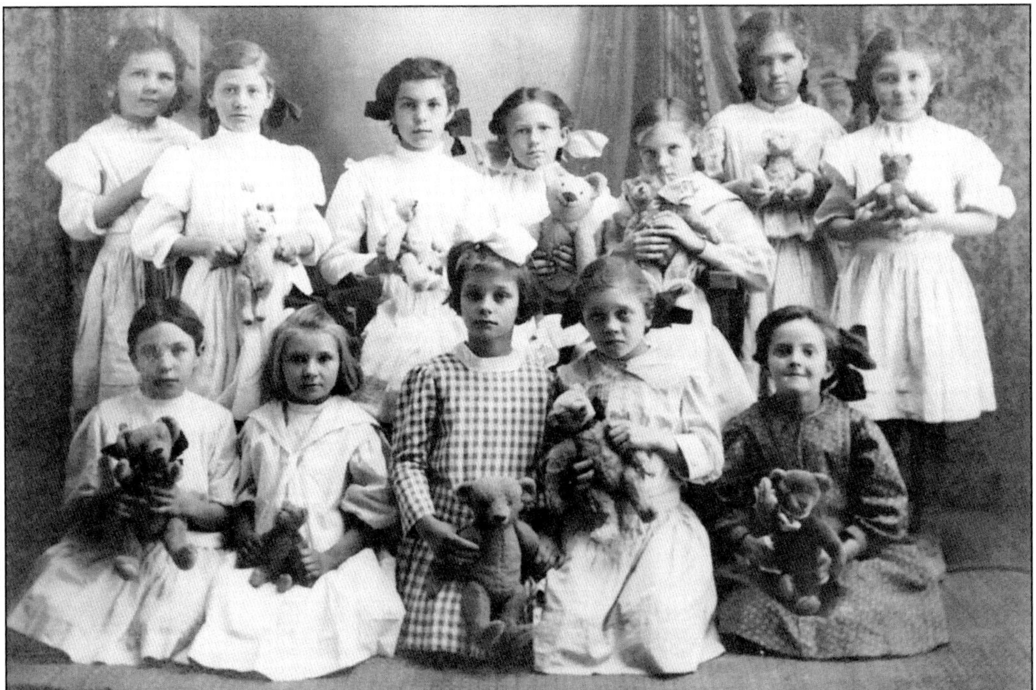

Teddy Bears All Fools Day was celebrated in Coachella in 1910. Alice Makasky and Julia Proctor are third and fourth from left in the first row holding their bears. (Courtesy of Louise Saunders.)

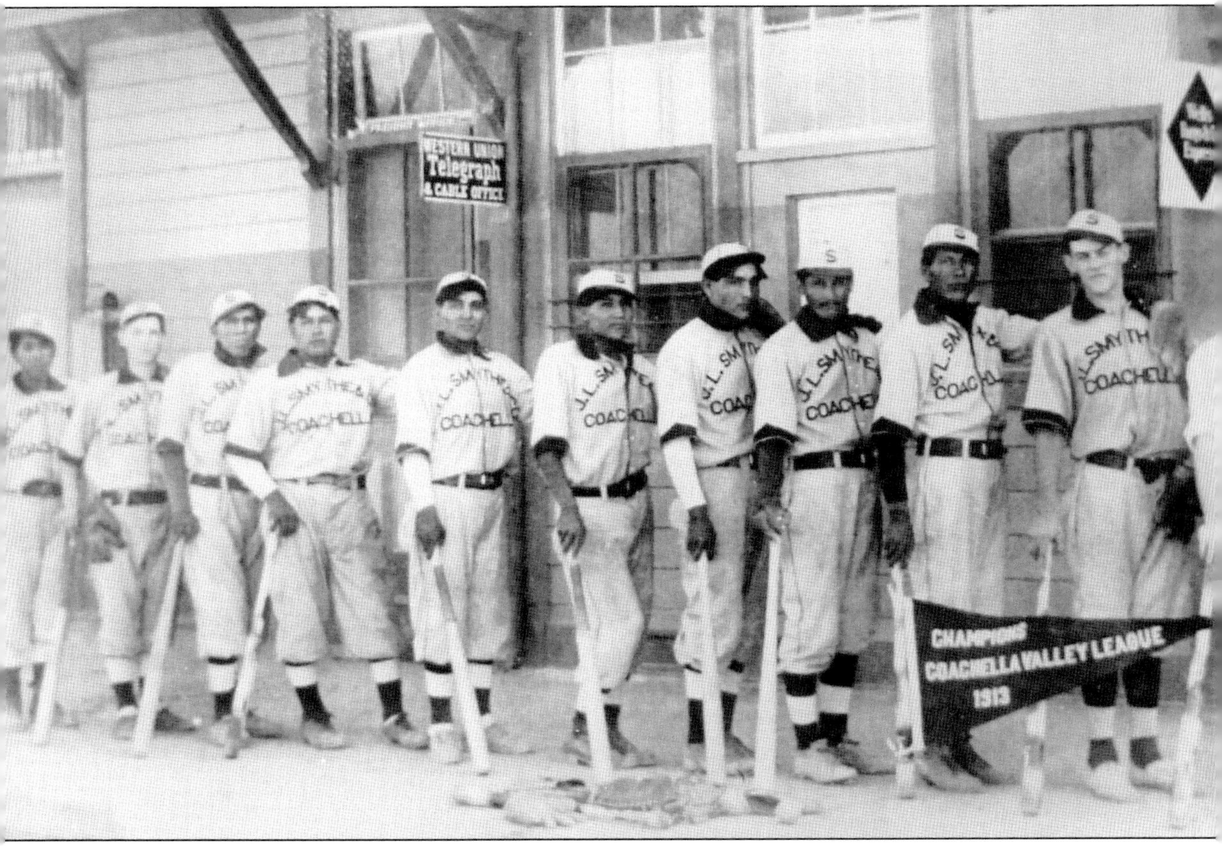

In 1913, J.L. Smythe's baseball team were the Coachella Valley League champions. Here, the team members pose in front of the Western Union office at the Coachella railroad siding. Most of the players on Smythe's team were local Desert Cahuilla Indians. At this time, some of the strongest baseball players in the Coachella Valley were Desert Cahuilla Indians. Baseball and softball became commonly played sports in the Coachella Valley and have been embedded into the desert community life. Many of the Desert Cahuilla play baseball or softball growing up. Several of the reservations hold softball tournaments combining their love of the sport with their own cultural traditions and celebrations. The Native American tribes in the Coachella Valley have often sponsored youth teams to play in the local community baseball and softball leagues. (Courtesy of the Coachella Valley Water District.)

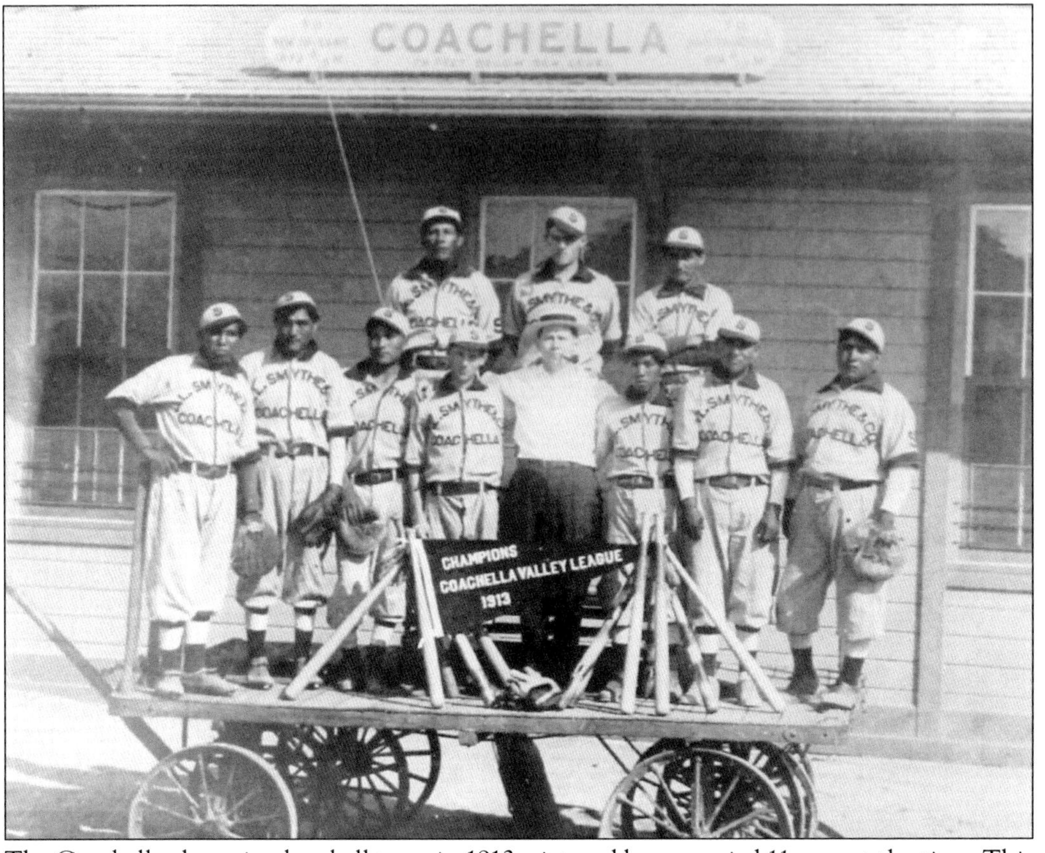

The Coachella champion baseball team in 1913, pictured here, carried 11 men at the time. This photograph of the team was taken at the Coachella railroad siding. (Courtesy of the Coachella Valley Water District.)

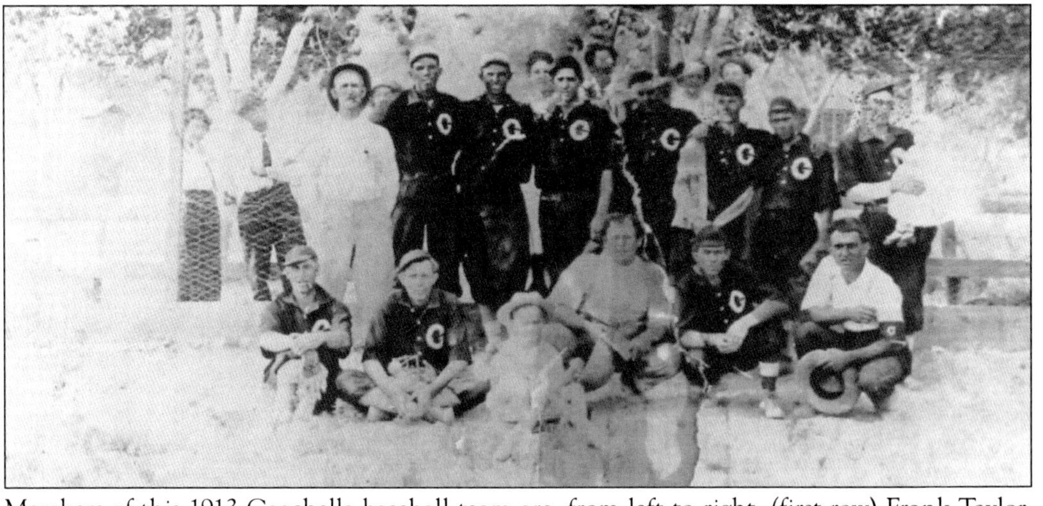

Members of this 1913 Coachella baseball team are, from left to right, (first row) Frank Taylor, Peterson, mascot Ray Thomas, Mert Cawthon, and Art Thomas; (second row) E.L. Young, M.C. McDonald, three Burdick brothers, Clarence Lund, Ralph Thomas, and A. Lyle Pearson, holding one-year-old Jessie Pearson. (Courtesy of the Coachella Valley Water District.)

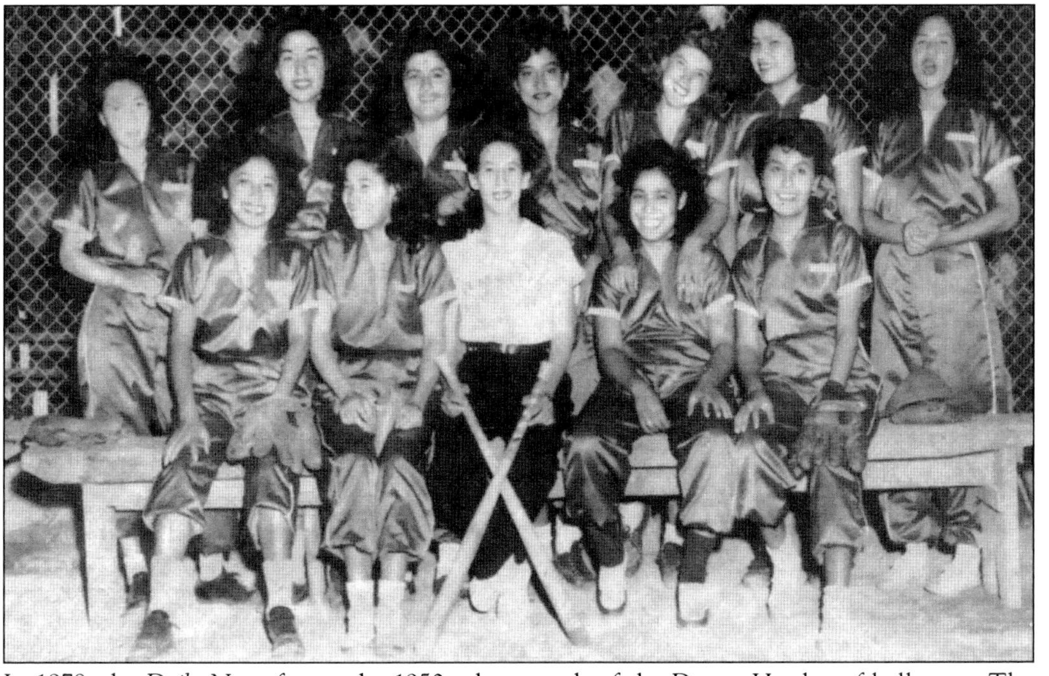

In 1978, the *Daily News* featured a 1950s photograph of the Desert Hawks softball team. The players pictured above are, from left to right, (first row) Katie Gonzales, Lupe Moreno, Dolores Moreno, and two unidentified; (second row) Gloria Moreno, Beatrice Vega, Dolly Escoto, Betty Dega, Loretta Vega, Helen Villa, and Josephine Rodarte. The Desert Hawks, seen below, are, from left to right, (first row) Mary Palazzo, Dolly Escoto, and Betty Vega; (second row) Gloria Moreno, unidentified, Loretta Vega, Beatrice Vega, Betty Porras, Josephine Rodarte, and Rosemary Carrillo. (Both, courtesy of Louise Neeley.)

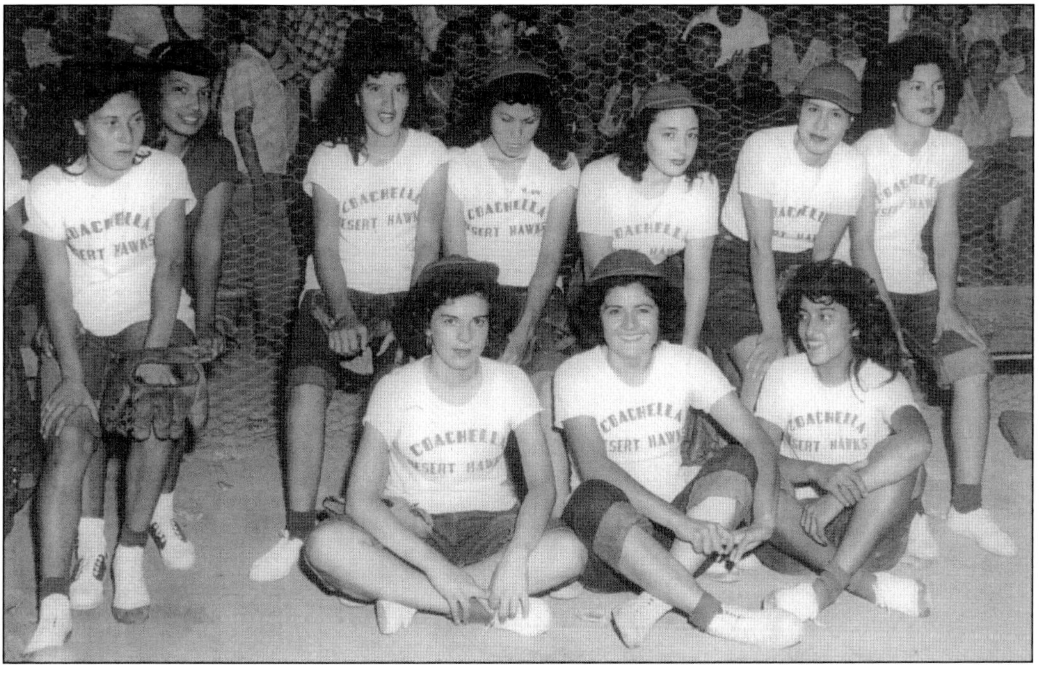

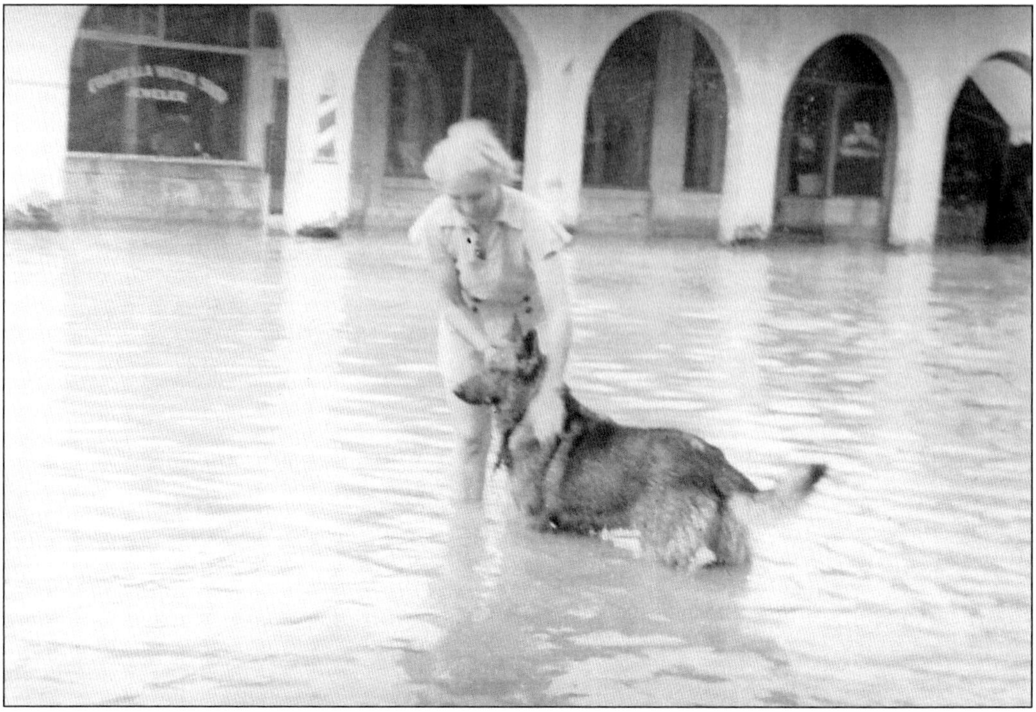

This photograph, taken during a 1940s flood, shows an unidentified woman petting a dog in the flooded street. She is standing in front of the Coachella Watch Shop. The photograph below shows flooding in a residential area. Two boys wade through the floodwaters. High water was a common occurrence until the completion of the extensive water wash system to help divert and control floodwaters. Flash floods do continue to be an annual danger to valley residents and cause major damage to property each year. (Both, courtesy of the Coachella Valley History Museum.)

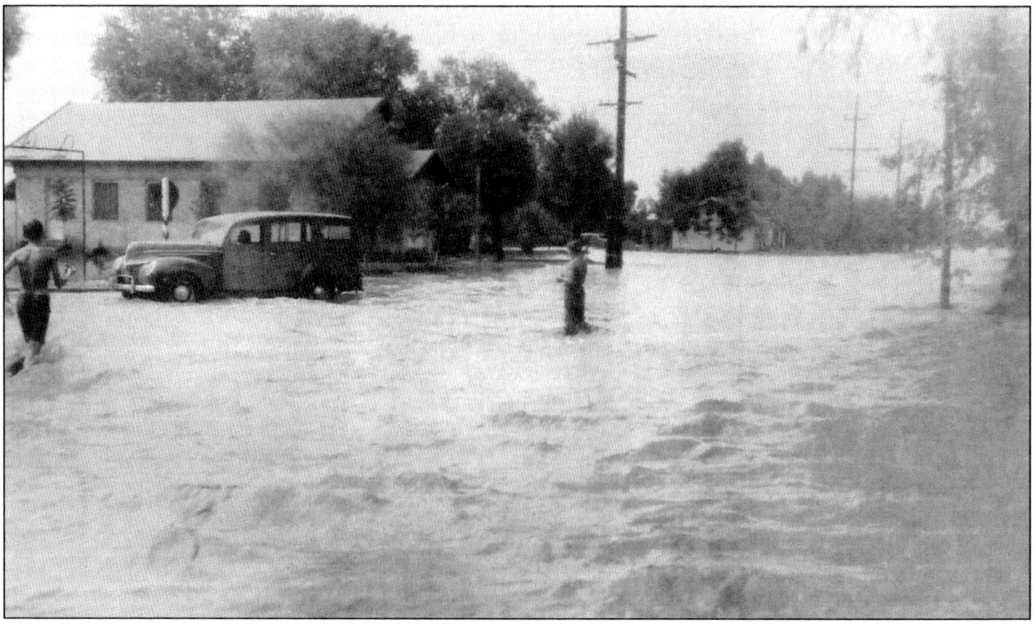

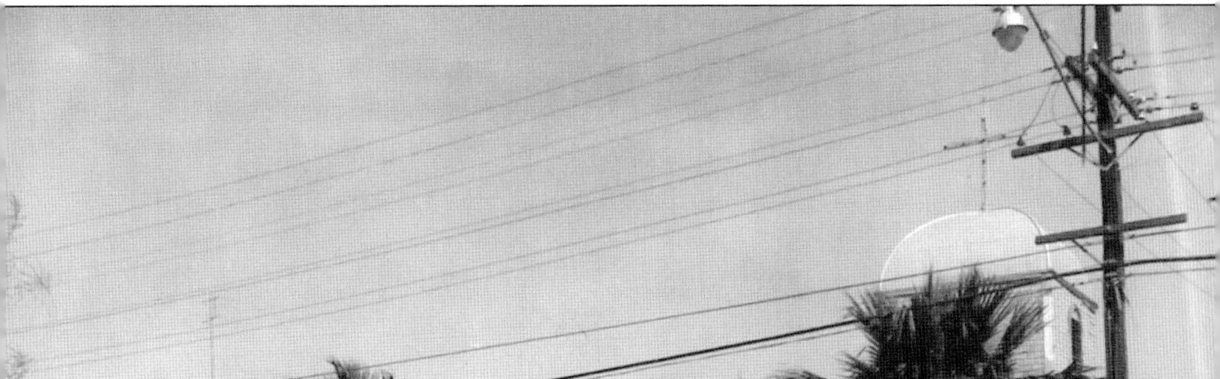

This 1960s photograph shows Our Lady of Soledad Catholic Church. This Roman Catholic church was located at First Street and Vine Avenue. Several denominations had churches in Coachella. Churches like the Coachella Church of Jesus Christ and Friends of Jesus Church also served as a place to continue cultural traditions. The Friends of Jesus Church was built at 85490 Avenue 50 by Japanese American Christians in 1929 at the urging of Japanese Christian social reformist Kagawa Toyohiko. Church members also established a Japanese language school in the same building. This church became a social and cultural focal point for local Japanese families, providing a place for them to continue practicing their traditions and teaching their language to their children. This church remained active until 1942, when the local Japanese population was sent to internment camps. (Courtesy of the Coachella Valley History Museum.)

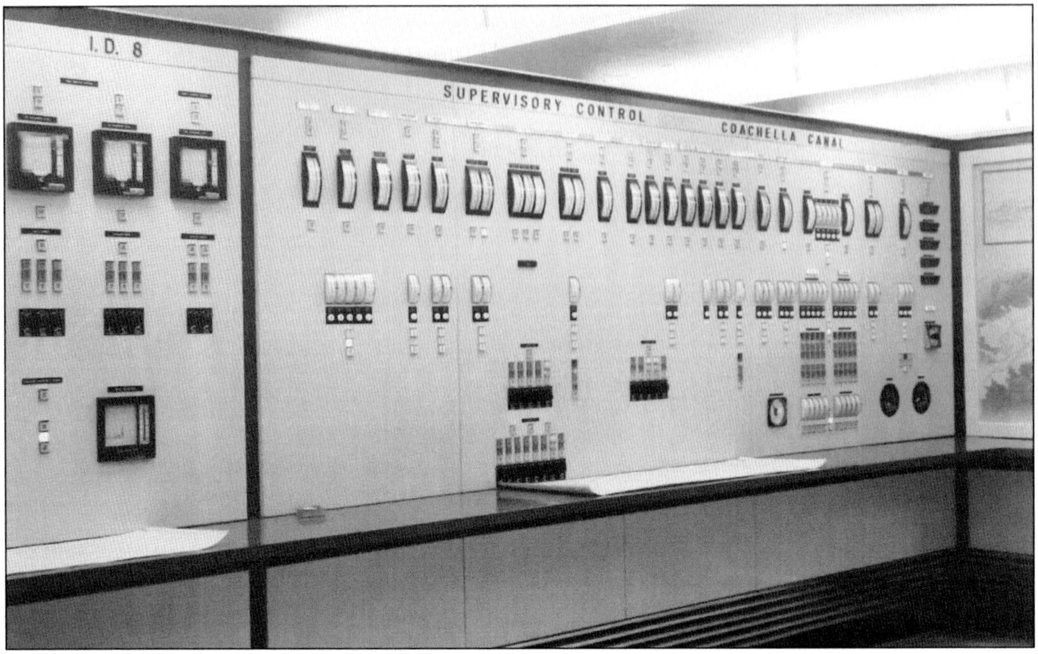

The Coachella Valley Water District was established in 1918. The company is regulated by state and federal agencies and is not governed by the California Public Utilities Commission. The company developed and maintains much of the Coachella Valley's groundwater supplies while providing drinking water and irrigation water for the local agricultural industry. The company provides services for the Coachella Valley and parts of Imperial and San Diego Counties. The 1970s photograph above shows a control panel at the Coachella Valley Water District. Below is the Coachella Valley Water District office in Coachella, also in the 1970s. (Both, courtesy of the Coachella Valley Water District.)

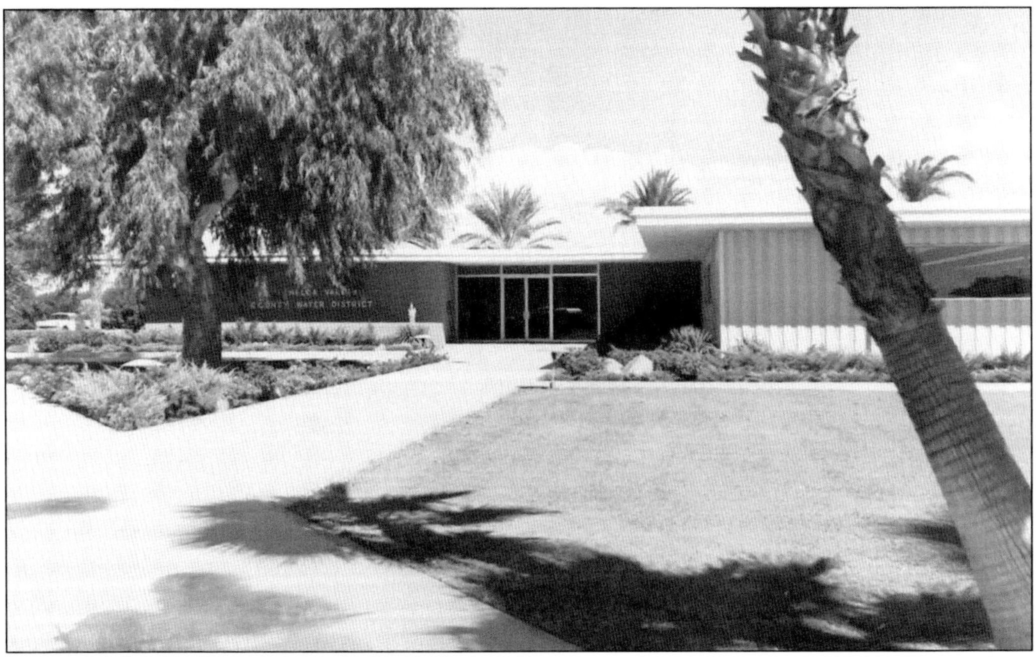

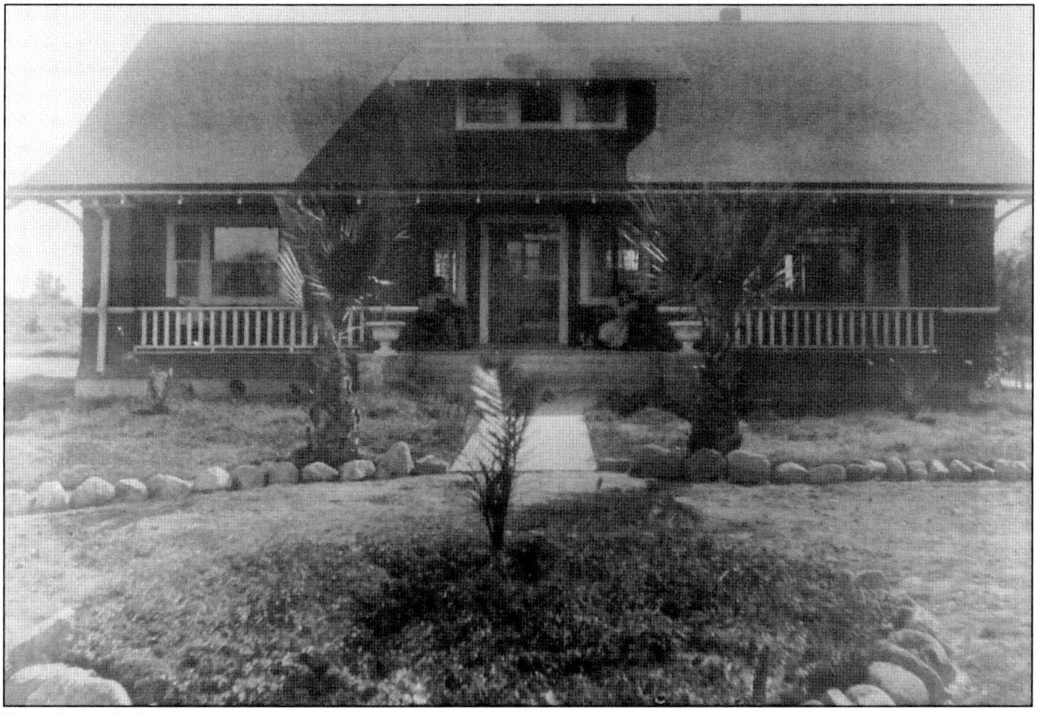

Ranch-style homes were prevalent in Coachella for the first couple of decades of the 20th century. With advanced technological developments in the agricultural industry and in transportation, there was demand to expand on the local architectural designs. This 1910s photograph shows an unidentified ranch house in Coachella. (Courtesy of the Coachella Valley History Museum.)

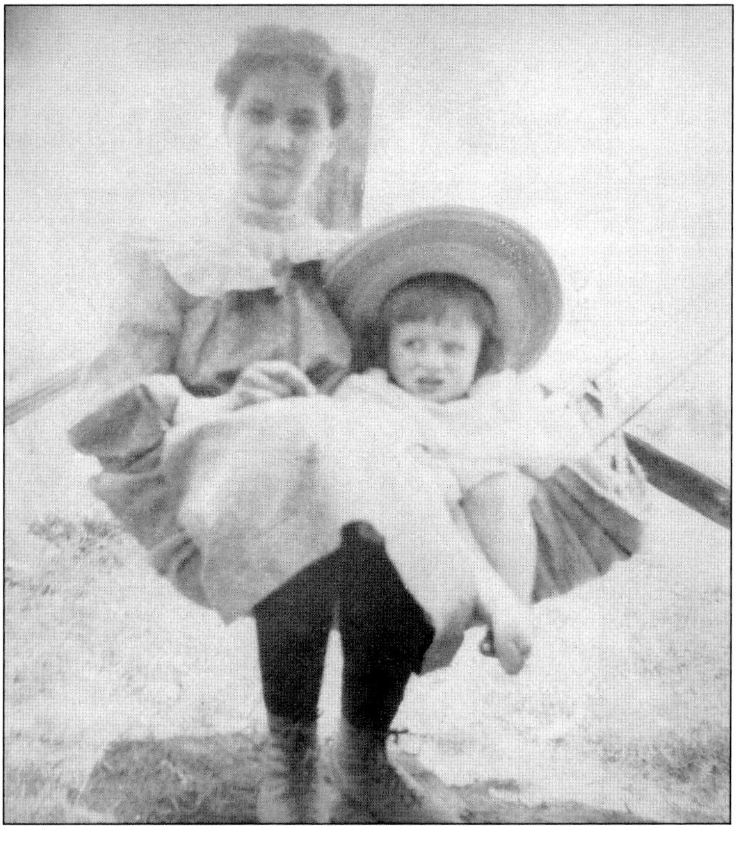

This 1903 photograph shows Reabock Lewis and Marina Cardinez in a swing. (Courtesy of the Coachella Valley History Museum.)

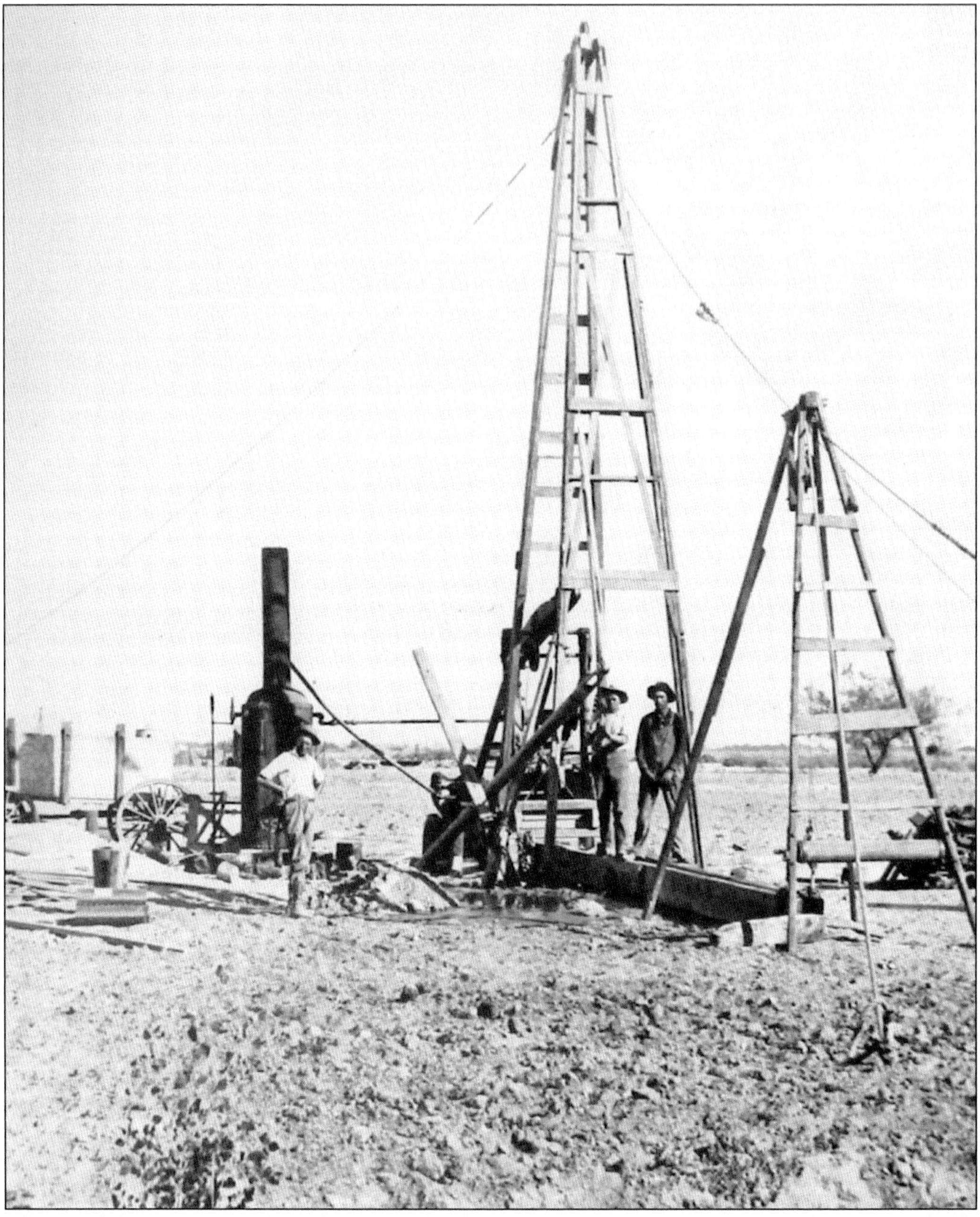

The need for water greatly influenced the development of communities, and the Coachella Valley was no different. Desert Cahuilla Indians, who lived in and near the Coachella Valley, were master well diggers. This photograph shows a well digging crew in Coachella in 1910. Well digging was vital to the establishment of Coachella and the surrounding area, where surface water was minimal. Prior to 1910, the water table in the Coachella Valley was relatively close to the surface. When Coachella Valley residents noted water table measurements that were lower than previous measurements, the Coachella Valley County Water District was formed in 1918. The water district's name was changed in 1979 to the Coachella Valley Water District. (Courtesy of the Coachella Valley History Museum.)

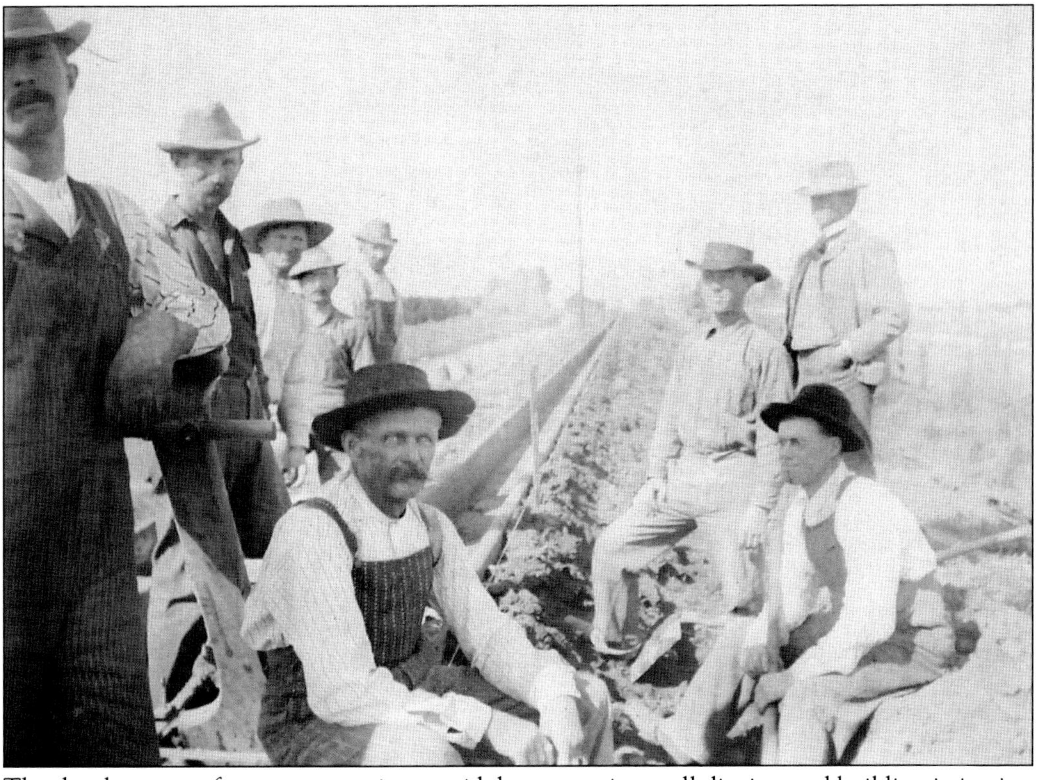

The development of water sources in an arid desert requires well digging and building irrigation systems to distribute water to the crops. This 1910 photograph shows a work crew posed next the concrete flume they are in the process of laying. Concrete flumes are used in the distribution of water. (Courtesy of the Coachella Valley History Museum.)

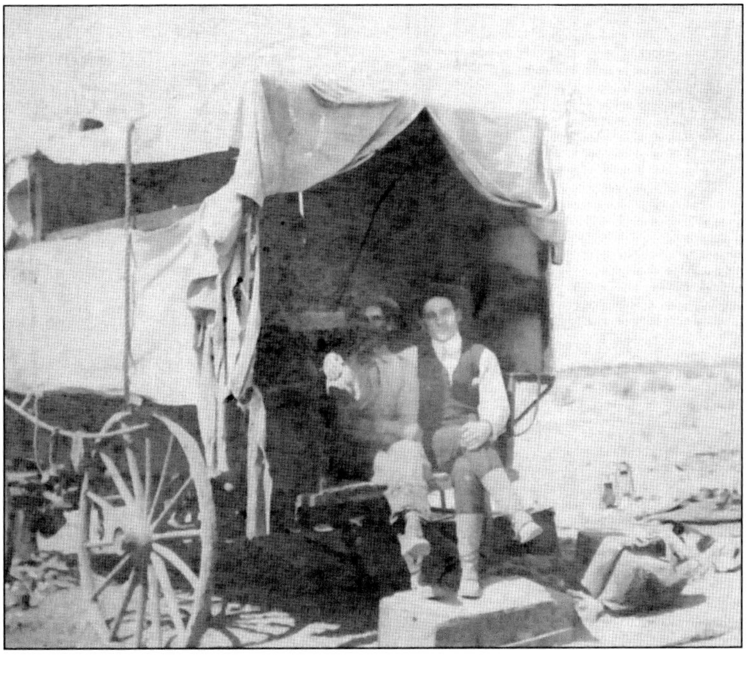

Cook wagons, as seen here, often traveled with work crews as they built infrastructure outside of town. This 1910 cook wagon was owned by A.H. Sandford and traveled with the well rig crew. (Courtesy of the Coachella Valley History Museum.)

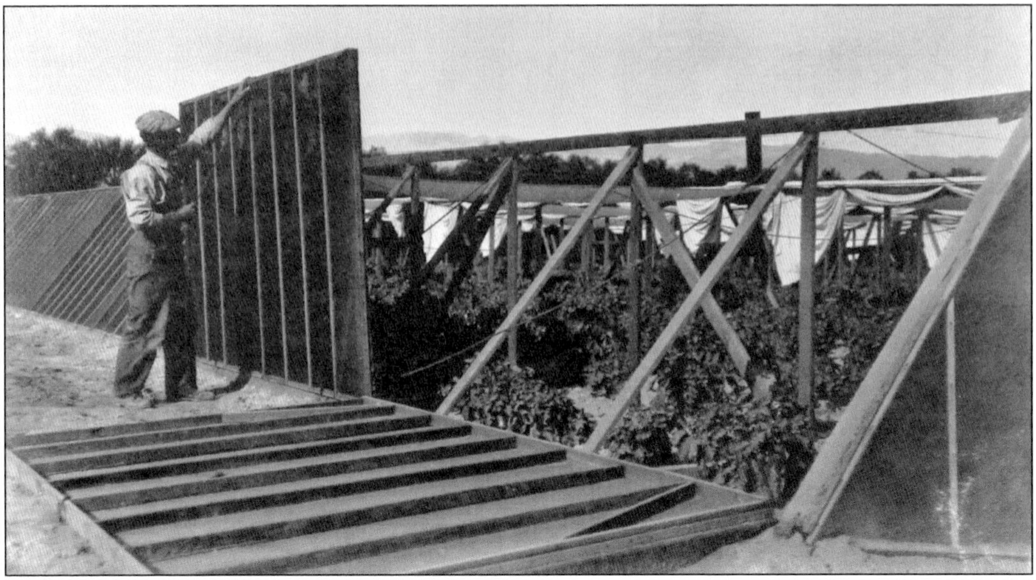

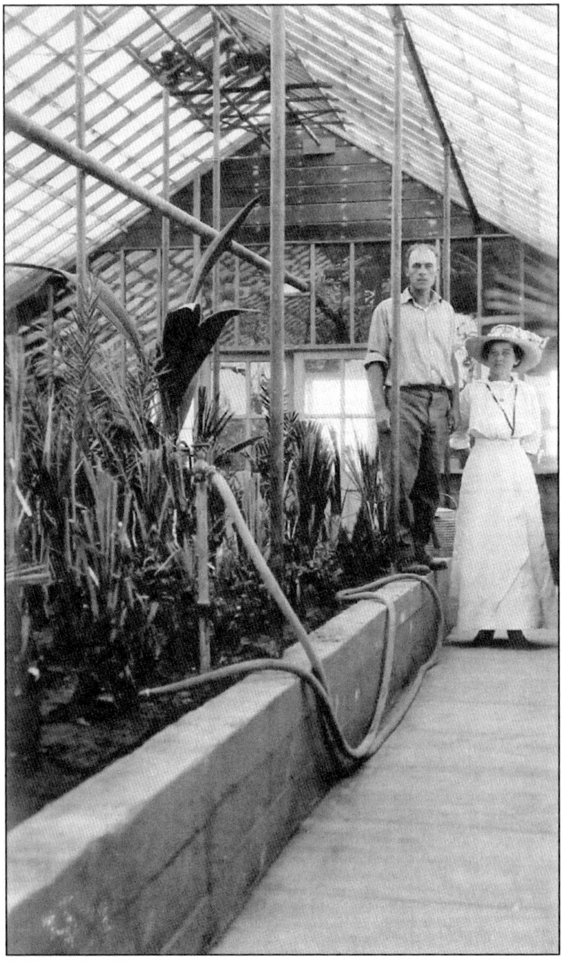

Diverting Colorado River water to the Coachella Valley enabled the development of various agricultural industries. The ability to grow crops year-round would further the drive to create an agricultural wonderland from a naturally arid desert land. Claude Hyde is pictured in 1915 building an enclosure for his eggplant crop. (Courtesy of the Coachella Valley History Museum.)

This photograph was taken at the Proctor ranch in Coachella in 1917. Hugh Proctor (left) and Alberta (Proctor) Hyde pose in the ranch's palm greenhouse. Steady water supplies allowed farmers to maintain larger crops. (Courtesy of the Coachella Valley History Museum.)

Five

Year-Round Crops

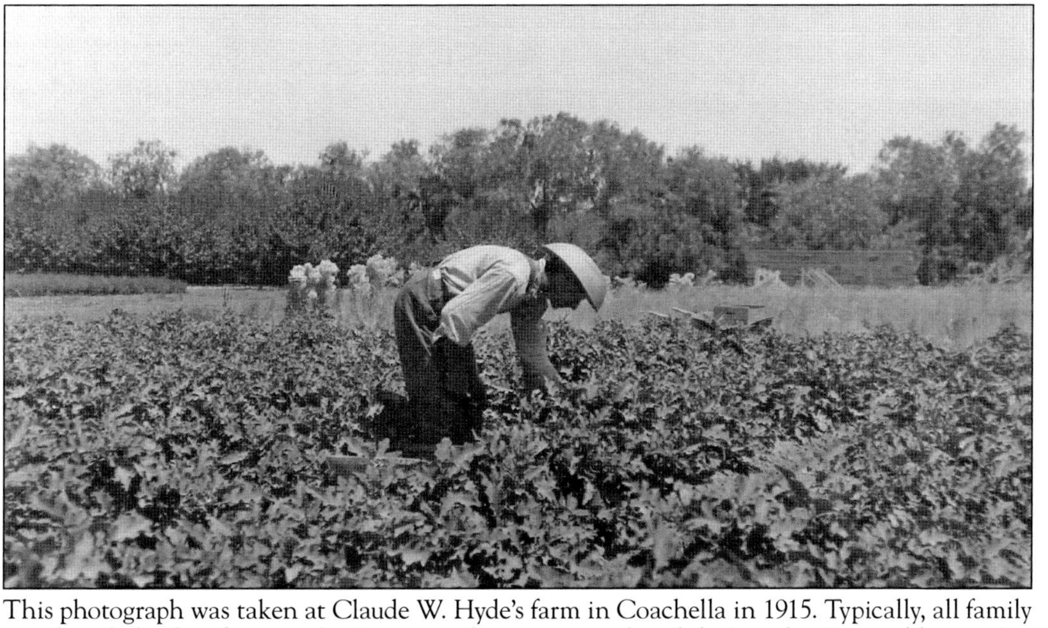

This photograph was taken at Claude W. Hyde's farm in Coachella in 1915. Typically, all family members helped to farm, and migrant workers were employed during planting and harvesting seasons. (Courtesy of the Coachella Valley History Museum.)

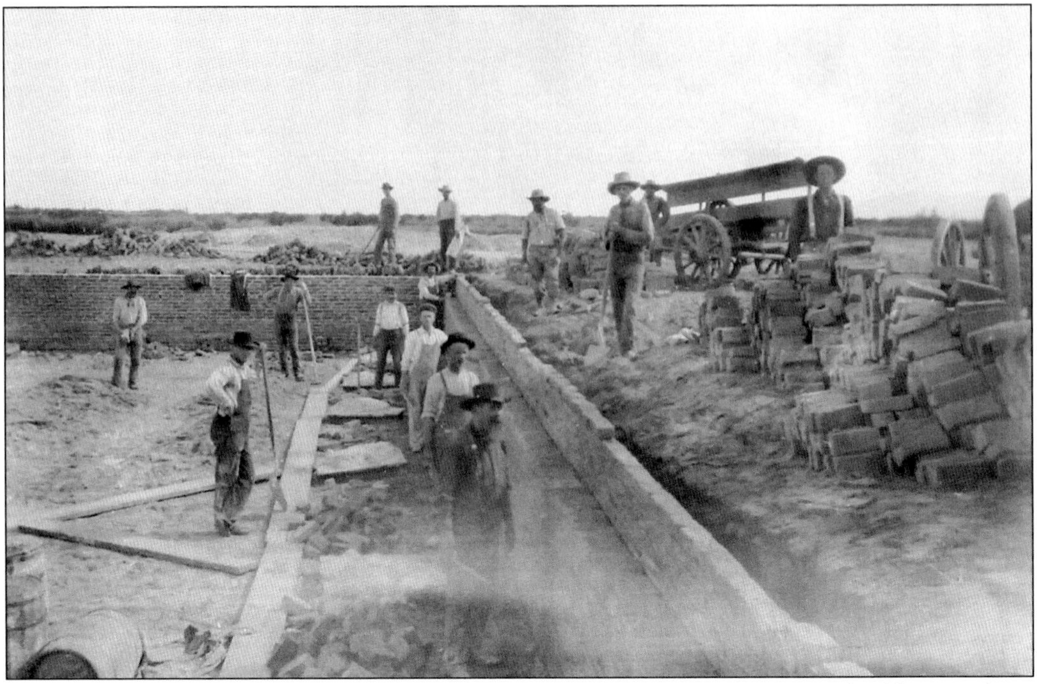

Here, workers are laying out the foundation for a building in 1915. Constructing buildings without backhoes and other heavy machinery, combined with the oppressive heat, made the process very physically demanding. (Courtesy of the Coachella Valley History Museum.)

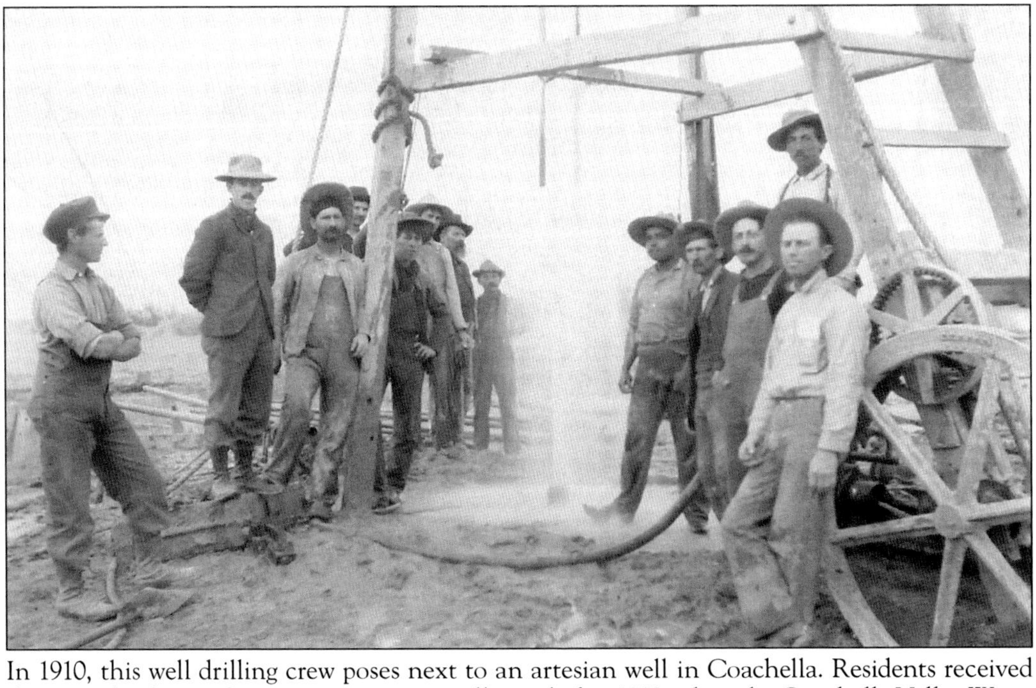

In 1910, this well drilling crew poses next to an artesian well in Coachella. Residents received their supply of water from private artesian wells until after 1918, when the Coachella Valley Water District was formed and began to develop water distribution systems. (Courtesy of the Coachella Valley History Museum.)

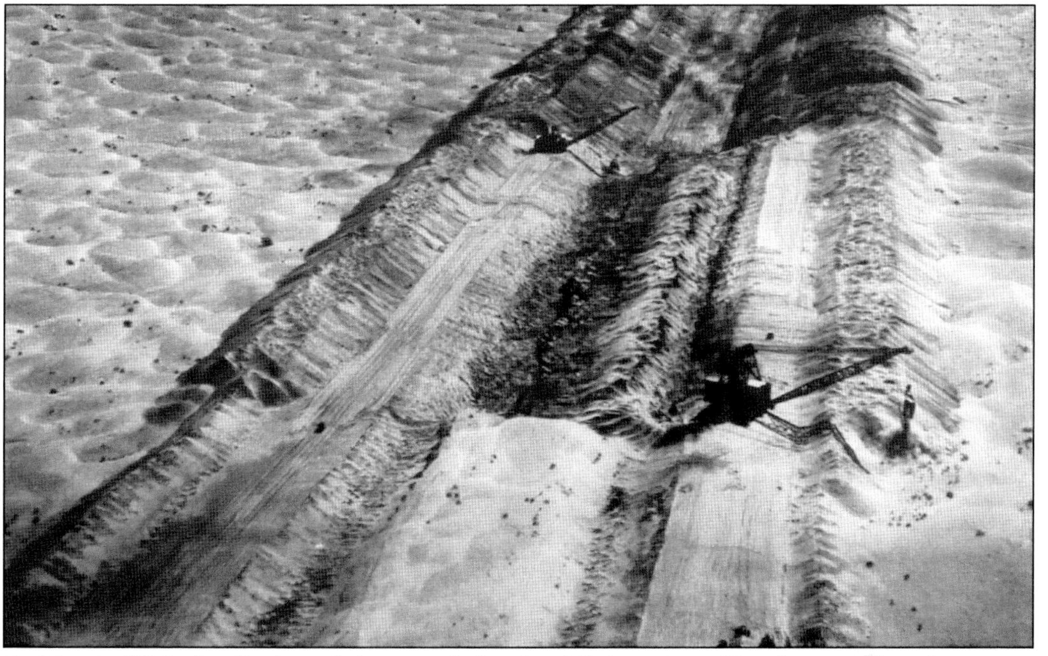

By March 1936, the digging of the trench for the All-American Canal was well underway, as seen above. The canal was finished in 1942 and was 80 miles long. It conveys Colorado River water to the Imperial Valley. A canal branch, called the Coachella Branch, was later completed in 1948–1949 and diverts water from the All-American Canal to the Coachella Valley. A crane is working on the canal at lower right. Pictured in the 1950s photograph below is a pipe-laying machine owned by Coachella Valley Concrete. Heavy modern machinery makes construction projects like laying pipes or digging canals easier. (Above, courtesy of the Coachella Valley Water District; below, courtesy of the Coachella Valley History Museum.)

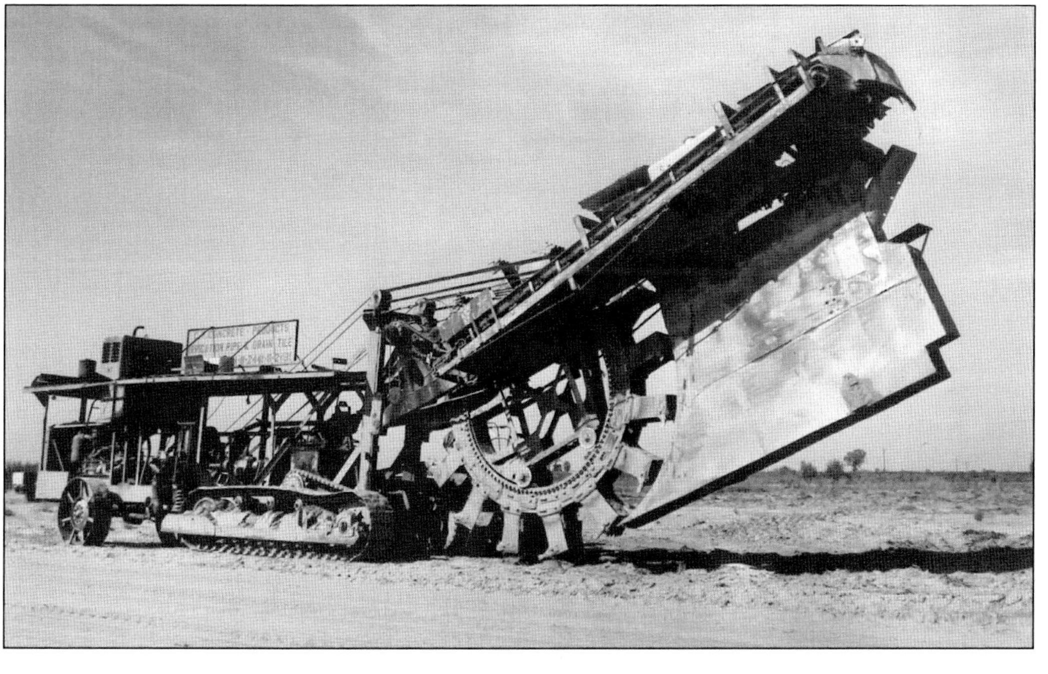

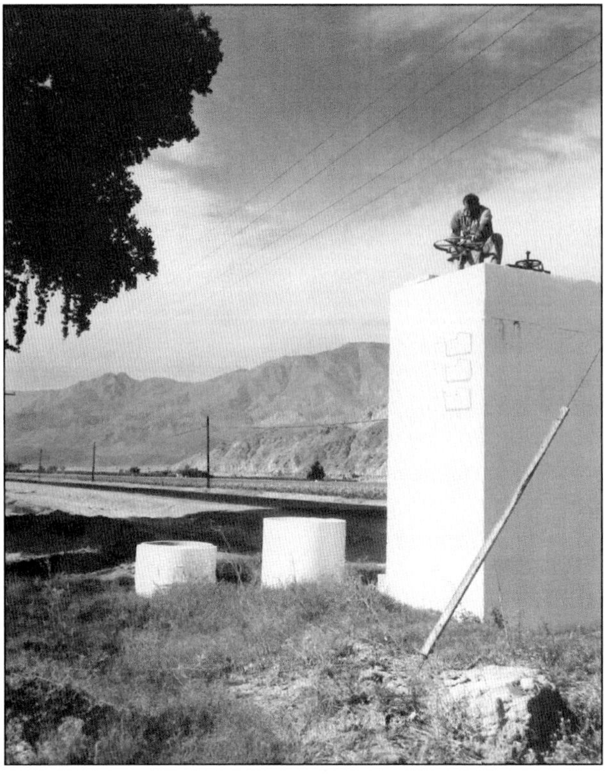

This photograph of Daryl Hammons, who was a Coachella Valley Water District employee, was taken in 1970. Hammons was opening an irrigation valve in Coachella to regulate the local irrigation system. The spillover pipes pictured next to where Hammons is working are common all over the valley's farming and ranching areas. (Courtesy of the Coachella Valley History Museum.)

The extensive irrigation systems in the Coachella Valley provide the water necessary for year-round growth of many crops, including the melon and barley fields pictured here. This photograph was taken in the 1960s at an unidentified farm in Coachella. The dryness of the soil can be seen between the crop rows. (Courtesy of the Coachella Valley Water District.)

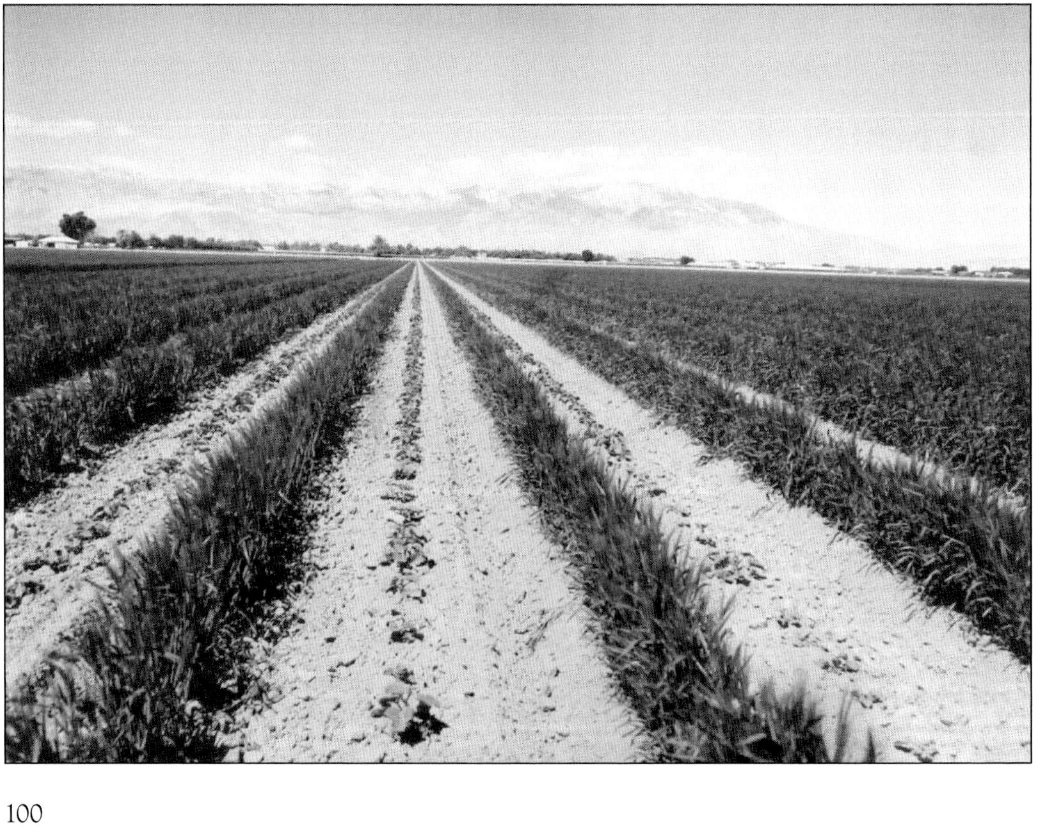

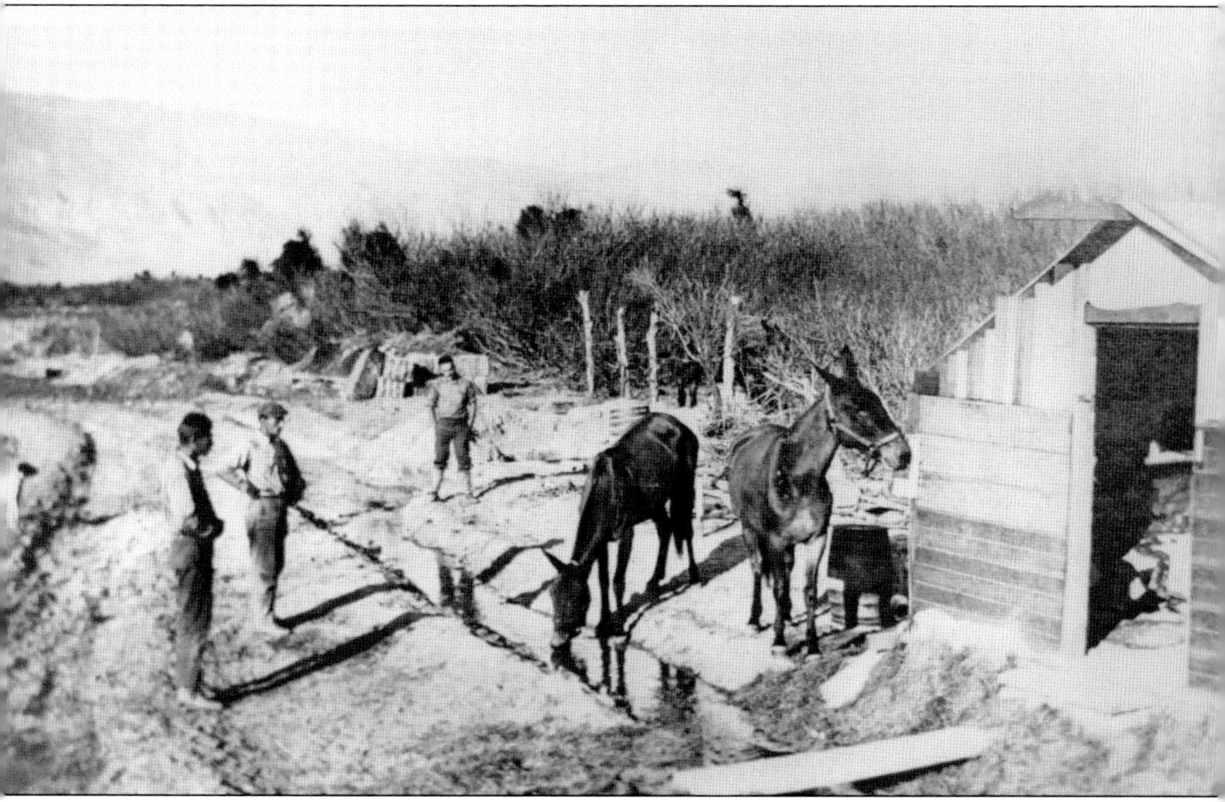

In the winter of 1915, E.N.T. Burnett works with his friends to set up his camp in the Coachella Valley. The men were photographed taking a break. Note that one of the mules is drinking out of the irrigation canal. Mules were often used in farming in the Coachella Valley. They were good workers and could tolerate the extreme heat better than horses. Clearing the land to ready it for planting had already been completed. Burnett became a fixture in the Coachella Valley communities. The Coachella Valley History Museum was fortunate in 2013 to receive a donation of two photo albums from the Burnett/Kimball family, which cover the early years of E.N.T. Burnett's life in the valley. (Courtesy of the Coachella Valley Water District.)

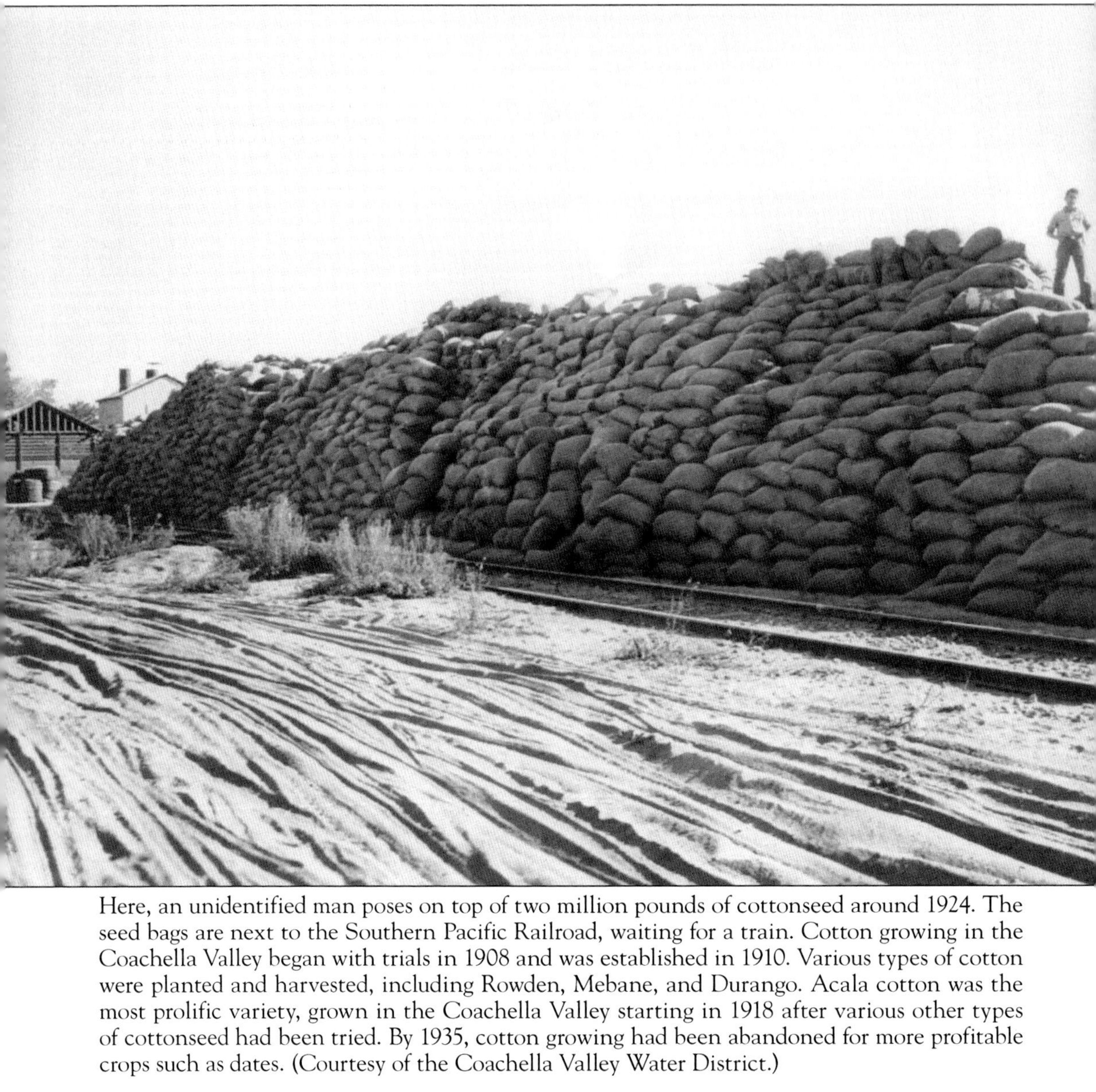

Here, an unidentified man poses on top of two million pounds of cottonseed around 1924. The seed bags are next to the Southern Pacific Railroad, waiting for a train. Cotton growing in the Coachella Valley began with trials in 1908 and was established in 1910. Various types of cotton were planted and harvested, including Rowden, Mebane, and Durango. Acala cotton was the most prolific variety, grown in the Coachella Valley starting in 1918 after various other types of cottonseed had been tried. By 1935, cotton growing had been abandoned for more profitable crops such as dates. (Courtesy of the Coachella Valley Water District.)

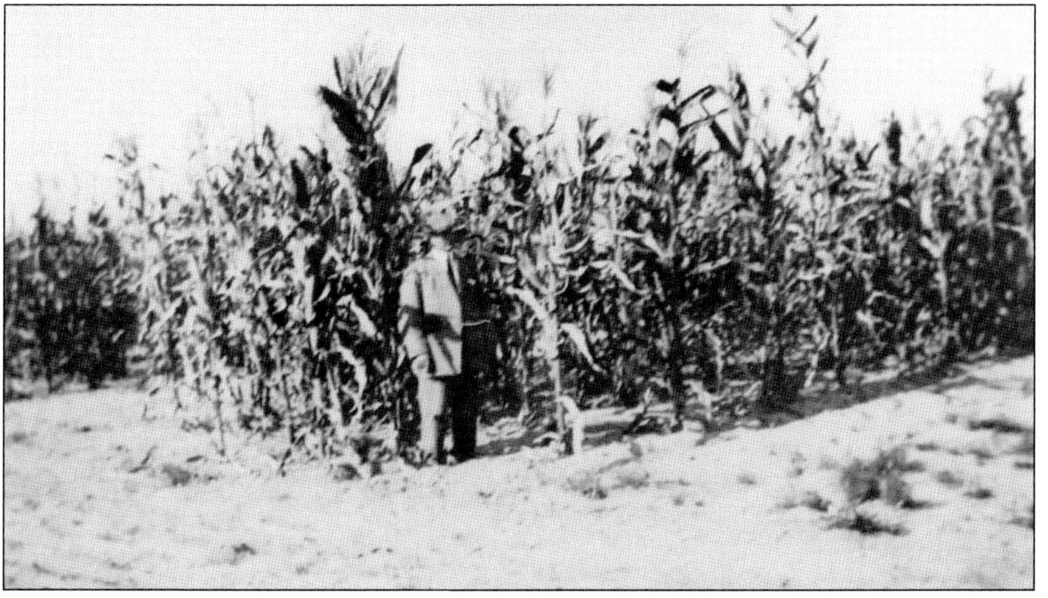

Above, an unidentified man is pictured in front of a cornfield in the Coachella Valley during the 1900s. The corn is much taller than the man. Below, two unidentified men ride in the wagon they used during a corn harvest. During the early 1900s, many farmers had their crops shipped to the Los Angeles area and sold there. The Coachella siding for the Southern Pacific Railroad was the primary shipping point for the valley's agriculture. (Above, courtesy of the Coachella Valley History Museum; below, courtesy of the Coachella Valley Water District.)

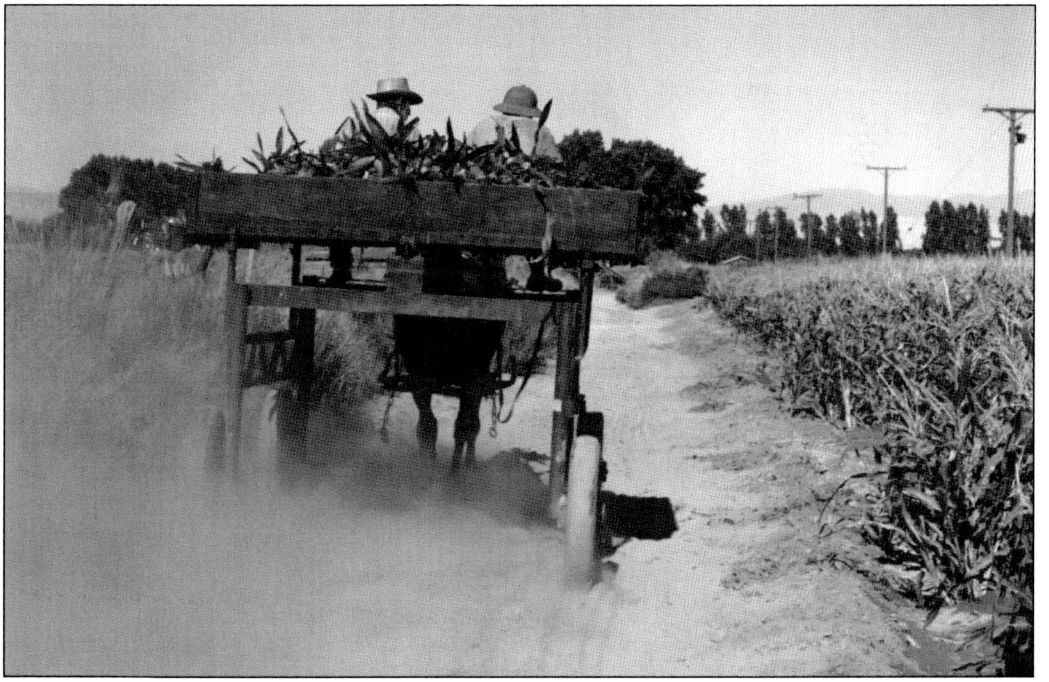

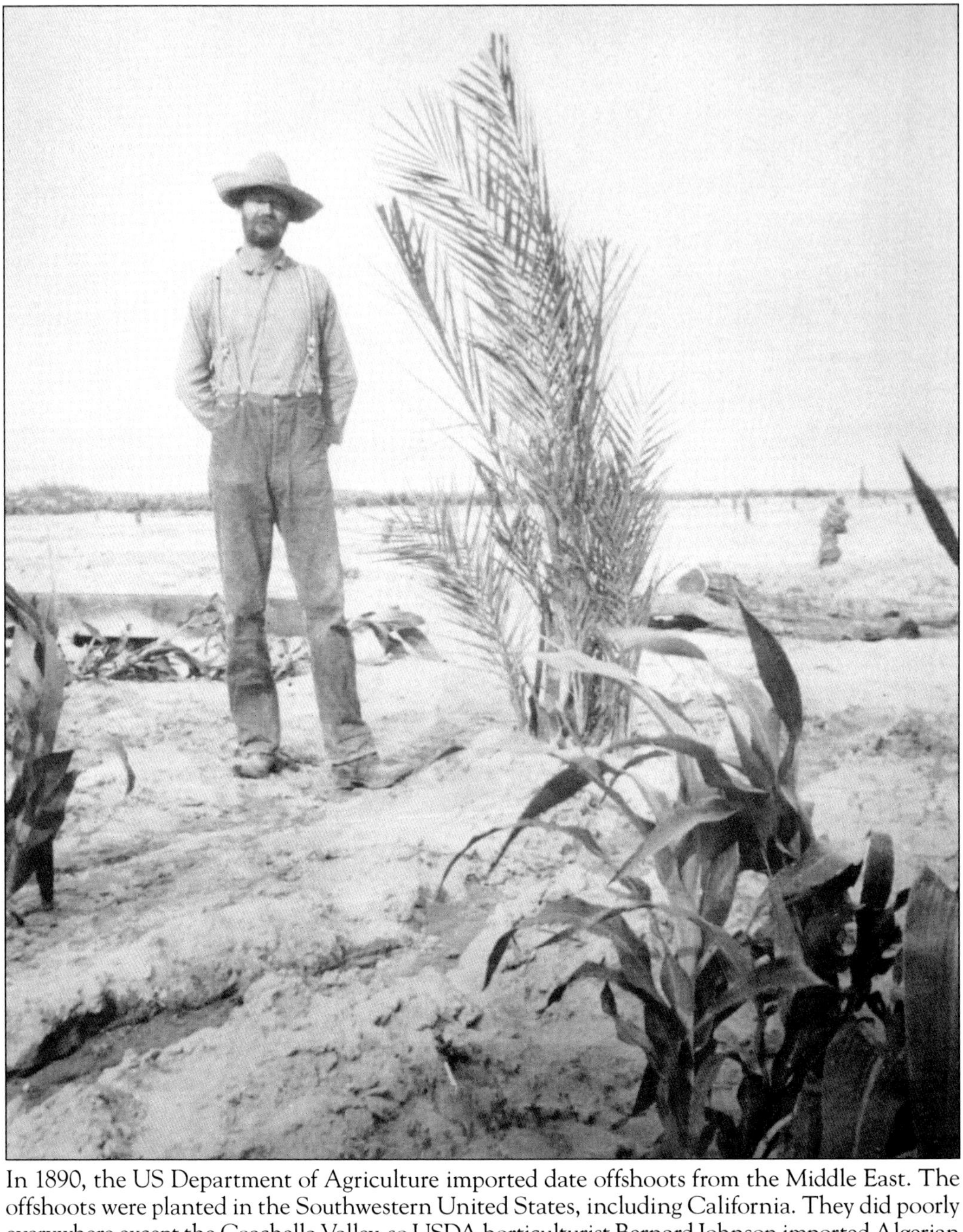

In 1890, the US Department of Agriculture imported date offshoots from the Middle East. The offshoots were planted in the Southwestern United States, including California. They did poorly everywhere except the Coachella Valley, so USDA horticulturist Bernard Johnson imported Algerian offshoots and planted them in Mecca in 1903. There were additional plantings from Algerian date offshoots in 1908 and 1912. This photograph shows Bernard Johnson, the father of the US date industry, standing next to a planted date offshoot in the Coachella Valley. The Coachella Valley date industry produces 95 percent of US dates. Date groves were spread throughout the Coachella Valley, but since the rapid development of residential and commercial properties, the groves have slowly been taken out. Despite the decline in groves, the valley remains the major producer of dates in the United States. (Courtesy of the Coachella Valley Water District.)

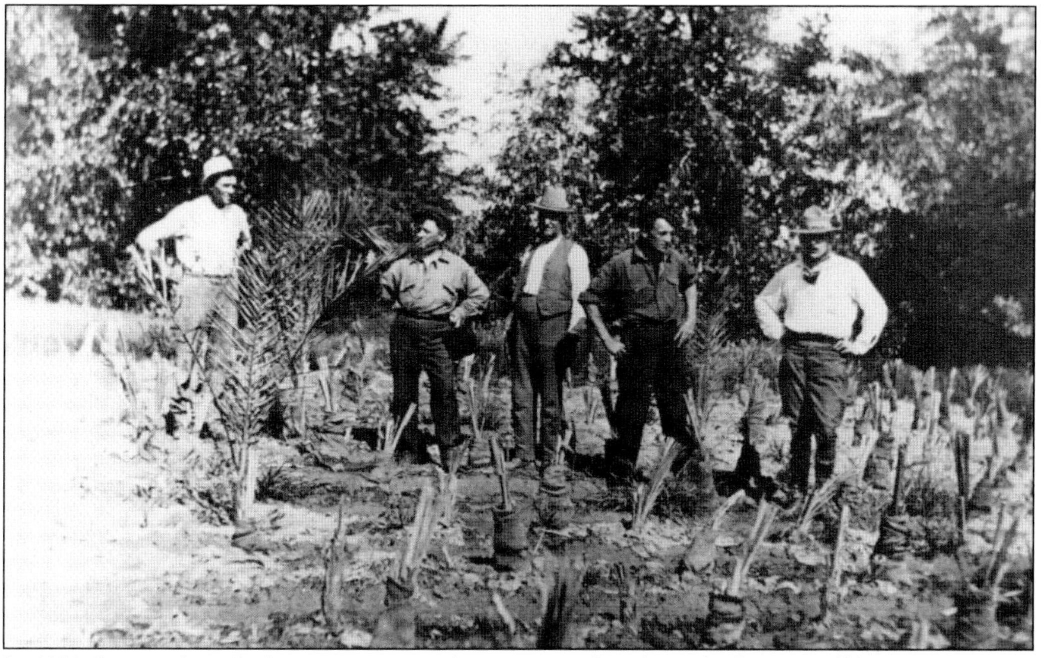

In 1914, five unidentified men are pictured inspecting the planted Algerian offshoots. Date trees are typically planted from offshoots, which are called suckers, from an adult date tree, rather than a seed. The female date trees are fruit-bearing, but require a male tree for the pollination process. (Courtesy of the Coachella Valley Water District.)

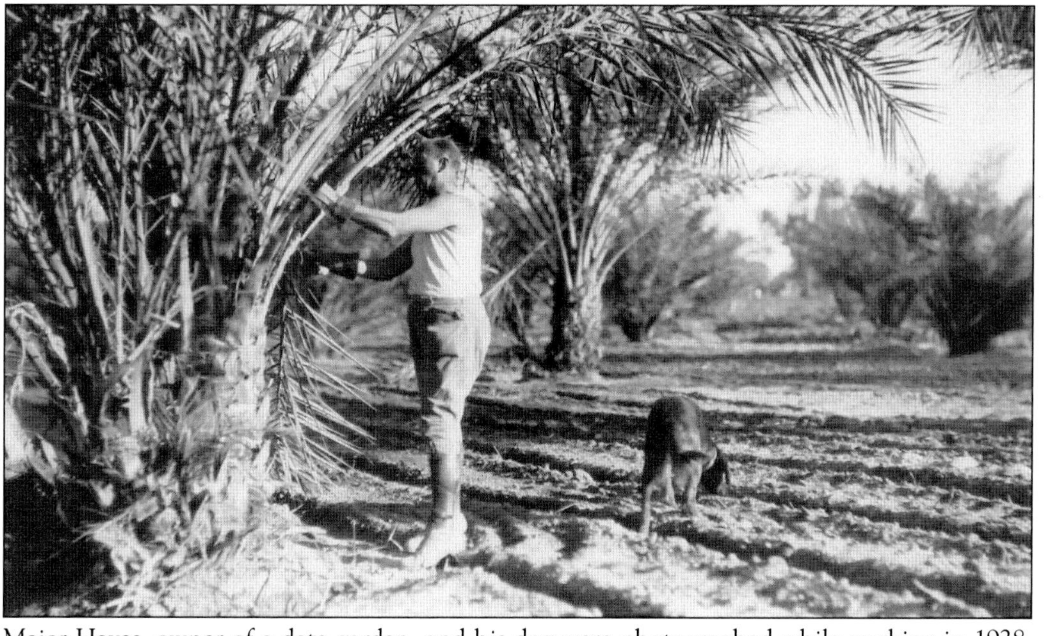

Major Hayes, owner of a date garden, and his dog were photographed while working in 1928. Having a date garden was common among non-ranchers in the Coachella Valley during the early 1900s. Coachella Valley homes in the 21st century typically have palms in their landscaping; however, date palms are less common due to the required upkeep. (Courtesy of the Coachella Valley History Museum.)

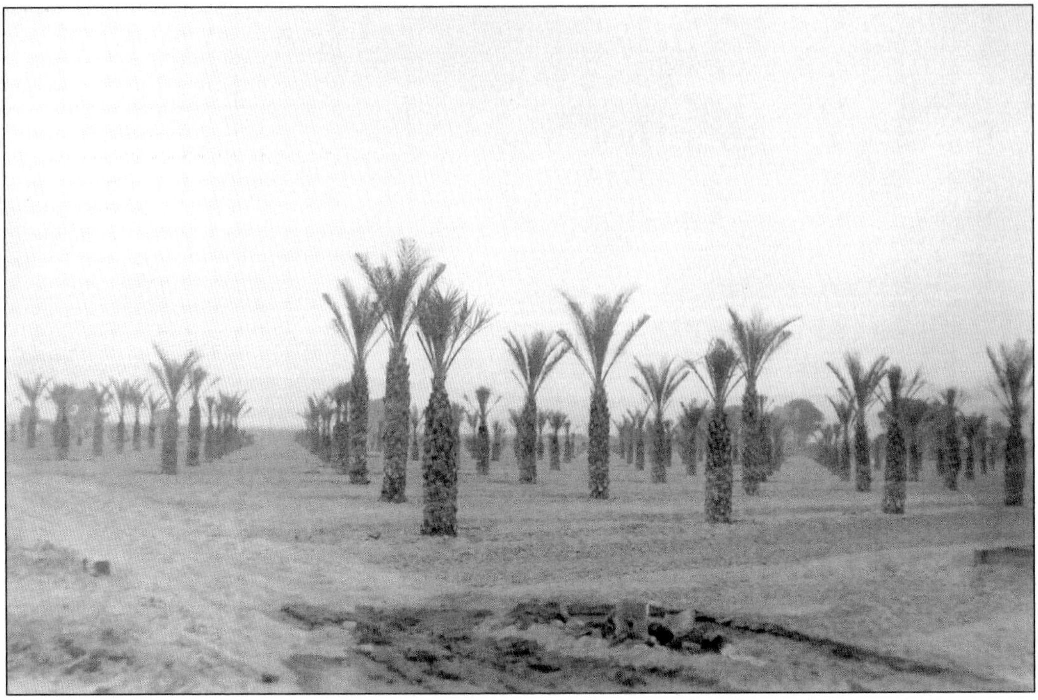

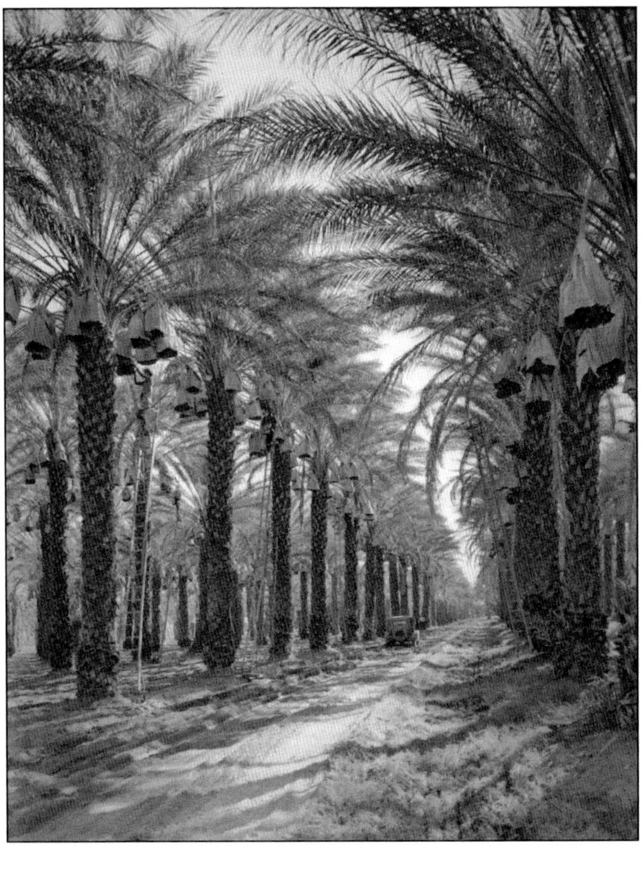

The above photograph shows the arid Coachella desert landscape organized in neat rows of date palms. In the 1920s, photographer Jack Klein took this photograph of a date ranch in Coachella. The photograph at left shows a date ranch in the Coachella Valley. The trees are full of dates, which grow in a cluster. Before the dates ripen, the farmers cover them with paper or bags to protect them from the intense heat and pests such as bugs and birds. (Above, courtesy of the Coachella Valley History Museum; left, courtesy of the Coachella Valley Water District.)

In the 1960s, a photographer captured this unidentified fieldworker picking green onions in Coachella. The top bar of the field's center pivot irrigation system can be seen in the background. The worker's only relief from the intense Coachella Valley sun is the oversized sombrero. (Courtesy of the Coachella Valley Water District.)

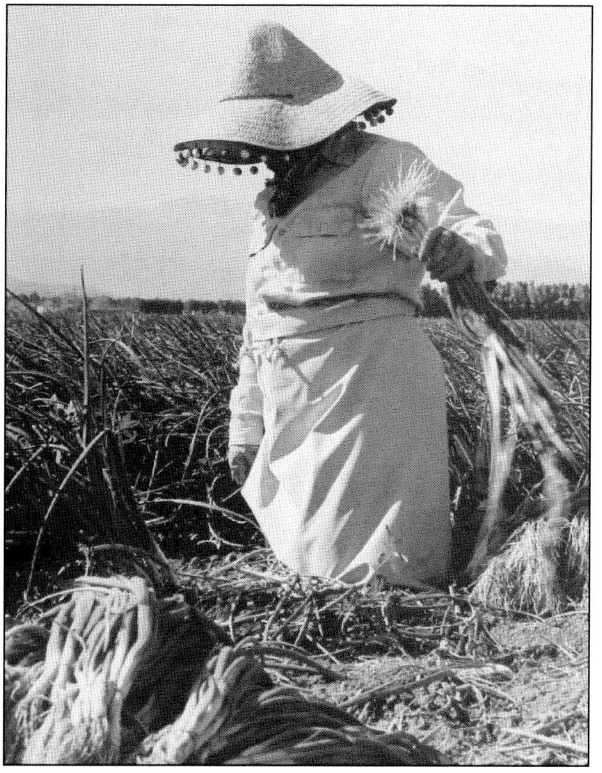

In the 1960s, an unidentified fieldworker loads cantaloupes into bins in a Coachella field. Most of the fieldworkers in the Coachella Valley are migrant workers. They move around with the changing harvesting seasons. Some of them are undocumented workers primarily from Central American countries. (Courtesy of the Coachella Valley Water District.)

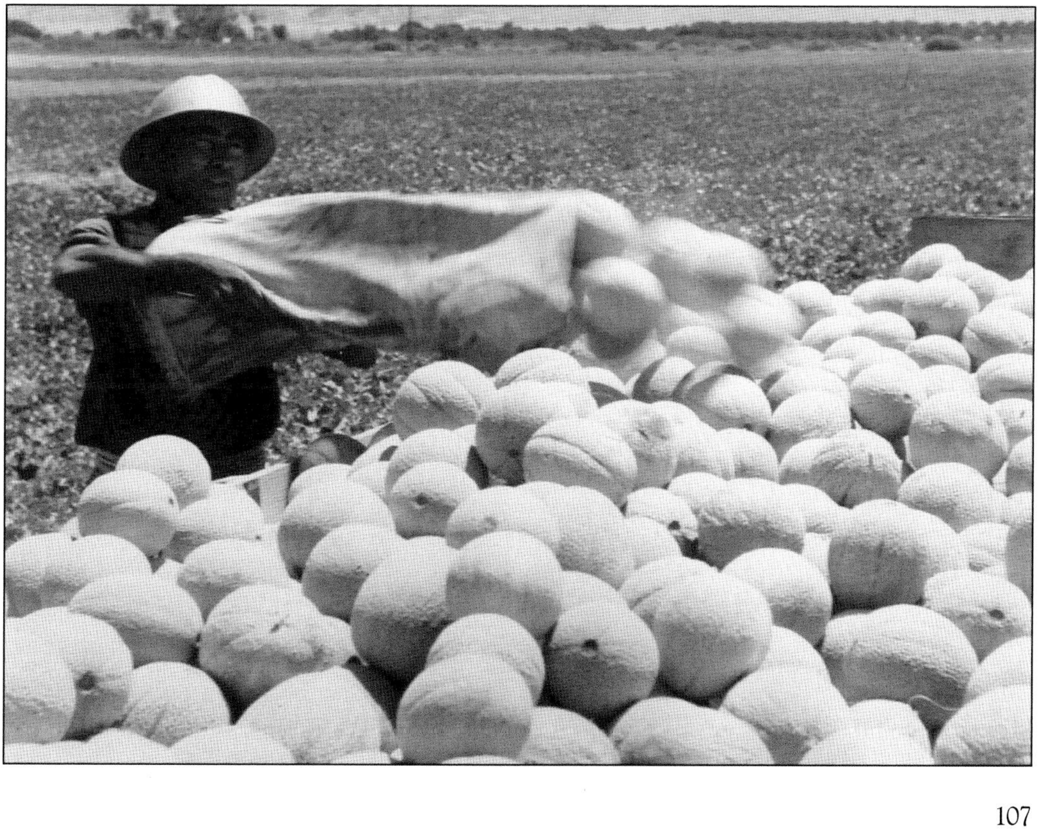

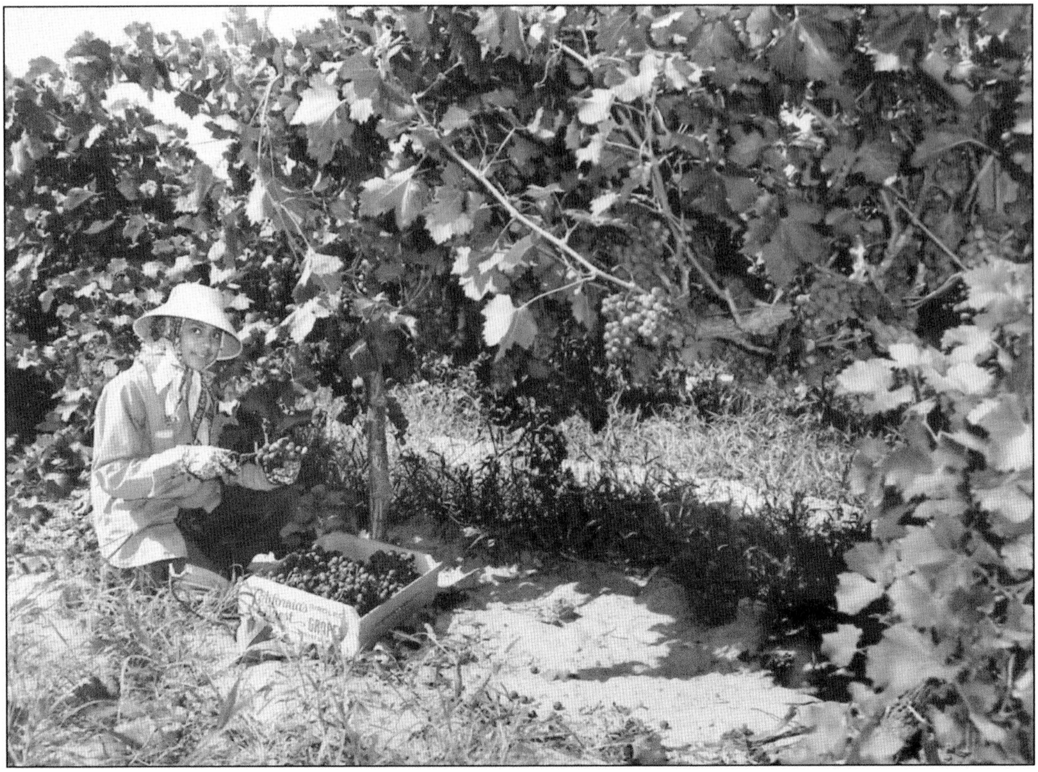

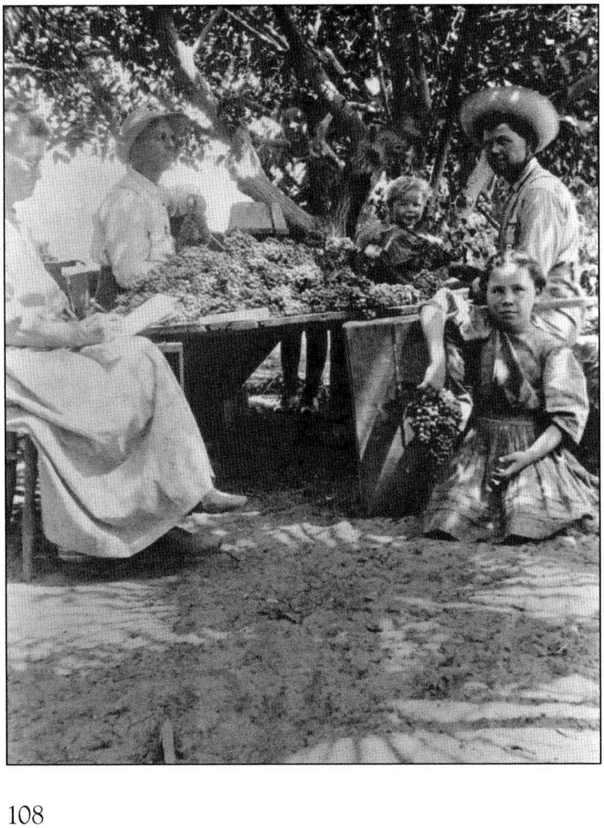

Grapes are one of the major crops grown in the Coachella Valley. The 1960s photograph above shows a fieldworker harvesting grape clusters from the vines. The wide-brimmed hat, scarf, long-sleeved shirt, and gloves are typical clothing for a fieldworker, protecting them from sunburn and pests. The Coachella Valley is home to several different types of spiders and scorpions. The photograph at left was taken at the Cheetah ranch during its grape harvest. The unidentified woman on the left appears to be counting the grape haul on the makeshift table while the man on the right waits. (Above, courtesy of the Coachella Valley History Museum; left, courtesy of the Coachella Valley Water District.)

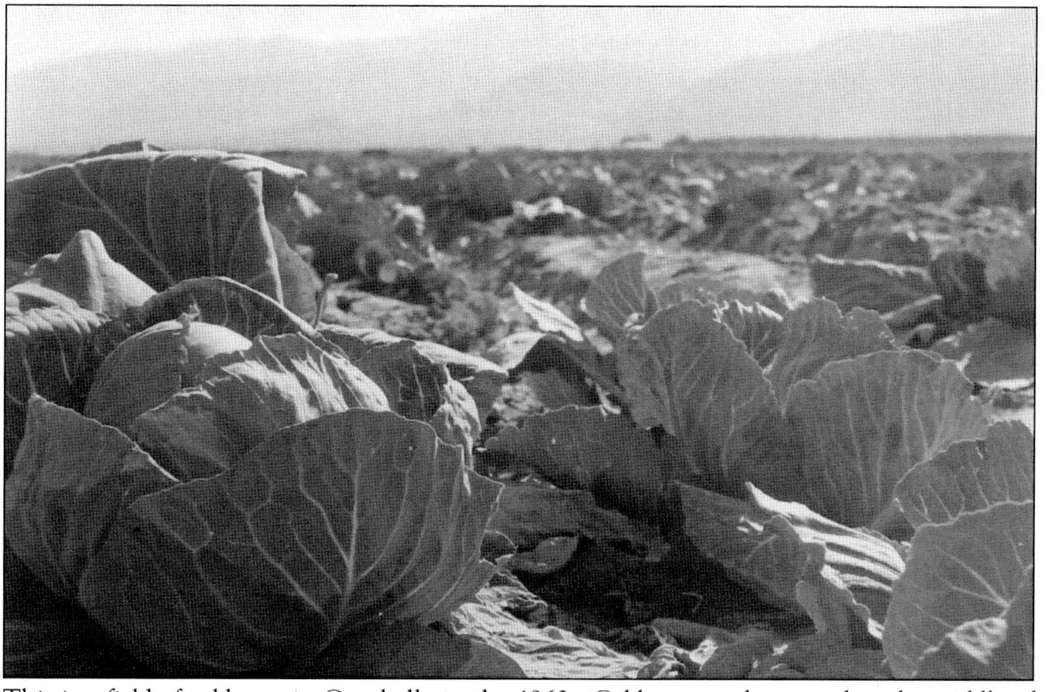

This is a field of cabbages in Coachella in the 1960s. Cabbages are harvested in the middle of summer. (Courtesy of the Coachella Valley Water District.)

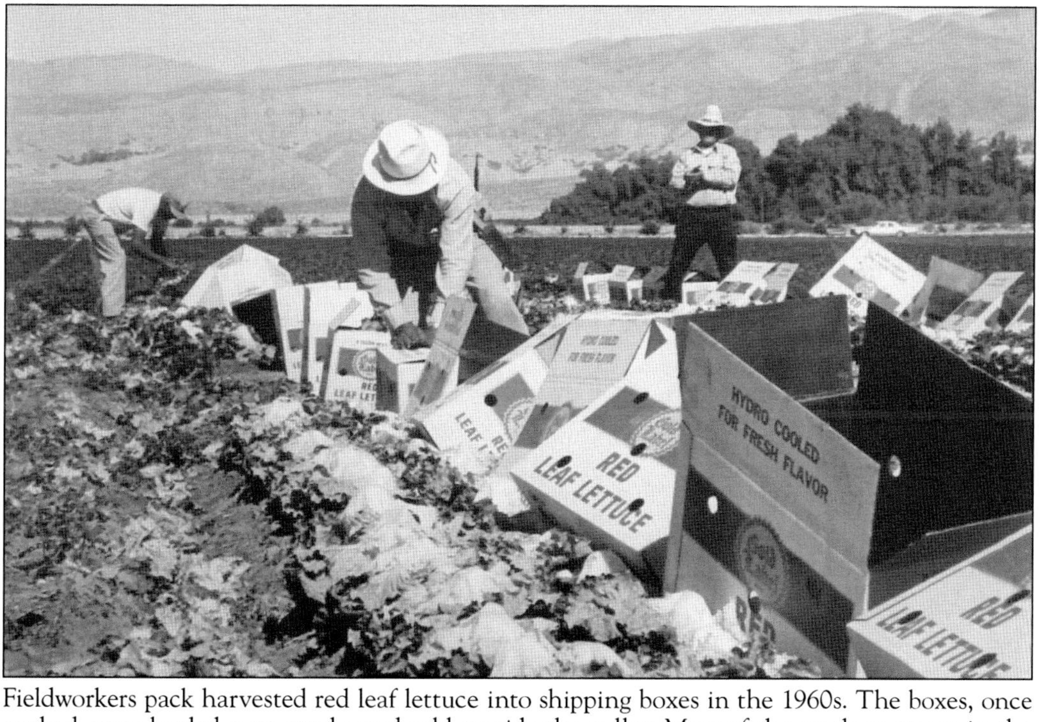

Fieldworkers pack harvested red leaf lettuce into shipping boxes in the 1960s. The boxes, once packed, were loaded onto trucks and sold outside the valley. Most of the produce grown in the Coachella Valley is sold to large groceries and shipped to other locales. (Courtesy of the Coachella Valley Water District.)

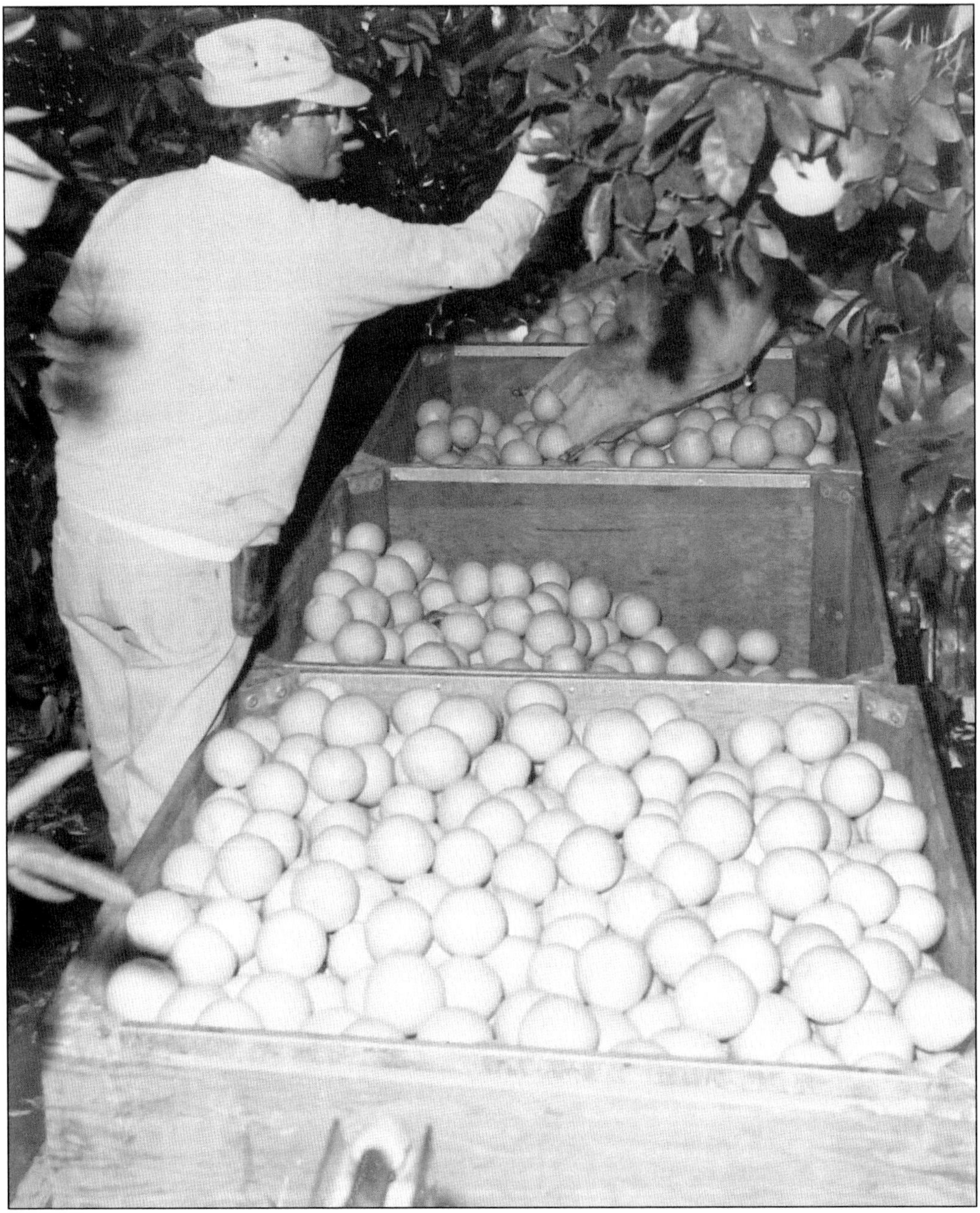

Here, an unidentified fieldworker is picking fruit and filling bins in a Coachella field. In the 1970s, when this photograph was taken, César Chávez and the United Farm Workers fought for improvements in the working conditions and rights of farm workers, in particular migrant workers. Migrant workers often had no rights, since many of them were undocumented. Unfortunately, some employers took advantage of this by paying wages far below the cost of living and having workers use tools that were dangerous. It was not until 1975 that the California Supreme Court ruled that the short-handled hoe was too dangerous and banned its use. After Chávez's death in 1993, California became one of several states that celebrate César Chávez Day each year on March 31. (Courtesy of the Coachella Valley Water District.)

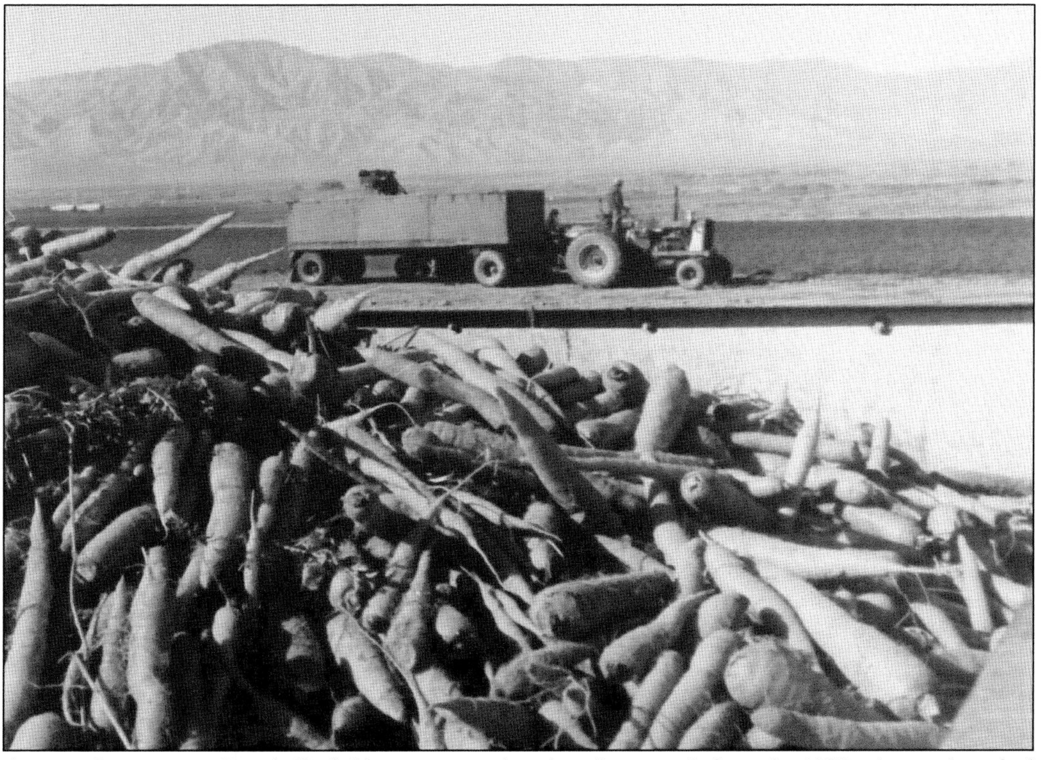

A carrot harvest in a Coachella field was captured in this photograph from the 1970s. An unidentified fieldworker can be seen driving the tractor in the background. The carrots would most likely be shipped outside the Coachella Valley. (Courtesy of the Coachella Valley Water District.)

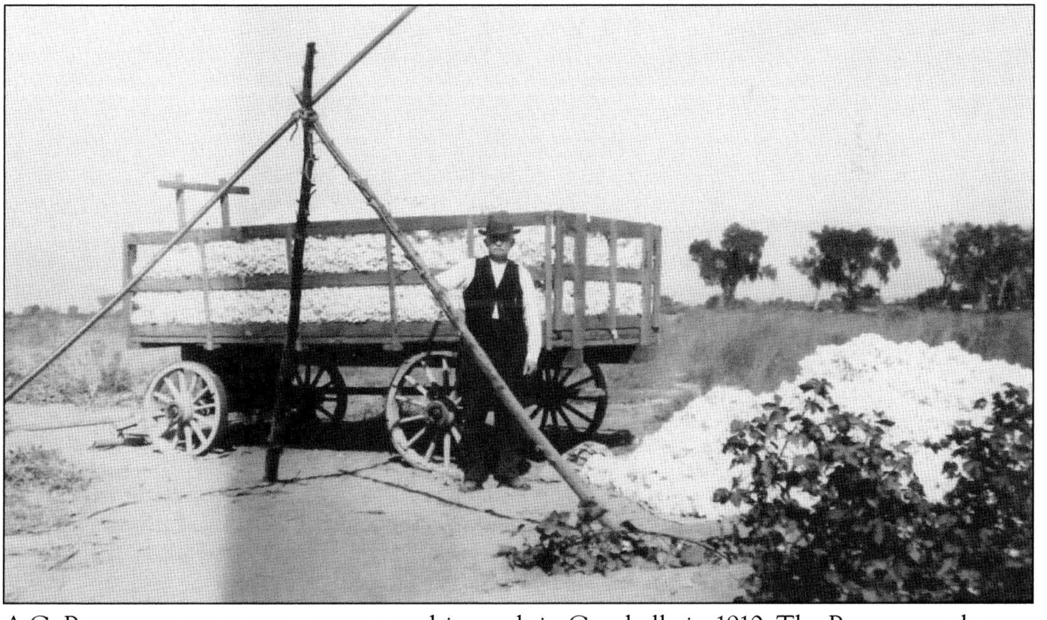

A.G. Proctor poses next to a wagon on his ranch in Coachella in 1910. The Proctor ranch grew cotton, which is what is in the wagon. There is still a mound of cotton on the ground to the right waiting to be loaded and shipped. (Courtesy of the Coachella Valley History Museum.)

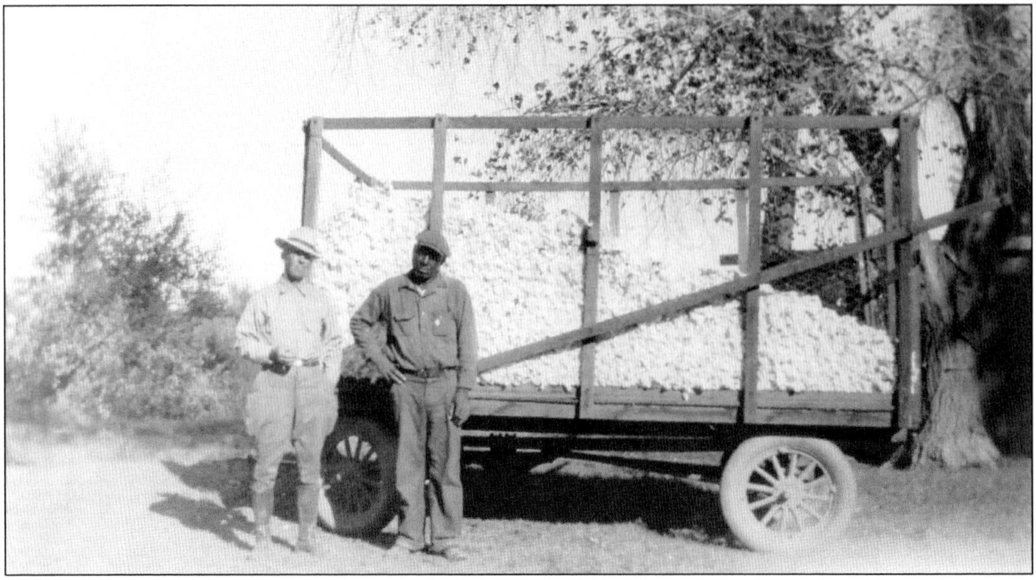

In Coachella in the 1930s, the Wool ranch was harvesting its cotton crop when the above photograph was taken. Ralph J. Wool (left) and an unidentified worker pose in front of a wagon filled with picked cotton. Another Coachella crop was onions, as seen in the 1910 photograph below of the onion harvest at the Proctor ranch. Workers pose next to onion-filled crates and filled wagons. The wagons transported the crated crop to packinghouses or the railroad siding in Coachella to be shipped outside the valley. (Both, courtesy of the Coachella Valley History Museum.)

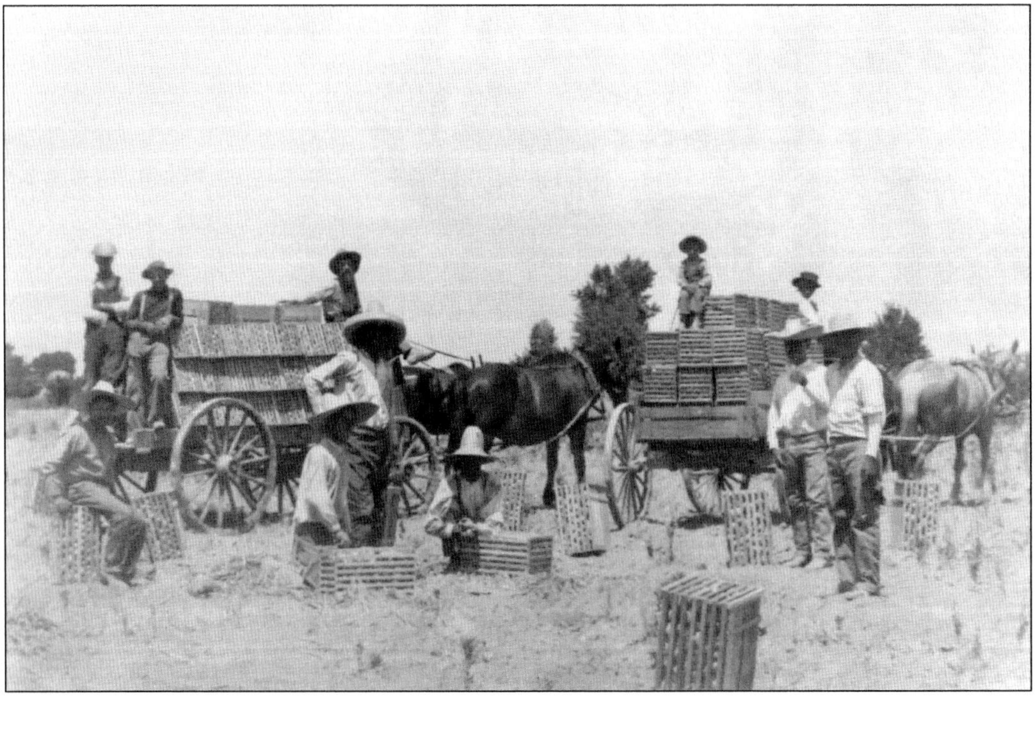

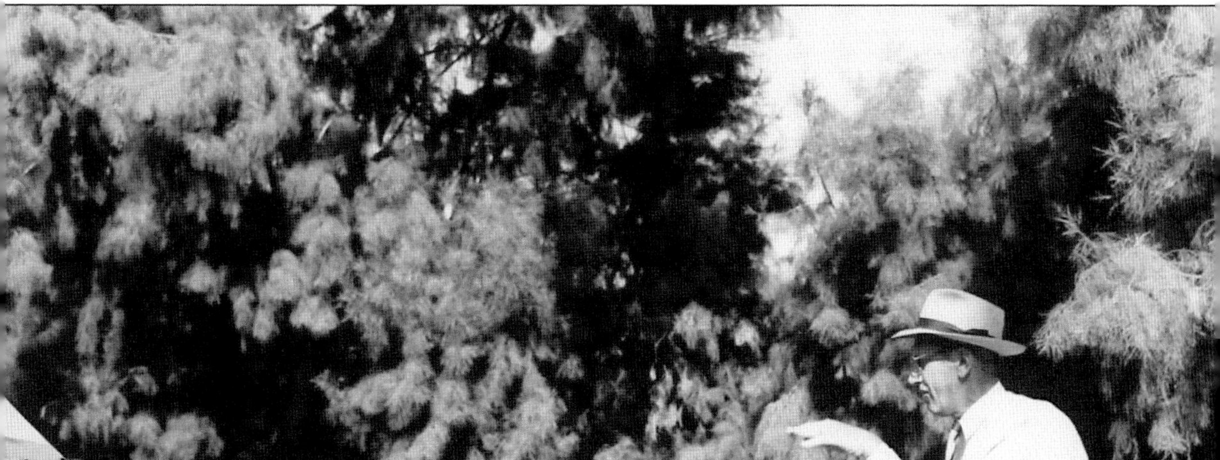

This photograph was taken in 1950 just as Pat Bennett threw a tree limb into the Imperial Irrigation District's new chipper. Clearing the natural desert underbrush was made easier by machinery. Early Coachella residents cleared the land by burning or cutting. The chips that are produced by the chipper could be recycled for use on playgrounds and in landscaping projects. The Imperial Irrigation District (IID) is one of the two power companies in the Coachella Valley; Southern California Edison is the other. They also provide water to residents and businesses in the Imperial Valley. The California Irrigation District Act established IID in 1911. (Courtesy of the Coachella Valley History Museum.)

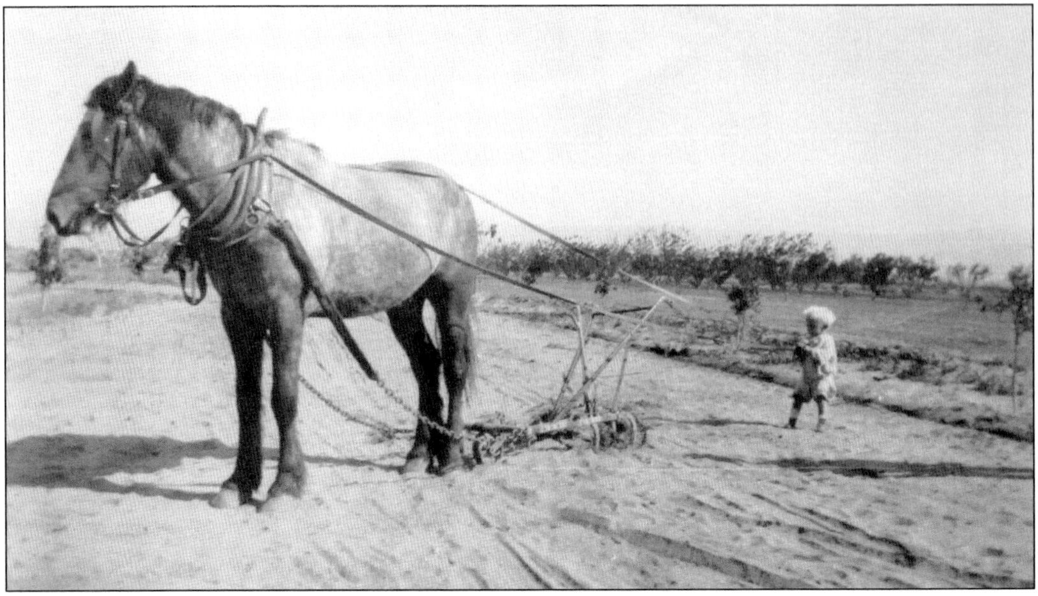

Bob Vote is pictured in 1918 pretending to walk the horse and plow. The horse stood calmly while the child had some fun. Some of the early farm children followed in their parents' footsteps in farming. The Golden Acre Farm in Thermal, which is owned and operated by the Kitagawa family, is one example. (Courtesy of the Coachella Valley History Museum.)

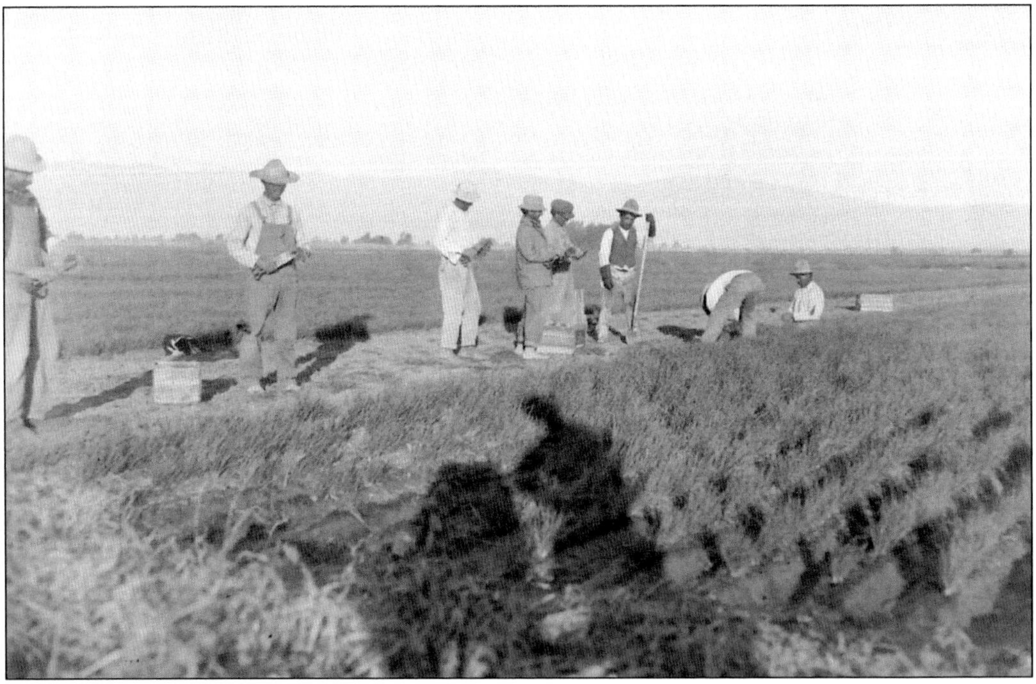

These unidentified fieldworkers are harvesting an onion field during the 1930s. It would be less than a decade before migrant workers from Mexico would participate in the Bracero Program (1942–1964), which allowed Mexicans to cross the border to work in the fields. The Coachella Valley was one of the places where *braceros* were employed. (Courtesy of the Coachella Valley History Museum.)

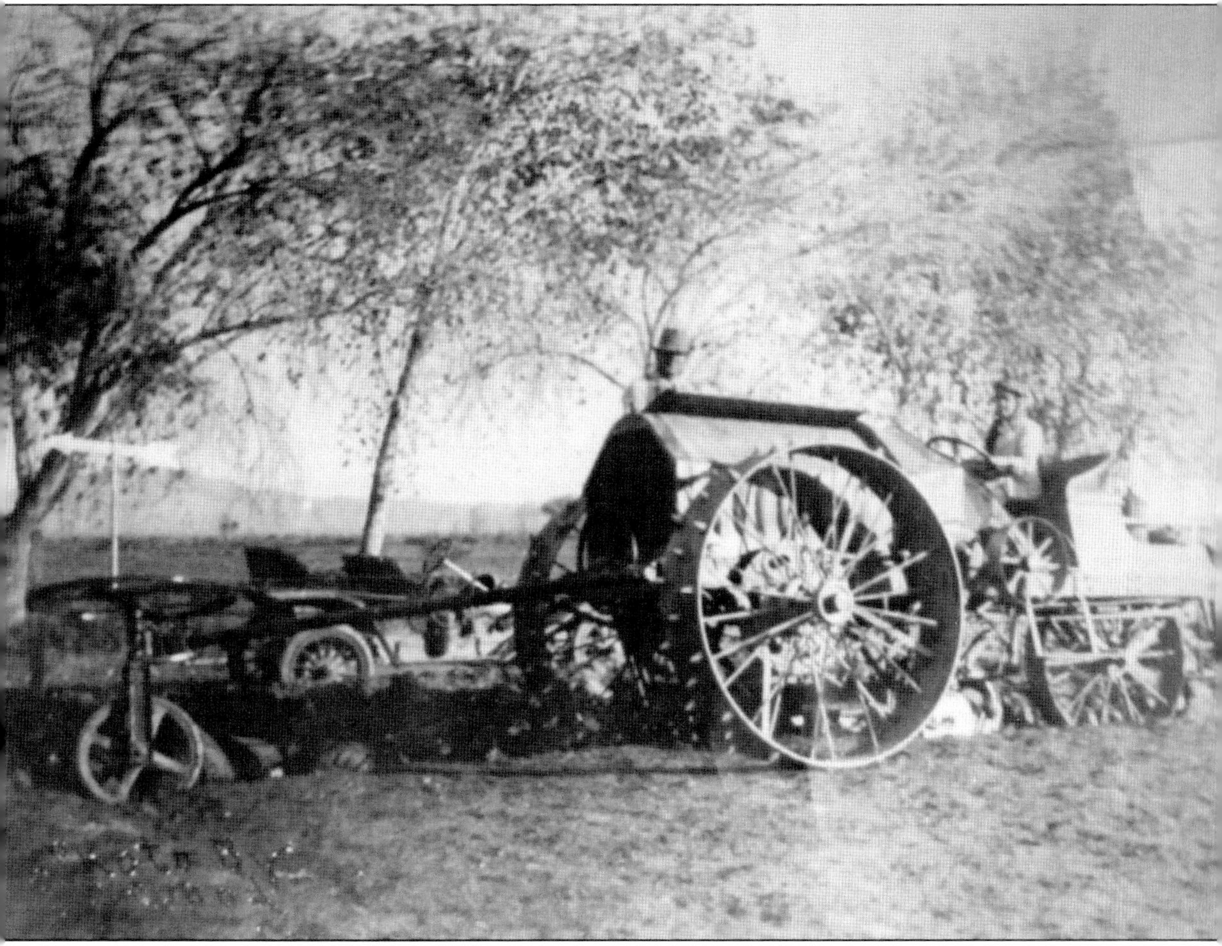

This photograph of a large tractor at a Coachella ranch was taken in 1912. Dr. Dorsey's ranch was located on Shady Lane. This behemoth of a tractor was a technological marvel during its time. The woman driving the tractor is Dr. Rebecca Lee Dorsey. Dr. Dorsey's career in obstetrics was mainly based in the Los Angeles area, where she opened her own practice, which thrived due to her success rate of healthy births. Part of her success has been credited to her use of sterilization, which she learned while in Europe. She has also been credited with delivering Earl Warren, who later became a chief justice of the US Supreme Court. Dorsey moved to her ranch in the Coachella Valley when she retired after 60 years of practicing medicine. She worked and ran a successful date ranch until her death in 1954 at the age of 95. (Courtesy of the Coachella Valley Water District.)

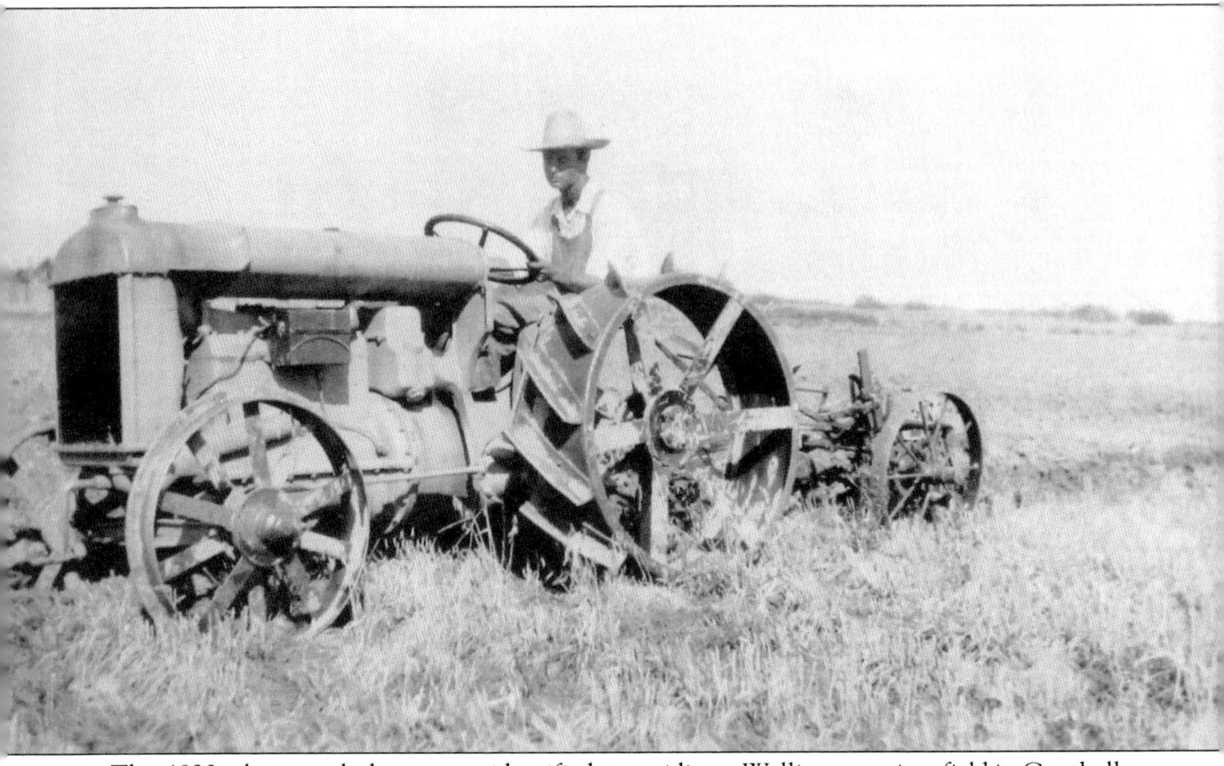

This 1920s photograph shows an unidentified man riding a Wallis tractor in a field in Coachella. The tractor has been identified as either a Cub Junior or a Model OK. The Wallis Tractor Company started in 1912, and in 1919 merged with the J.I. Case Plow Works Company. The Wallis Cub Junior (Model J) was available starting in 1917, while the Wallis Model OK was first available in 1923. These gasoline tractors were more efficient and faster than the previous steam-powered tractors. These particular Wallis tractors also had several forward gears and a reverse gear for faster and easier maneuverability. The use of tractors to plow the fields had essentially replaced the use of a horse-drawn plow on large farms. Farmers were able to plow fields in much less time with less help. Tractors, along with other technological advancements, revolutionized the agricultural industry. (Courtesy of the Coachella Valley History Museum.)

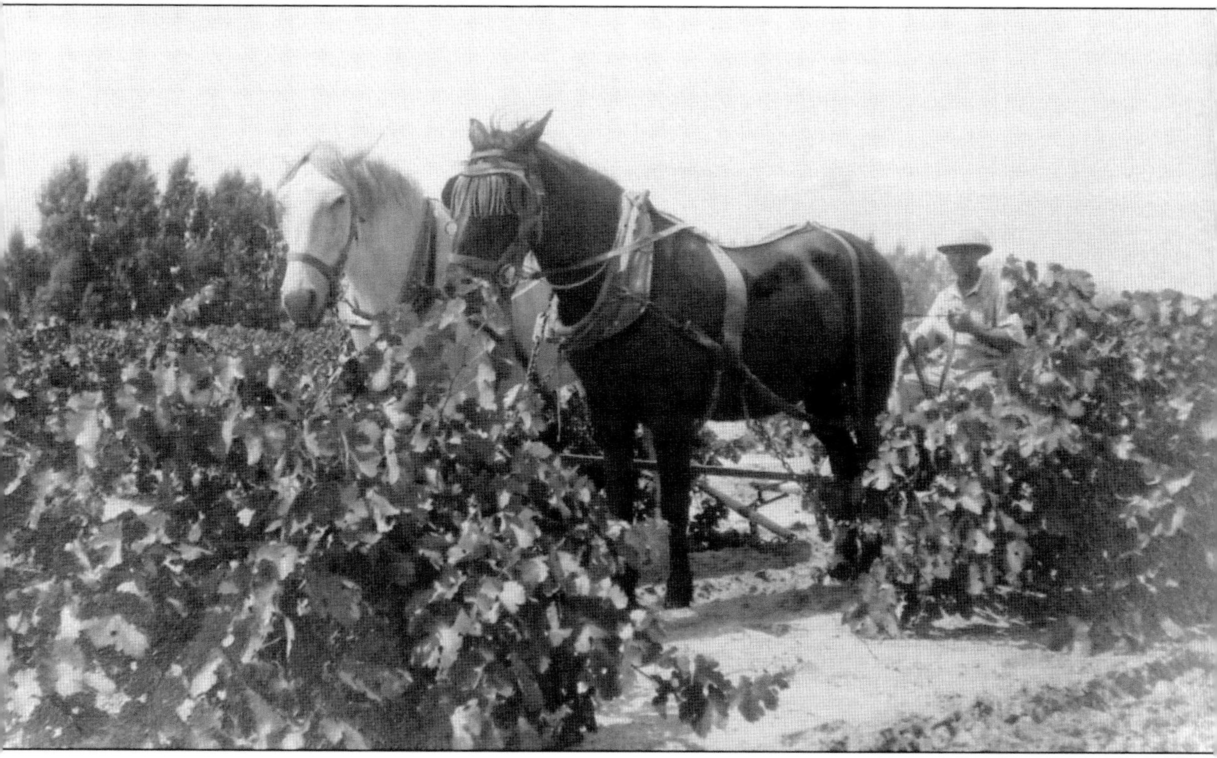

In 1918, Claude W. Hyde drives a horse-drawn plow on his ranch in Coachella after the year's harvest had finished. Hyde is cultivating his 1918 grape crop. The grapes grown in the Coachella Valley are used as table fruit to be eaten rather than for the production of wine, like the grapes in the Napa Valley area. Vineyards were initially grown all over the Coachella Valley, but by the 1990s, the progress of land development had left just the vineyards on the east side of the valley in place. Each year, when the grapes are ready to be harvested, migrant fieldworkers arrive, since grape picking is still done by hand. (Courtesy of the Coachella Valley History Museum.)

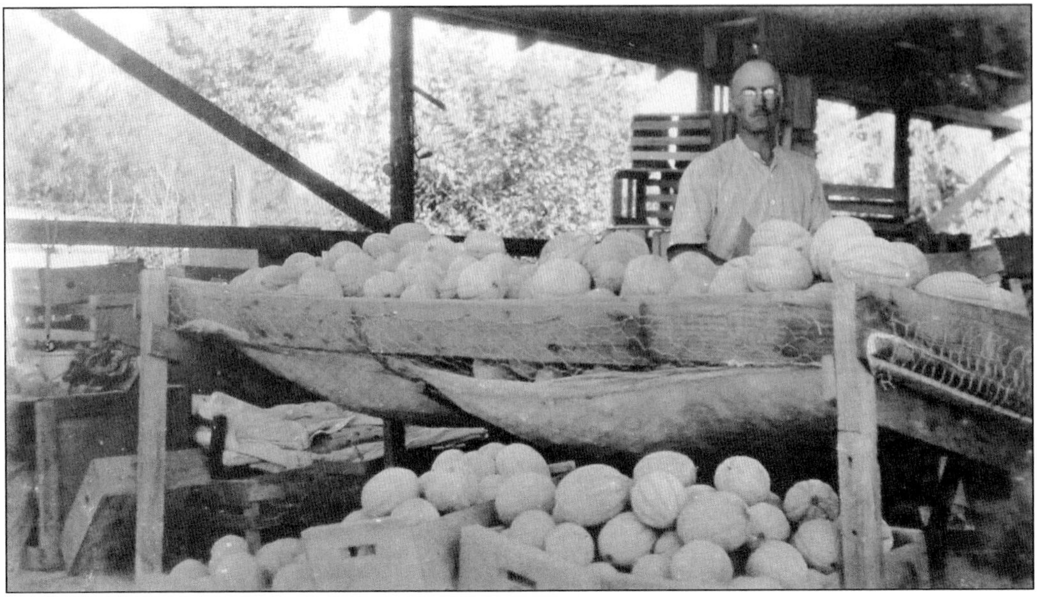

Robert Proctor is seen above packing cantaloupes in 1914. Proctor was working in one of the structures on his Coachella ranch as he prepared his crop for shipment. The cradles holding the cantaloupes held the melons until they were packed into shipping crates to be shipped by train or truck. Today, most of the produce shipped from the Coachella Valley is done by truck. The early 1900s photograph below shows the Crutchfield and Woolfolks Cantaloupe Shed. Horse-drawn wagons wait in front of the shed, where produce was packed and readied for shipment. (Above, courtesy of the Coachella Valley History Museum; below, courtesy of the Coachella Valley Water District.)

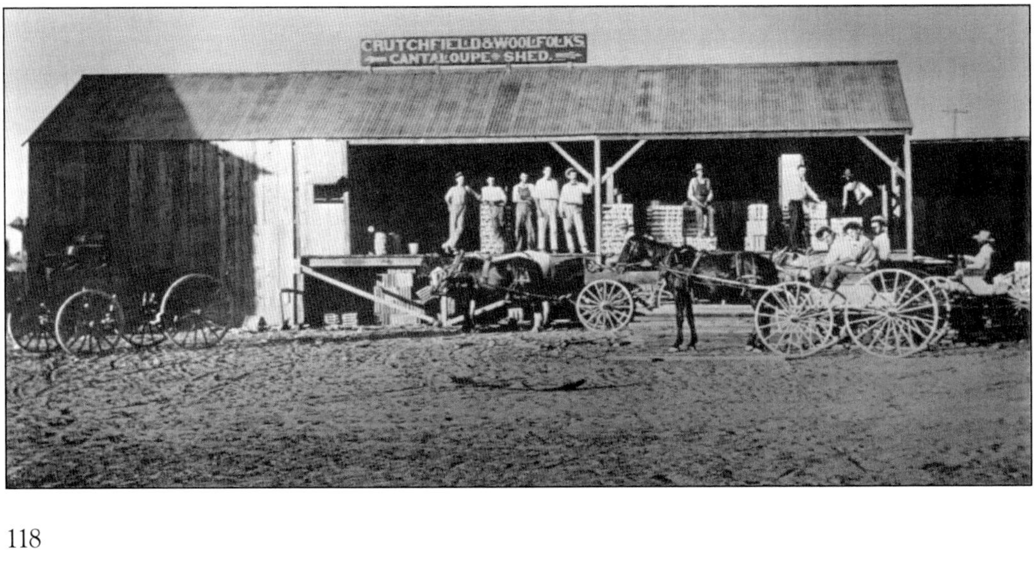

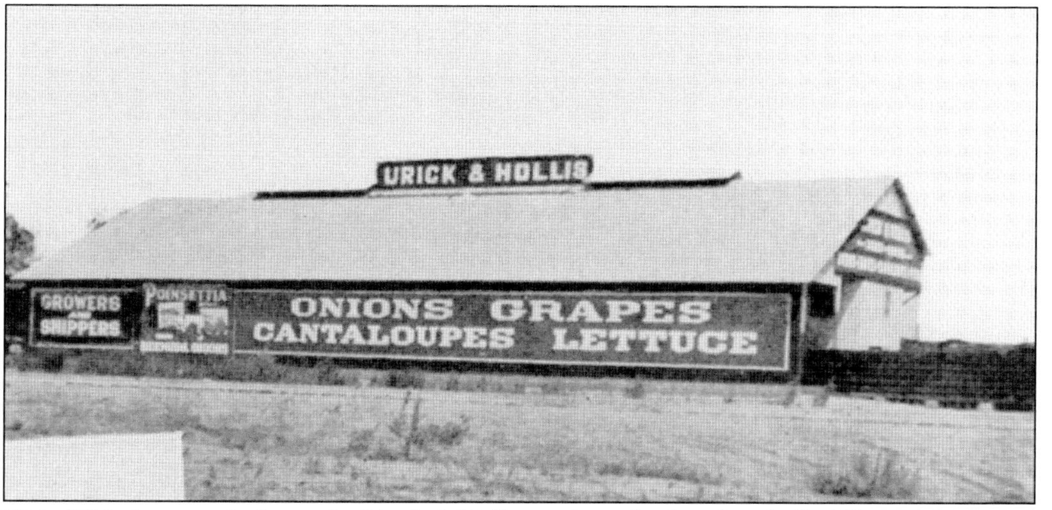

This 1926 photograph shows the Urick & Hollis packing shed in Coachella. There were several packing sheds available for farmers to take their crops to in order to get assistance with packing their produce for shipment. Often, the packing sheds were close to the railroad for easy transport to the railroad siding. (Courtesy of the Coachella Valley History Museum.)

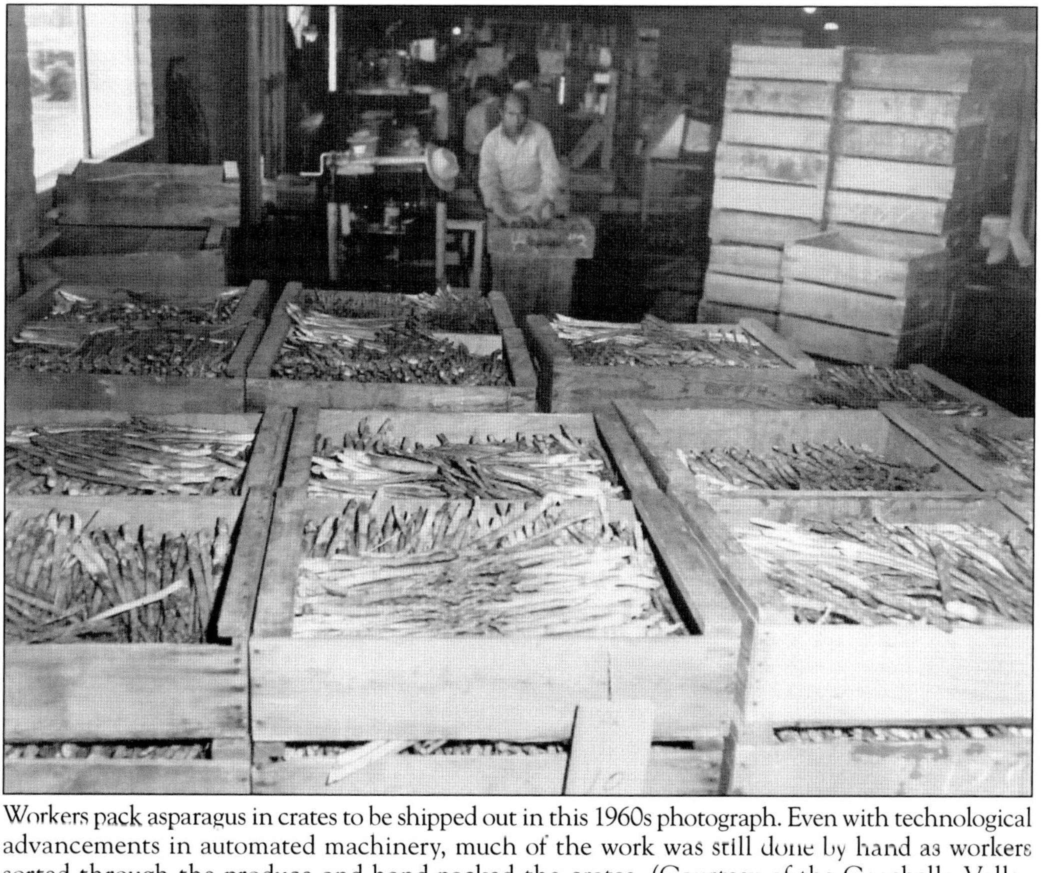

Workers pack asparagus in crates to be shipped out in this 1960s photograph. Even with technological advancements in automated machinery, much of the work was still done by hand as workers sorted through the produce and hand-packed the crates. (Courtesy of the Coachella Valley Water District.)

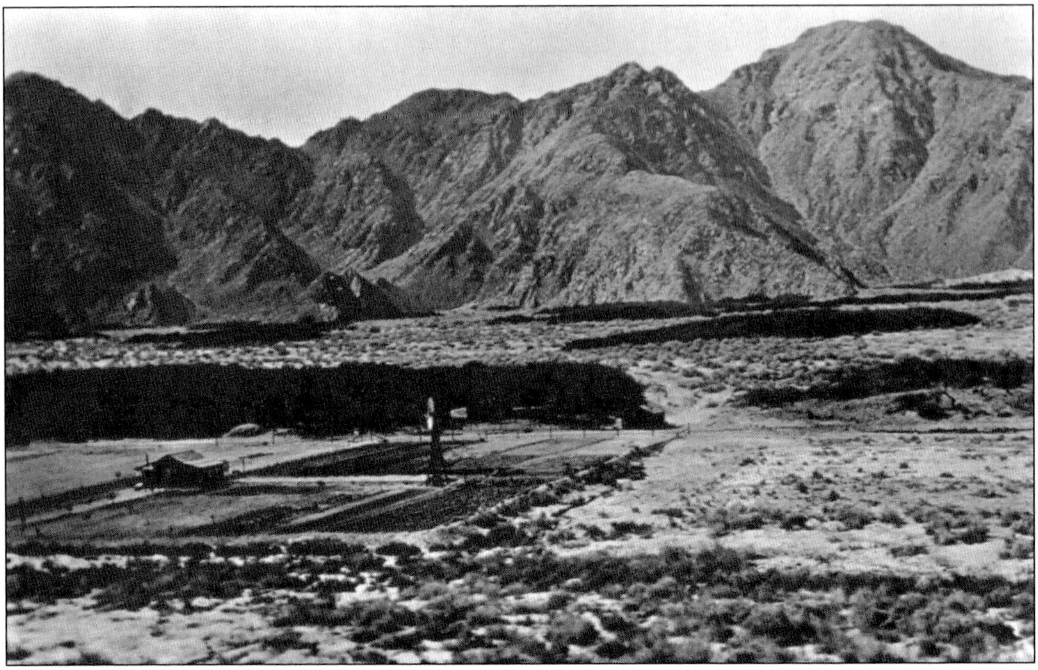

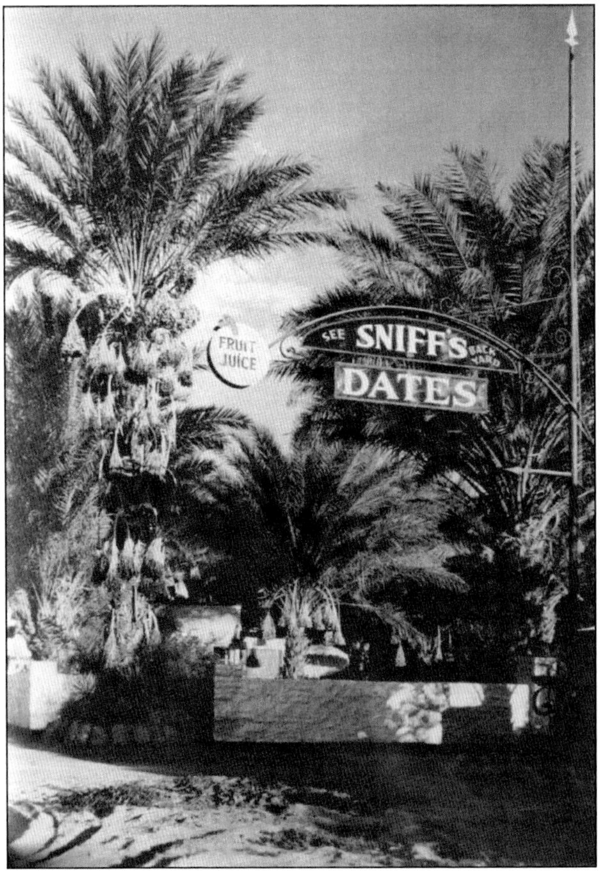

The Coachella Valley Water District took this photograph of the Blair ranch. William P. Blair started this ranch in 1909 in Indian Wells. However, by 1916, a flood had destroyed most of the ranch. The Tennis Gardens of Indian Wells are just west of where the Blair ranch was. (Courtesy of the Coachella Valley Water District.)

Sniff's Backyard Dates Garden was just west of Indio. Visitors could view the surrounding date garden while shopping at the store. Sniff's sold dates, fruits, and various other products. Like most date gardens, Sniff's had date shakes available for purchase. (Courtesy of the Coachella Valley Water District.)

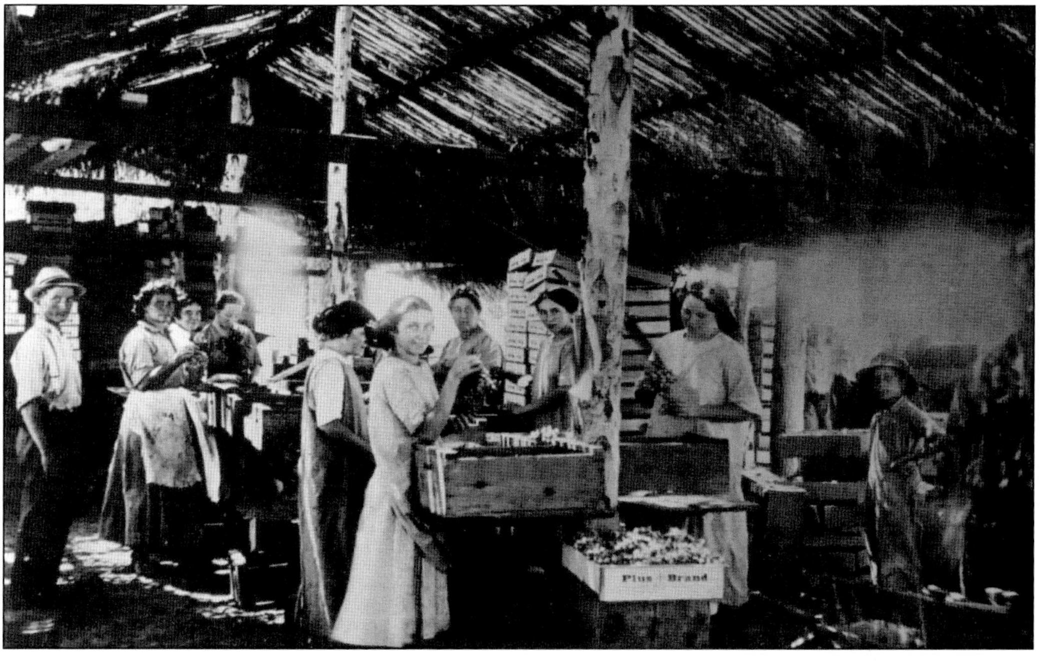

The above photograph was taken inside the Edmunds Date Packing Shed. Many of the workers in the packing sheds were women, as can be seen in these two photographs. Prior to child labor laws, children also worked in the packing sheds to help bring in additional income for their families. Workers sorted the dates before placing them into the packing crates for shipment. The below photograph was taken inside an unidentified packinghouse. The workers, all women, wear white uniforms, much like nursing uniforms. (Both, courtesy of the Coachella Valley Water District.)

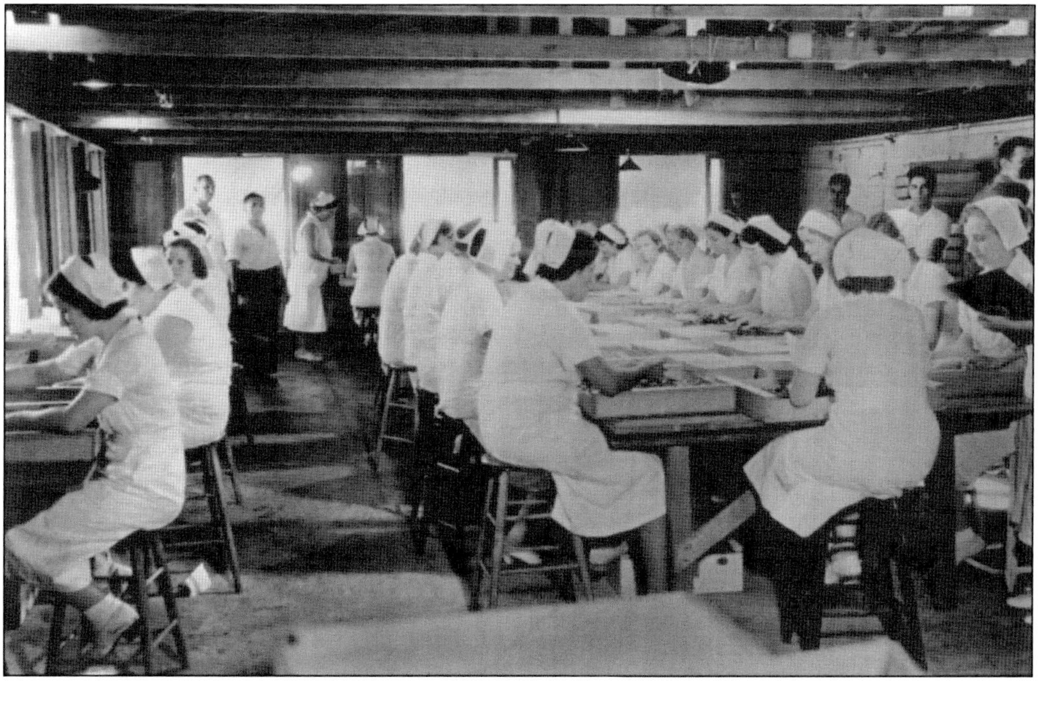

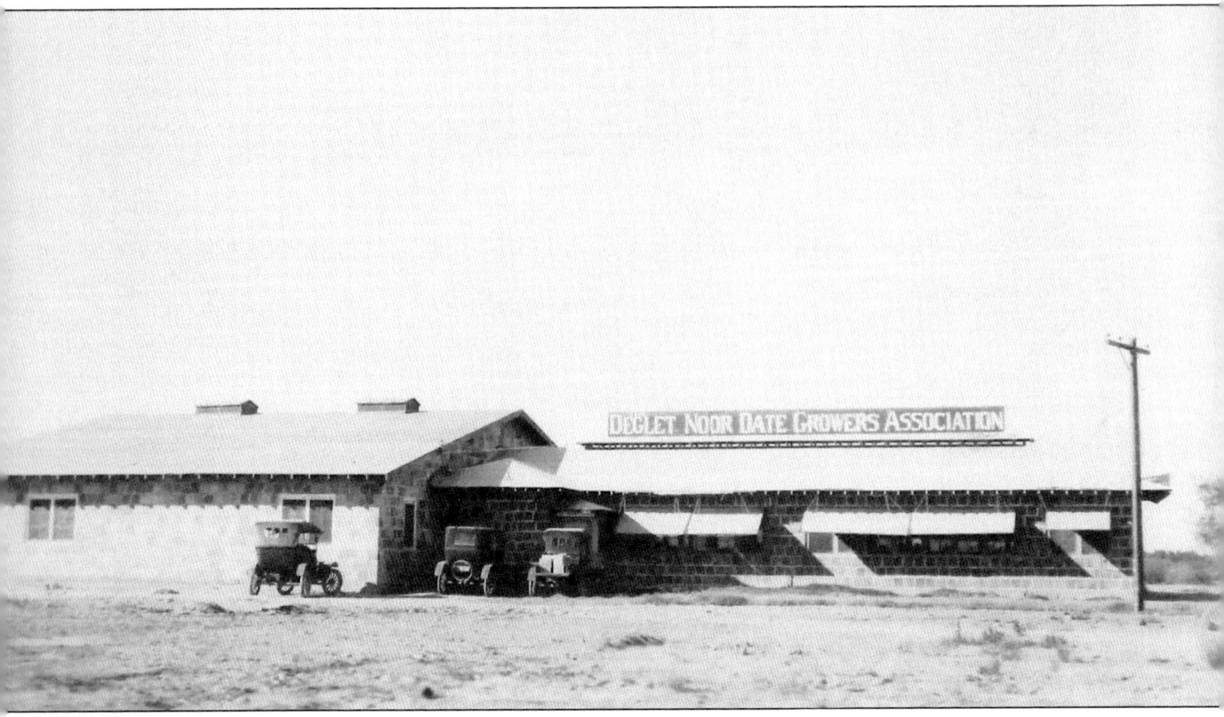

The Deglet Noor Date Growers Association Building, located in Indio, is pictured in the 1920s. This was the building the association built after outgrowing its leased building in Coachella. The Deglet Noor Date Growers Association was started in 1919 in an effort to control the quality of Deglet Noor dates. The building pictured here was the association's cooperative packinghouse. By 1932, the organization's name was changed to the California Date Growers Association. Dates were hand sorted into grades to maintain consistent quality. There was also a sales room in the packinghouse. The association continued to operate until the 1970s, when it was disbanded. Today, the US Food and Drug Administration and the US Department of Agriculture make quality regulations. (Courtesy of the Coachella Valley History Museum.)

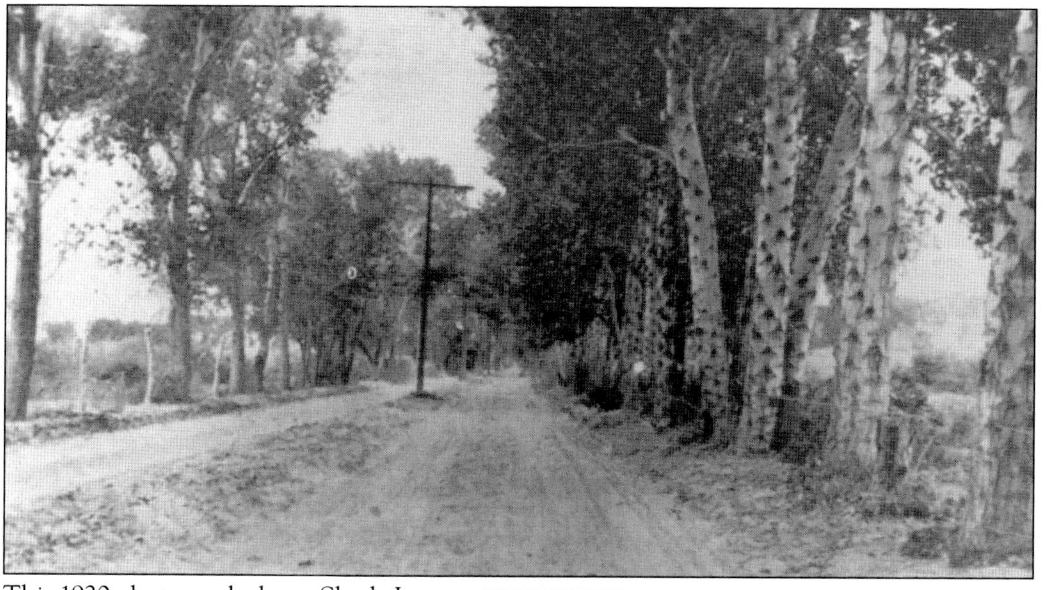

This 1920 photograph shows Shady Lane in Coachella. The agriculture industry affected not only jobs and the economy but also the landscape of the area. The arid desert with immense vegetation-free sections of land mixed with dense brush-covered sections changed to cleared land with agriculture fields and designed landscaping. (Courtesy of the Coachella Valley Water District.)

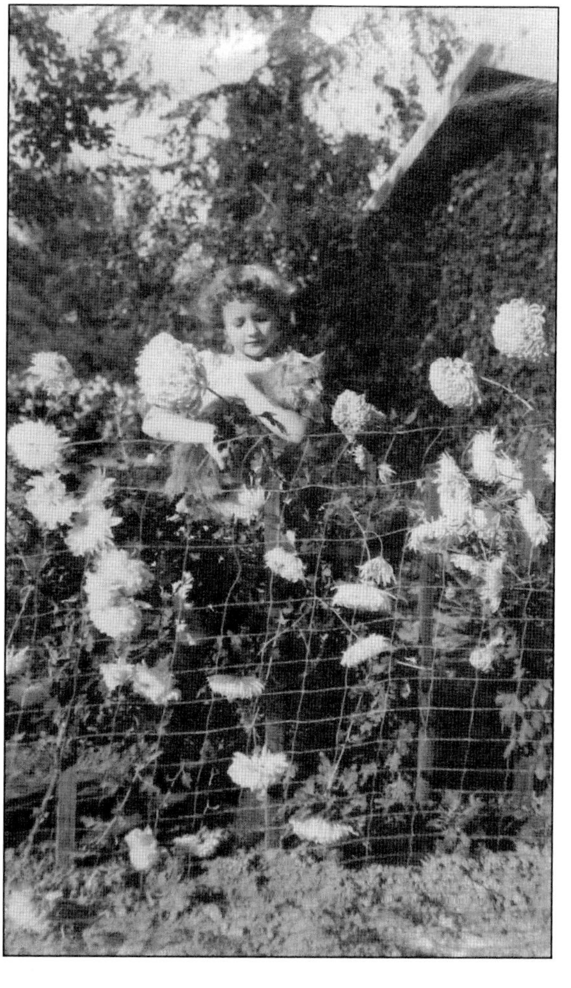

This photograph was taken in 1923 of Coachella resident Margaret Proctor holding a cat while visiting the Hyde ranch in Coachella. The desert landscape was a stark contrast to the lush, flowery garden around her. (Courtesy of the Coachella Valley History Museum.)

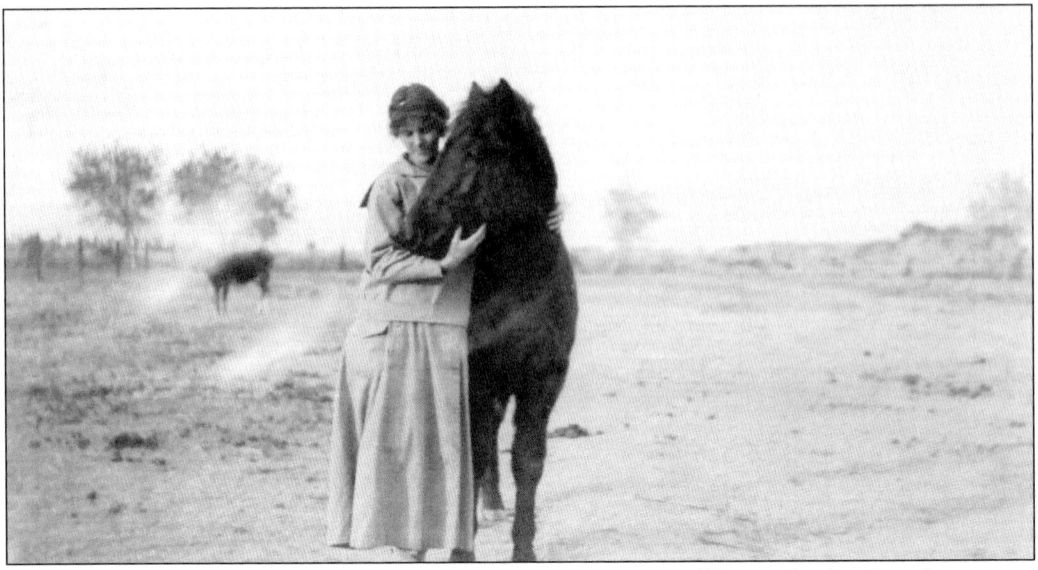

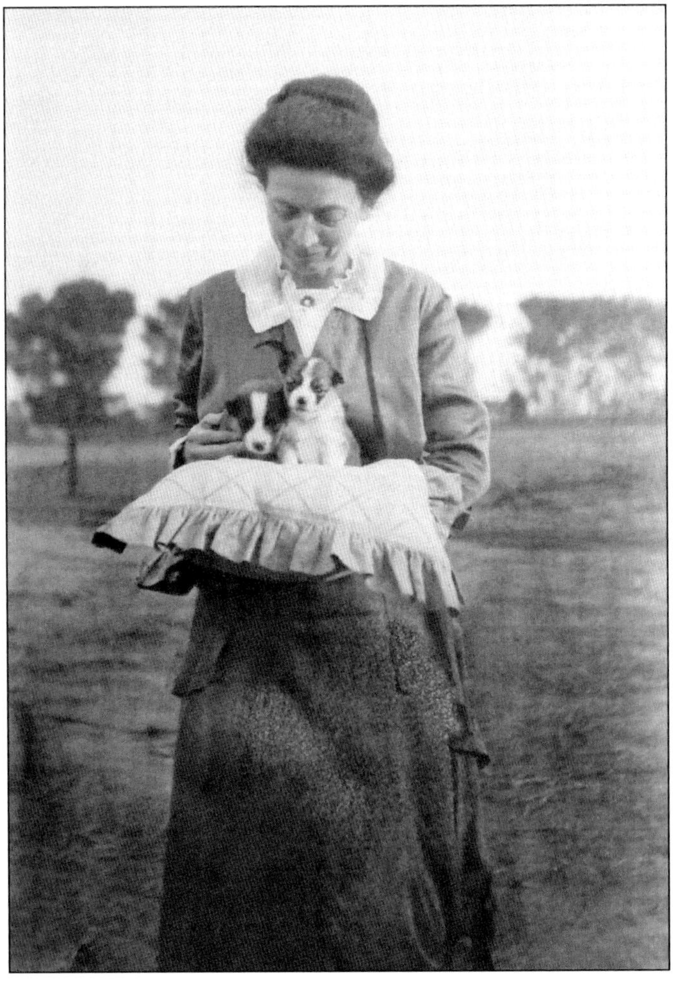

Those who lived in the Coachella Valley shaped the development of the city of Coachella. The above photograph shows Katherine Gridley Teagle and a horse in Coachella in 1914. The agricultural fields can be seen behind her. The photograph at left was taken in the same year and shows Alberta (Proctor) Hyde holding puppies Ricky and Allen. Despite the hard life that comes with living in an arid desert, the people of Coachella flourished and developed throughout the decades. (Both, courtesy of the Coachella Valley History Museum.)

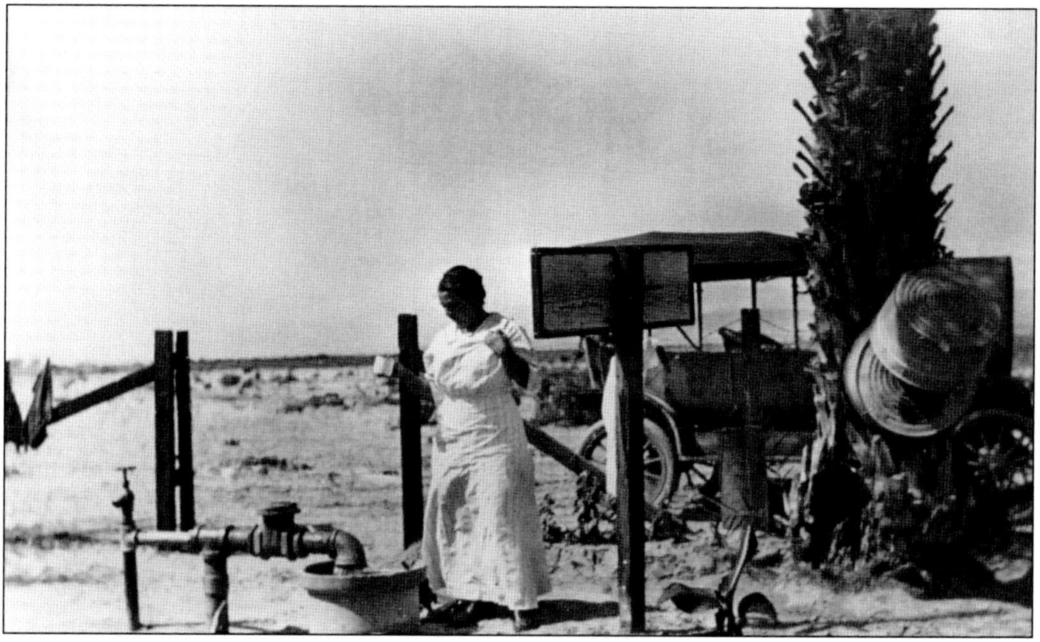

Mrs. Drummond is pictured above at the Date Station in Indio. The stark fields can be seen in the background. Drummond appears to be getting water from the irrigation pipe in front of her. She was the wife of Bruce Drummond, who was the superintendent of the USDA Date and Citrus Experiment Station from 1907 to 1923. Bruce Drummond also assisted local farmers in growing the new date crops. In contrast, the 1918 photograph below shows a group of unidentified young adults smiling and relaxing as they pose with a car for the camera. This photograph was taken in Coachella. (Both, courtesy of the Coachella Valley Water District.)

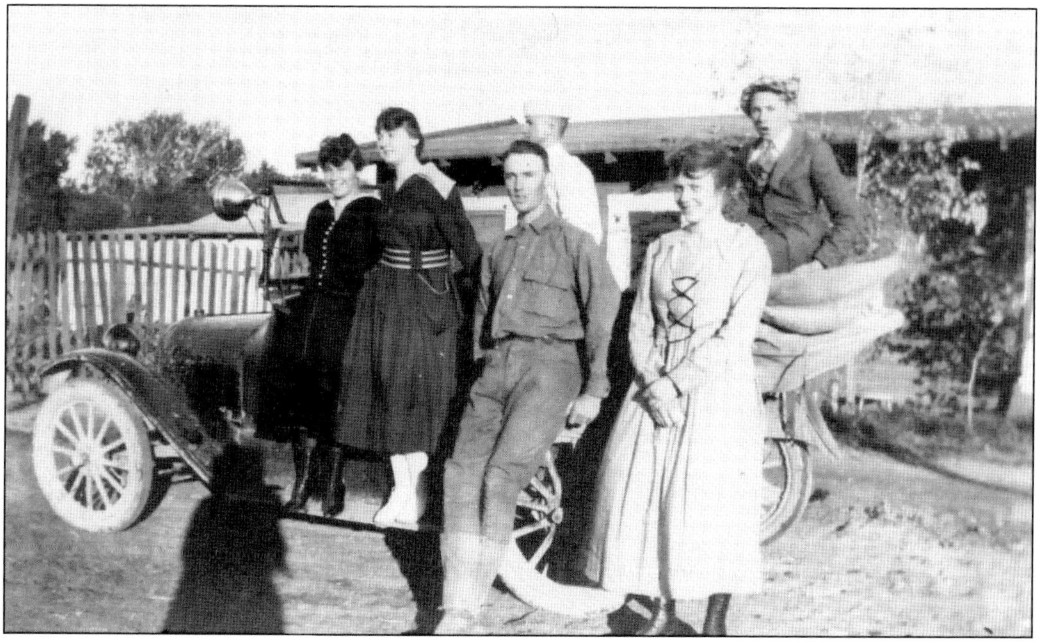

Bibliography

Coachella Valley Historical Society Inc. *The 2012 Periscope: Strength Through Unity, The Woman's Club of Indio, 1912–2012.* Indio, CA: Coachella Valley Historical Society Inc., 2012.

Department of Parks and Recreation, State of California. The Resource Agency. *Building, Structure, and Object Record #33-5792.* Resource Identifier CRM TECH 184-1. April 28, 1995.

Hornbeck, David. "The Salton Sink before the Great Flood of 1905." www.imperialgroup.info/PDF/HornbeckSaltonBefore1905030906.pdf

Laflin, Patricia B. *Coachella Valley, California: A Pictorial History.* Virginia Beach, VA: Donning Company, 1998.

———. *The Periscope: The Salton Sea, California's Overlooked Treasure.* Indio, CA: Coachella Valley Historical Society Inc., 1995.

Mitchell, Kathleen Ann. *Submarines, Salsa, and Pottery Shards: A Narrative History of Coachella, California.* Riverside, CA: University of California, Riverside, 1991.

Nordland, Ole. *Coachella Valley's Golden Years.* Indio, CA: Desert Printing Company, 1978.

Postlethwaite, R.H. *The Coachella Valley and Its Date Industry.* Coachella, CA: V.V. Green, 1938.

Soltys, Richard J. *Coachella Valley: Yesterday, Today and Tomorrow.* La Quinta, CA: Richard J. Soltys Productions, 2003.

INDEX

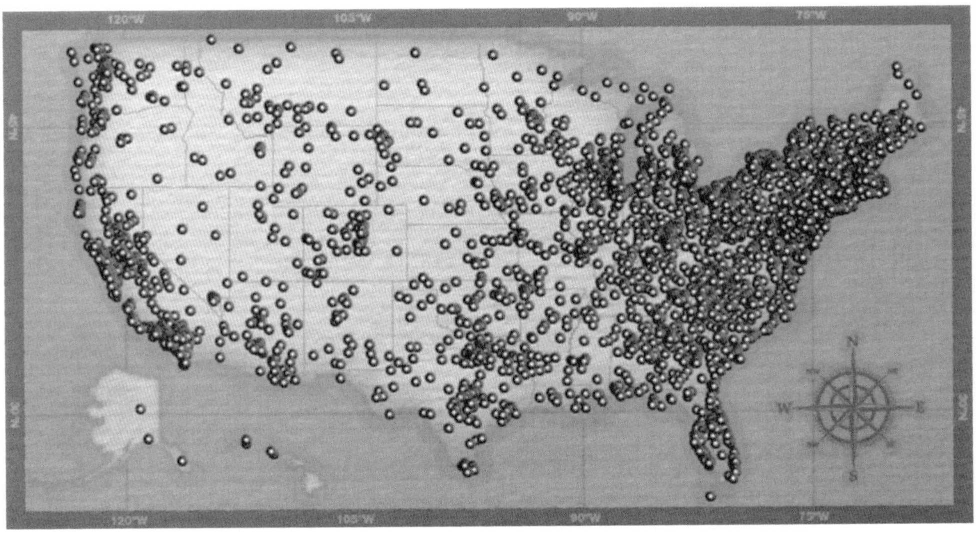